THREE RIVERS REGIONAL LIBRARY SYSTEM

3 3400 50057 1784

D1479831

Three Rivers Regional
Library System
Gilchrist County Public Library
P.O. Box 128
Trenton, FL 32693

FIRST FAMILIES IN RESIDENCE

LIFE AT THE FLORIDA GOVERNOR'S MANSION

Early morning at the Florida
Governor's Mansion. *Florida's
Finest* greets visitors of all
ages as they enter the mansion
grounds. The mansion foundation
commissioned Tallahassee artist
W. Stanley (Sandy) Proctor in 1978
to create this bronze sculpture to
celebrate Florida's children.

FIRST FAMILIES IN RESIDENCE

LIFE AT THE FLORIDA GOVERNOR'S MANSION

BY ELLEN J. UGUCCIONI

Governor and Mrs. Jeb Bush welcomed back former first ladies to the governor's mansion on November 2, 2005. On this rare occasion, many of Florida's former governors and their families gathered to pay tribute to all eleven of the outstanding women who resided here since 1957, and the docents who served with them.

Standing, from left to right:
First Lady Columba Bush,
Governor Bob Martinez,
Governor Wayne Mixson,
Governor Reubin Askew;
Seated from left to right:
First Lady Mary Call Collins,
Governor Jeb Bush,
First Lady Mary Jane Martinez,
First Lady Margie Mixson,
First Lady Donna Lou Askew.

Copyright © 2006
The Florida Governor's Mansion Foundation, Inc.

All rights reserved. No part of this publication may be reproduced, stored
in or introduced into a retrieval system, or transmitted in any form or by any
means (electronic, mechanical, photocopying. recording, or other) without
written permission from the publisher.

Published 2006
Printed in Florida, in the United States of America

First edition
ISBN 0-9654772-1-5

Book design by Dee Dee Celander, Celander Creative
50th Anniversary photography by Ray Stanyard Photography
Printing by Boyd Brothers, Inc., Panama City, Florida

Information about the Florida Governor's Mansion, its programs and tours
can be found at the following website: www.floridagovernorsmansion.com.
Correspondence may be addressed to the attention of
the Mansion Curator at:

Governor's Mansion
700 North Adams Street
Tallahassee, Florida 32303

Details, from top to bottom:
USS *Florida* fruit bowl
set before 18th century
knifeboxes in the state dining
room; lighted garlands line
the private stairwell during the
second Bush term; holiday
décor in the Florida Room
during the Martinez era.

CONTENTS

Governor Jeb Bush and First Lady Columba Bush

INTRODUCTION

GOVERNOR AND MRS. JEB BUSH

My family and I have been profoundly honored to call the Florida Governor's Mansion home during the past eight years. We are deeply grateful to all Floridians for allowing us the opportunity to live, work, and serve in the "People's House." Like the many families who had this privilege before us, Columba and I immediately set out to make the most of our stay by continually working hard on behalf of all Floridians. ¶ The governor's mansion holds countless memories for Columba and me, our family, and our guests—memories of promoting the importance of education, memories of hosting unique art exhibitions, holiday celebrations, dinners with friends, memories of excited school children touring the mansion for the first time, memories of events recognizing the achievements of our African-American and Hispanic communities, and memories of quiet evenings and weekends at home with our children. ¶ In early January of 2007, we will leave the governor's mansion; however, the memories we made in the mansion will remain with us forever. It will then be time for the newly elected governor and family to begin creating their own mansion memories, starting with the traditional inaugural open house. ¶ The celebration on January 2, 2007, will mark fifty years since Governor LeRoy Collins and his wife Mary Call hosted the first inaugural open house at the newly built governor's mansion. Since 1957, the mansion has evolved, with each family adding character to the home with their own special touches. ¶ Twenty-first-century technology has enabled us to provide unlimited access to the governor's mansion. Students, teachers, and residents interested in learning more about the mansion and Florida's history can do so by logging onto our e-mansion website, www.floridagovernorsmansion.com. ¶ It has truly been an honor and a privilege serving as the governor and first lady of Florida and living in the People's House. We are proud of our achievements, yet humbled by the experience, and thank all Floridians for giving us such a remarkable opportunity. ¶ We hope you enjoy this commemorative book and also enjoy gaining insight into the Florida Governor's Mansion and the families who called it home.

Jeb Bush

Governor of Florida

Columba Bush

First Lady of Florida

Ambassador and Mrs. Alfred Hoffman, Jr.

FOREWORD

AMBASSADOR AND MRS. ALFRED HOFFMAN, JR.

The governor's mansion. Even the phrase has a bit of irony and mystique about it. As Americans, we bestow the privilege of living in these lovely, historic homes to the duly elected chief executives of our states for a finite amount of time. Yet we, the electorate, expect that the lights will always be on, the doors will always be open, the grounds will always be manicured, and all will be in order when we arrive for our mansion visit. What does that say about our collective sense of civic pride, not to mention our desire that the best that our states have to offer be accessible to all of us? Residents of most states visit their governor's mansions by the thousands each year, and the cycle is repeated from one generation to the next. An invitation to visit the governor's mansion in and of itself brings with it a great sense of honor and distinction. And well it should! Physical buildings such as these have a symbolic value which transcends the ordinary and makes such visits really quite extraordinary. ¶ In Florida, we are fortunate to have a governor's mansion which was carefully planned a half-century ago, through the collective efforts of many capable visionaries. Changes have occurred quite naturally over the decades, but the integrity of the residence has remained intact and carefully preserved. Each and every first family in residence has thoughtfully and tirelessly added to the character of the home and to our state. We are proud to have chaired fundraising for the Florida Governor's Mansion Foundation during the creation of the new Florida Library in 2006 in the final year of the Bush administration. At Governor Bush's suggestion, this library will highlight Florida books by Florida authors. It is the first such addition to the residence in over twenty years, and it will reflect the emphasis which our governor and first lady have placed upon literacy and education during their tenure. It is our hope that their legacy project, like the Florida Room before it, will become another favorite spot within the mansion, utilized and appreciated by future residents and citizens alike, one generation after another. ¶ So please, enjoy this commemorative book. Enjoy the new Florida Library. After all, it's your governor's mansion. Happy anniversary!

Alfred Hoffman, Jr.
United States Ambassador to Portugal

Dawn Hoffman
President, Florida Governor's Mansion Foundation

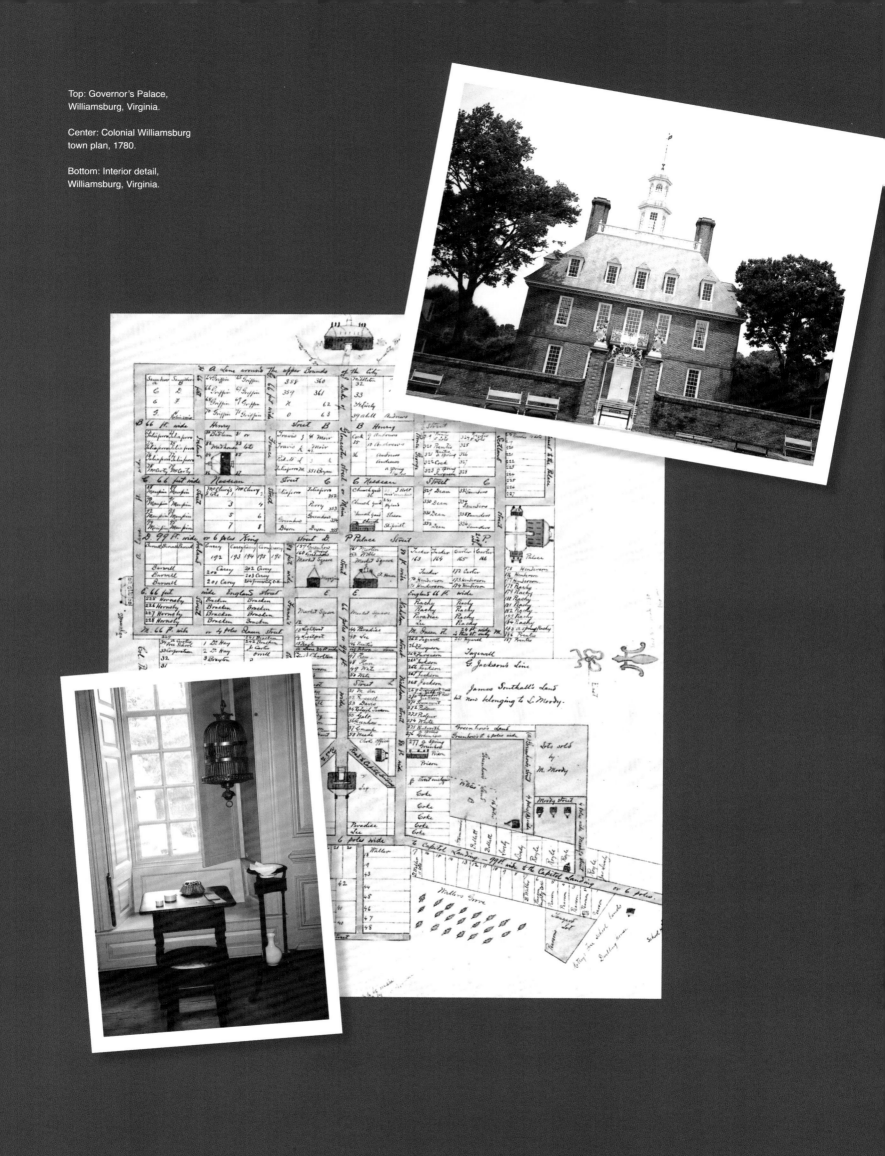

Top: Governor's Palace,
Williamsburg, Virginia.

Center: Colonial Williamsburg
town plan, 1780.

Bottom: Interior detail,
Williamsburg, Virginia.

PREFACE

Even in the nascent American colonies, not yet separated from England, institutional architecture mattered. The colonial leaders desired buildings that characterized stability and created a sense of permanence imbued with symbol, understood by all. Apart from the capitol, the next most venerated seat of government was the residence of the colony's leader. Centuries-old traditions have passed down to us the expectations we seek in a building of this stature. The colonial Governor's Palace in Virginia's capital of Williamsburg begins to tell the story of the standards we have come to expect from a building grand enough to house the principal leader of government. ¶ The Williamsburg Governor's Palace, completed in 1722, was sited in a strategic, highly visible location and was of a size and substance that set it apart from adjacent buildings. A textbook example of Georgian architecture, the palace was approached through a formally landscaped forecourt, adding anticipation when approaching the splendid entrance hall. The hierarchy of spaces was critical in underscoring its premier importance to the colony. ¶ Almost two centuries later those hierarchical principles would manifest themselves in the design for an executive mansion in an exotic, previously remote location in what became the southernmost state in the union. The first building constructed for the exclusive use of Florida's chief executive was built in 1907, with Governor Napoleon Bonaparte Broward its first occupant. This impressive *tour de force* of Greek Revival architecture served its residents well, but sadly was ultimately judged obsolete because of the inflexibility of its spaces to accommodate larger crowds and its serious physical deterioration. Following the original mansion's demolition in 1955, the present governor's mansion was designed and built on the same site. ¶ The current governor's mansion was completed in 1957, and its first residents were Governor LeRoy and Mary Call Collins. Immediately after he assumed office, Governor Collins led the state through the frequently divisive and painful racial integration process. His terms of office also coincided with the beginnings of the Cold War, a time when anxieties ran high. The very real possibility of cataclysmic global war influenced every aspect of life, and most certainly the life of the governor. Floridians held their collective breaths. The new mansion transcended its role as a home and became a refuge and a symbol of stability for all Floridians. ¶ The mansion became home, albeit temporarily, for a series of notable Florida governors who balanced their lives as chief executives with their responsibilities as husbands and fathers. They came from a variety of circumstances, some affluent and others from more modest backgrounds. Each family had their own special moments, their own significant recollections, and a reverence for the time they spent in the "People's House." ¶ This book focuses on the mansion as a place of refuge and sanctuary where the first families were allowed to be themselves. The children living at the mansion were left with indelible impressions of a time when they too were under close scrutiny, but managed to be children in spite of it. ¶ Through successive administrations the state of Florida has weathered innumerable storms, both literally and figuratively. Throughout those years, the Florida Governor's Mansion bore witness to those events and remains a tangible symbol to inspire and endure. The lives led at the Florida Governor's Mansion by its distinguished residents provide a candid insight into their personalities, allowing us a very special glimpse into the world of the men, women, and children who have made the well being of Florida their uppermost priority.

Part One

THE PLACE

CHAPTER ONE

A NOTABLE BEGINNING

A Commingling of Cultures; Conflict and Resolution

he state of Florida entered the union in 1845. The Spanish who thrilled at the land's beauty had discovered it some three centuries earlier in 1513. Because they arrived in the Easter season, they called it "Flowery Easter" (*la Pascua Florida*). Over the years, *la Florida* would see the flags of the Spanish, French, British, and finally the United States fly over its land (and, albeit for a short time, the Confederacy's Stars and Bars also waved).

Castillo de San Marcos, constructed as a heavily fortified garrison by the Spanish in 1672, has weathered more than three hundred years in St. Augustine, Florida.

The efforts of the Jesuit and Franciscan priests continued, and by 1675 there were some forty missions serving twenty-five thousand Indians in Florida and Georgia.

COVETED *LA FLORIDA*

As a peninsula with long coastlines on both the east and west, with the Atlantic Ocean on one side and the Gulf of Mexico on the other, Florida was strategically positioned for encounters with seafarers who made their way to its shores. Spain's first contact with Florida is generally associated with the voyage of Juan Ponce de Leon in April 1513, although new scholarship suggests even earlier contacts. Through successive decades and other European expeditions, the settlement of *la Florida* began in earnest.

The observations of the conquering armies characterize a land unique among others, with its antediluvian alligators, towering moss-draped oaks, and perpetually blooming flowers in every hue. They begin to set the image of a fantastic world that would survive for centuries of occupations. The expeditions of Hernando de Soto, beginning in 1539, added to the mystery and fantasy associated with the new land. De Soto arrived on Florida's Gulf coast to begin a four-year expedition that took him through Florida as well as nine other southern states. Arriving in what is present-day Tallahassee, de Soto celebrated the first Christ's Mass (the Feast of the Nativity of Our Lord) by Europeans in the New World on December 25, 1539.

The battle for control of this mystery-shrouded Florida was intense. The English, French, and Spanish all had designs on the land that held an important military position to protect shipping routes along the northern Gulf coast and through the Bahamas Channel. Frenchman Jean Ribault came to Florida in 1562 to claim the land for France. Landing at the mouth of the St. Johns River, he continued his explorations, moving north, and established a short-lived fort on the Carolina coast.

In 1564 another French expedition, led by René Goulaine Laudonnière, brought some three hundred colonists to Florida and established Fort Caroline, near present-day Jacksonville, the first attempt at a permanent settlement. Ribault had returned to France but came back to Fort Caroline, bringing desperately needed supplies and another five hundred men to shore up the French presence.

While Spain had yet to found permanent settlements in Florida, they saw it as *their* territory. With that territory threatened, the Spanish monarchy sent Pedro Menéndez de Avilés to remove the French. In August 1565, Menéndez arrived at Fort Caroline and, when offered little resistance, easily took the fort. Ribault, who had sailed to engage Menéndez, wrecked on the shore. Laudonnière, left at the fort, fled into the woods. Both were slaughtered when caught. From then on, Florida belonged to Spain, and to Spain alone.

Menéndez built a settlement at St. Augustine, and the Spaniards embarked on a zealous campaign to convert the native populations to Christianity, establishing a series of mission towns throughout the Southeast. Battles for conquest continued for decades as the British stepped up their involvement. In 1586 Francis Drake led a raid against St. Augustine. An attack in 1668 under the command of Robert Sears led to the construction of the Castillo de San Marcos in 1672, a heavily fortified garrison. The efforts of the Jesuit and Franciscan priests continued, and by 1675 there were some forty missions serving twenty-five thousand Indians in Florida and Georgia. Constantly embattled, however, the Spanish mission system was effectively destroyed. By 1702, the missions were all but abandoned.

In 1763, after almost two hundred years of Spanish rule and influence, Britain, Spain and France signed the Treaty of Paris, which ended the French and Indian War (1754–1763) and forced the French out of North America. Because Spain had supported the French, Britain demanded reparation. In exchange for the island of Cuba, captured earlier by the British, the Spanish traded Florida to Britain.

THE DIVISION OF EAST AND WEST

Upon their arrival, the English established two separate colonies: East and West Florida. The west was administered from Pensacola and the east from St. Augustine. The area encompassed by the two Floridas was enormous. East Florida extended from the Georgia border south to the New Smyrna Colony in what is now Volusia County, with the Atlantic Ocean on the east and the Apalachicola River on the west. West Florida extended west from the Apalachicola River to the Mississippi River and included parts of modern-day Alabama, Mississippi, and Louisiana.

Opposite top: The reconstructed Franciscan Church at Mission San Luis in Tallahassee, Florida. A commemorative Mass is currently held each December in the church.

Opposite bottom: Seminole warrior Osceola, one of only two historical figures to appear within the mansion's 47-piece USS *Florida* presentation silver collection. The other figure is Juan Ponce de Leon, who discovered "*la Florida*" on March 27, 1513.

East Florida was blessed with fertile soil perfectly suited to the propagation of crops, particularly indigo, sugar, and citrus. The British brought colonists to this new land with promises of land grants. Colonists not only farmed the land but also served to defend its borders. Agricultural trade flourished between the new colony and the island nation, introducing the exoticism of Florida to the English.

West Florida was less amenable to planting, with its sandy soil and thick stands of pine trees. Its economy was principally based on the fur and timber trade. Both East and West Florida depended on the labor of imported slaves and indentured servants.

The British lost Florida as a consequence of the American War of Independence. East Florida was loyal to the Crown and contributed to the war as best it could. In West Florida, Spanish forces, drawn into the conflict by the intervention of their French allies, defeated the English at Pensacola. By 1783, the English recognized the independence of the thirteen colonies, and Florida was returned to Spanish control. While their brief twenty-year tenure left no lasting political legacy, the English agricultural legacy that promoted the cultivation and export of a variety of products, especially citrus and timber, continues today.

A United States Territory and "Old Hickory"

The interior regions of the state became more populated. Many who sought their fortunes here were displaced Indians and runaway slaves who sought refuge in the area. They brought to Florida a cultural diversity that has influenced the state ever since.

Particularly vulnerable to disease, the Native American populations in Florida suffered greatly during the initial European contact. Thousands perished. Skirmishes between the remaining natives and the new settlers—Spanish, English, and American alike—were frequent and violent. The inevitable showdown came during the First Seminole War in 1818 when President James Monroe appointed Major General Andrew Jackson from Tennessee to subdue the Seminole Indian population.

Jackson had earned a formidable reputation as a warrior during the War of 1812, especially for his victory over the British during the Battle of New Orleans in January of 1815. As commander of the southern division of the United States Army, Jackson in 1818 led more than three thousand men, capturing the territory from St. Marks to Pensacola and destroying Indian settlements along his route. The First Seminole War culminated with the 1823 Treaty of Moultrie Creek. The treaty required the Seminole Indian tribe to move south to some four million acres of land around present-day Ocala.

By then, Spain recognized the extent of U.S. control over its lands. In February 1819, Secretary of State John Quincy Adams and Spain's representative Luís de Onís met in Washington to negotiate a boundary settlement between the United States and Spain. Their negotiation led to the signing of the Adams-Onís treaty that gave Florida to the United States. The actual transfer of sovereignty occurred in July 1821 when the United States acquired Florida as a territory. When the Stars and Stripes was raised in Pensacola, Andrew Jackson was there, but no longer as Major General Jackson. On March 20, 1821, President James Monroe had appointed him the first American territorial governor of Florida.

One of the men closely associated with territorial Florida, Richard Keith Call, shared an important affiliation with Andrew Jackson. (One hundred years later the legacy of both Andrew Jackson and Richard Call figure prominently in our story of the governor's mansion.) Call joined Jackson's army as a volunteer and accompanied him in both Florida campaigns and in the Battle of New Orleans, becoming his aide and earning the rank of general. He later established a law practice and served on the Florida Legislative Council (1822–1823). In 1824 Call was elected the territorial delegate to Congress. At that time, only white males of at least twenty-one years of age who had been residents of the territory for at least three months were allowed to participate in the vote.

While territorial delegates were not allowed a vote in the Congress, Call lobbied for naval construction, roads, bridges, and internal improvements. Then, in 1825, Call resigned his position to become the "Receiver of Public Monies for Florida" and began construction of his palatial Greek Revival residence he

General Andrew Jackson, Florida's first territorial governor.

named the Grove. Eighty years later, Florida's first governor's mansion would be constructed on Call's land, directly to the south of the Grove. Call served as territorial governor from 1836 to 1838 (appointed by President Andrew Jackson) and again from 1841 to 1844.

Just months after his appointment as territorial governor, Andrew Jackson completed the establishment of a provisional government and, considering his mission completed, resigned in November 1821. President Monroe appointed Judge William P. DuVal to succeed him. Jackson returned home to his prospering plantation in Tennessee and began the transformation of his log farmhouse into the impressive mansion he named the Hermitage.

ONE CAPITAL FOR ALL

The British division of Florida into east and west with two capitals continued, for all practical purposes, through Florida's territorial period. In 1822 Congress established a single territorial government, but in reality Florida continued to be divided both administratively and geographically. The Territorial Congress declared that its annual meeting would alternate between St. Augustine and Pensacola.

The first Legislative Council was scheduled to meet on June 10, 1822, in Pensacola. The council was delayed until July 22 to achieve a quorum. The representatives from St. Augustine were forced to travel around the Florida Keys in a long and treacherous voyage. One drowned while others simply never arrived. During the next year's session, with itineraries reversed, the members of the Pensacola delegation encountered the same difficult journey.

In 1823 Governor DuVal sought some common ground. He assigned two representatives, one from St. Augustine and one from Pensacola, to find a suitable location midway between the two former capitals. At the time, Florida's settlements were concentrated in the north, though in the center of the territory (known as Middle Florida), enormous plantations were being built around the farming of cotton, tobacco, and sugar, along the St. Johns River valley. They agreed to a place called Tallahassee, the location of an Apalachee Indian village of gardens and council houses (Tallahassee means "old fields" in the Apalachee language). Tallahassee officially became the seat of the territorial capital on March 4, 1824. In their report, John Lee Williams from Pensacola and William Simmons from St. Augustine declared, "a more beautiful country can scarcely be imagined: it is high, rolling, and well watered, the richness of the soil renders it so perfectly adapted to farming, that living must ultimately be cheap and abundant."

In 1830 Andrew Jackson (nicknamed Old Hickory) was the seventh president of the United States and signed the Indian Removal Act. It was the death knell for Florida's native population, who were required to move to reservations in the western United States. By 1835, Florida's native population consisted mostly of the Seminoles, former Creeks who had been driven south from their lands in Georgia and Alabama. Because they refused to move, the Second Seminole War broke out, spreading into south

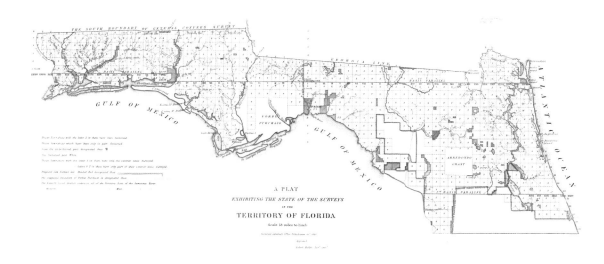

Opposite: Richard Keith Call, early territorial governor and great-grandfather of future First Lady Mary Call Collins. The Grove property, on which Call built his home, originally included the land upon which the first and current mansion now sit.

A plat exhibiting the division of East and West Florida in the state surveys of 1840, by William James Stone (1798–1865).

Florida to Lake Okeechobee on the north and the Everglades on the south. Forts were established around Florida, including Fort Foster in the Big Cypress and Fort Dallas in what is now Miami. Fort Dallas became the base of operations for soldiers pursuing Indians into the Everglades. The Second Seminole War finally came to an end in 1842, after almost seven long years of fighting and bloodshed. Even then, the territory wanted the remaining small numbers of Seminoles to leave for areas set aside in present-day Oklahoma. Those that refused disappeared into the Big Cypress and the Everglades.

Settlers soon replaced the displaced Indians. To encourage the settlement of Florida, in 1842 the federal government passed the Armed Occupation Act that offered settlers from northern states a 160-acre parcel of land at no cost. The only requirements for ownership were that five acres of land be cleared, crops planted, and residency maintained for at least five years. Any man who was head of a household, or a single man over the age of eighteen and able to bear arms, was eligible for the program. The Occupation Act transformed the land as hundreds came to make Florida their permanent home.

STATEHOOD: A DELICATE BALANCE

Florida's statehood, though, was delayed until two critical qualifications could be met. Entry into the United States required that territories have a population of at least sixty thousand, and that the nation's distribution of slave-owning and nonslave-owning states be kept in balance. The friction over slavery that resulted in the Civil War had already begun, and in order to maintain the peace, Congress required equal representation between the two positions. President Andrew Jackson was committed to Florida's statehood, and ultimately Florida, as a slave state, entered the United States paired with Iowa, a nonslave state. Finally, that great day came as Florida became the twenty-seventh state in the union on March 3, 1845.

William D. Moseley was the state of Florida's first elected governor (1845–1849), winning out of a field of four candidates that included former territorial governor Richard Keith Call. On June 25, 1845, Moseley was sworn in on the steps of the newly built capitol. Moseley's inauguration and Florida's statehood were cause for grand celebration, setting the tone and protocols for the many inaugural ceremonies to come. Only the death of President Andrew Jackson tempered the joy-filled ceremony. He had died just weeks earlier on June 8, 1845, but the news of his death was delayed for at least two weeks because of primitive communications. Jackson was revered in Florida, having greatly assisted the young territory in achieving statehood. Many of the participants at the inauguration wore black armbands in his memory. Florida would remember Jackson in a variety of meaningful ways, including the naming of Jacksonville.

The new governor's address that day stressed the sovereignty of the states, referring to the federal government as having "strictly limited powers." The Stars and Stripes, with its one new star, was raised over the capitol, along with the new state flag of blue, orange, red, white and green horizontal stripes inscribed with the words "Let Us Alone." (Florida's antagonistic banner was summarily retired soon thereafter.) Florida's position as a slave state and its perceived independence from federal control foreshadowed ominous consequences when years later the first shots fired on Fort Sumter initiated the War Between the States.

The first State Seal of Florida after statehood. This State Seal replaced the earlier Territorial Seal. It was in use from 1846 until 1868. This glass seal was one of thirty-one state seals commissioned for the ceiling of the United States House of Representatives in 1857. The artist, J. A. Oertel, lived in several southern states, including Florida.

A Divisive and Devastating War

By 1850 the population of Florida had grown to some 87,000. Of that number 39,000 were African-American slaves while another 1,000 were free blacks. When Abraham Lincoln was elected president of the United States in 1860, the long-simmering conflicts over slave ownership boiled over, and South Carolina seceded in December 1860. Less than a month later, Florida became the third state to secede from the union. Governor Madison Starke Perry presided over the General Assembly that on January 10, 1861, voted 62 to 7 in favor of secession. Richard Keith Call, one of the dissenters, exclaimed these prophetic words: "You have opened the gates of Hell, from which shall flow the curses of the damned which shall sink you to perdition." The Civil War began three months later.

An estimated fourteen to fifteen thousand Floridians took up arms in the Confederate Army, and some twelve hundred men, mostly from east Florida, fought for the Union. Because Florida was less populated than other southern states, the war's devastation was far less catastrophic. Tallahassee was the only southern capital east of the Mississippi not captured by federal troops (Confederate soldiers repelled Union troops at Florida's Battle of Natural Bridge toward the end of the war). The Stars and Bars of the Confederacy continued to fly over Florida's capitol until May 20, 1865, when hostilities ended. The bitterness and passion some Floridians felt at the defeat were evidenced by the suicide of Governor John Milton, who believed "death would be preferable to reunion."

The long road back to normalcy was begun in a vacuum of leadership, first with Milton's suicide, then with the assassination of President Lincoln. President Andrew Johnson was left with the Herculean task of reconstruction, and in Florida he appointed a former federal judge from Key West, William Marvin, as provisional governor. Following a constitutional convention at which the laws of Florida were brought into harmony with those of the United States, another gubernatorial contest elected David Walker.

Those initial years following the Civil War were fraught with divisiveness, as the Congress pushed suffrage for African-American citizens, while President Johnson opposed it. Florida was so strongly behind President Johnson that federal troops were stationed in Florida to maintain the peace. Ultimately, with the passage of the Fourteenth Amendment to the Constitution (ratified by Florida on June 9, 1868), establishing the inalienable rights of citizens regardless of color, the pursuit of normalcy could proceed.

Resuming the Peace

Despite the turbulent Reconstruction years, Florida made progress, particularly as settlers began moving southward. It became exceedingly clear that the state's development depended on transportation systems. In 1881, under the leadership of Governor William D. Bloxham, over four million acres of land were sold to saw-and-tool manufacturer Hamilton Disston. With Disston's $1 million purchase, the state acquired the capital to make public lands available and to attract railroads.

As the nineteenth century ended, Henry B. Plant from Connecticut would bring his railroad, hotels, and steamship lines along the Gulf coast and into central Florida. Henry M. Flagler would do the same on the east coast. Flagler, a partner with John D. Rockefeller in Standard Oil, developed a multi-million dollar empire of railroad, shipping, hotel, and land development from St. Augustine on the north as far south as Miami (1896) and eventually Key West (1912).

Modern Florida begins with the mobility of the nation. The prosperity and economic freedom of the American people following the First World War would transform the state, as the real estate boom of the mid-1920s put Florida on the map. Florida's evolution as an idyllic vacationland, retirement oasis, agricultural powerhouse, technological leader, and key state in national political races has earned it a powerful position in the nation.

The residents of the Florida Governor's Mansion played vital and influential roles in that transformation. Our story will serve as witness to the men, and their families, who have held the most trusted role in Florida's government, a role in which history is made.

CHAPTER TWO

A GREAT AND GRACIOUS HOME

The First Executive Mansion

he territorial legislature first met in Tallahassee in 1824 inside a rudely fashioned log hut. Two years later the cornerstone for a two-story brick statehouse was laid. The Legislative Council occupied the upper story, while the executive and judicial branches occupied the lower. Tallahassee experienced phenomenal growth during those territorial years and by 1835 had grown to 1,500 residents as a combination government town and merchant center. In 1839 a new and larger capitol was erected (today the center

section of the restored Old Capitol building). ¶ Though capitol construction progressed, Florida's governors were left to maintain their own personal residences. In 1903 under the administration of Governor William Sherman Jennings, the legislature was convinced that it was time to build a suitable home for the chief executive. One can't help but think that Jennings's wife, May Mann Jennings, provided the governor with great encouragement to lobby for the building of an executive mansion.

Top: First Lady May Mann Jennings photographed in a white satin crepe inaugural dress, trimmed in lace she made herself, including the butterfly perched in tulle in her hair.

Bottom: Governor William Sherman Jennings.

Top: The first governor's mansion, designed by Jacksonville architect Henry Klutho, was completed in 1907. It graced the address known as 700 North Adams Street for almost fifty years.

Bottom: Governor Napoleon Bonaparte Broward and his family on the steps of the original mansion. Elizabeth Broward, sitting on the lap of her mother, was the first child born to an incumbent governor. Currently, a monogrammed object belonging to the Broward family rests upon an antique cellarette in the state entrance hall. The sterling silver, filigree bowl was donated by retired Supreme Court Justice B.K. and Mrs. Roberts during the Graham years.

JENNINGS'S DREAM, CALL'S LAND

Mrs. Jennings was in the vanguard of women who sought greater roles for their gender at the beginning of the twentieth century. May Jennings fought for women's suffrage, conservation of the natural environment, reservations for the Seminole tribe, and compulsory education. She was also instrumental in founding a state library in Tallahassee and creating a state park service. In her book *May Mann Jennings: Florida's Genteel Activist*, biographer Linda D. Vance remarks that at Jennings's death in 1963 she was "Florida's most impressive and successful female citizen."

Unfortunately, disagreements about location delayed the mansion plan for two years, and Governor and Mrs. Jennings did not have the distinction of becoming its first residents. At last, in 1905 the legislature appropriated $25,000 "for the Acquisition of a Site, and the Erection, Building and Furnishing of a Mansion Thereon for the Governor of the State of Florida." With the appropriation of funds also came the creation of a Governor's Mansion Commission to oversee and advise on the project. The commission members included the governor, the comptroller, and three citizens.

The last obstacle was the acquisition of the land. The legislature specifically prohibited the use of the money for purchase of land, so the building site had to be in public, not private, hands. Though a location owned by the city of Tallahassee was suggested, the city's reluctance to part with the land resulted in another solution. Tallahassee banker George Saxon agreed to donate four lots at the city's northern boundary—land formerly owned by territorial governor Richard Keith Call. At last, all was in place for the construction of 700 North Adams Street, the Florida Governor's Mansion.

BROWARD: TRANSFORMING FLORIDA

The beginning of the twentieth century for all of America was a time of rampant and unrelenting change. The inventions of Thomas Edison, Henry Ford, and Alexander Graham Bell created an unheard-of

Governor Napoleon Bonaparte Broward

mobility and communication. Rural, agrarian America was transformed into an industrial nation of cities, though eventually suburbia exploded as more and more Americans sought a more rural respite from their work lives. Great social tumult also marked the times, as civil rights and justice were sought for all Americans. The going was tough, but change was inexorable. Nowhere was change more evident than in the state of Florida.

Napoleon Bonaparte Broward from Duval County was elected governor in 1905. Broward launched a progressive agenda that literally changed the face of Florida. In south Florida and elsewhere, he initiated a campaign to drain the wetlands through a system of canals emptying into the Atlantic Ocean and Gulf of Mexico. The canals (their irreparable environmental damage then unknown) opened up thousands of acres to development. Broward's programs included road construction, the establishment of social services and child labor laws, tax reform, the institution of railroad regulations, and a unified system of higher education.

Before moving into Florida's first executive mansion, Governor Broward and his wife lived in a rented home on Monroe Street, close to the capitol. He and his wife, the proud parents of eight children, must have been particularly delighted with the prospect of larger quarters.

THE FORMIDABLE AND FLUID KLUTHO

The choice for the architect of the new governor's mansion was Henry John Klutho (1873–1964) from Jacksonville. By 1905 Klutho had acquired a formidable reputation, leading the rebuilding of Jacksonville after a devastating fire in 1901 that destroyed over 1,700 buildings in only eight hours. Klutho today is remembered as a leading proponent of the Prairie School style of architecture.

Toward the end of the nineteenth century, some American architects sought a departure from the purely historicist styles practiced by so many of their colleagues schooled in the École des Beaux-Arts reverence for the past. When a catastrophic fire occurred in 1871 in Chicago, the city became a mecca for practicing architects. One particularly influential firm, Adler and Sullivan, was beginning to explore the nature of materials and their potential expression in high-rise construction. A young apprentice to the firm, Frank Lloyd Wright, would learn from their mastery and become America's most famous architect, employing a new and personal style that has become known as the Prairie School. The term was coined to describe this radical new departure from traditionalist styles, with its origins in the Midwest.

Henry Klutho grew up in Illinois and would have been much exposed to the modern style making inroads in Chicago. While his first formal study came at a business school, he soon attended a drawing academy in St. Louis, where his passion for architecture was ignited. Klutho moved to New York in 1884, further honing his skills in the design of buildings. In 1898 Klutho studied in Europe for a year, acquiring intellectual depth and a firsthand knowledge of the world's great architectural masterpieces.

Henry John Klutho, architect of the original mansion.

The fire in Jacksonville led Klutho to spend the rest of his life in Florida, creating a portfolio of work that has earned him lasting fame. In a recent monograph of Klutho's work, author Robert C. Broward said: "His buildings are the best examples of Prairie School left in the country. In my opinion, his work will be important a hundred years from now, when few other buildings, even those being put up downtown [in Jacksonville] right now, will still be standing."

Even while Klutho was at the cutting edge of architectural design, moving toward a new style of purely American architecture, he was offered the commission for the Florida Governor's Mansion. He was a master at defining the appropriate form that a building should take to accomplish not only its basic role as shelter, but its symbolic role as well.

A look at one of Klutho's Jacksonville commissions bears this out. The Carnegie libraries are well known throughout the nation, as literacy was the chief philanthropic preoccupation of billionaire industrialist Andrew Carnegie. His gifts to cities at the beginning of the twentieth century resulted in some of the nation's finest landmarks. In 1902, following Jacksonville's fire, Carnegie offered $50,000 for a new library.

The commission went to Klutho. In his design for the Jacksonville Free Library at 101 East Adams Street, Klutho drew upon the Greek Revival style for a building that acted as a repository of knowledge. In many respects the building is similar to his design for the governor's mansion. The Greek temple front consists of a portico of double height with Doric columns that carry a pediment, and Klutho adheres to the strictest of symmetry, balancing the elevated, projecting portico with two wings on either side. The choice of limestone as the basic building material is in keeping with the permanence and timelessness of the institution itself.

A TEMPLE OF WOOD

While he designed his own residence in the Prairie School style, Klutho also had the utmost respect for design that resonated in the collective consciousness of the public. Klutho once remarked:

> Design is of paramount importance. A project should be so designed as to indicate its function. A church, a school, a hospital, a public building, or an office building should each be recognizable as such. A project should be made to harmonize with its environment.

With this view central in his mind, it comes as no surprise that Klutho would choose the same Greek Revival design for the first governor's mansion in Tallahassee.

The design demanded an architecture of permanence, one that harked back to the ancient ideals of the democratic tradition. For that reason a mansion designed almost as a Greek temple, though built of wood, was the choice for the "People's House." An expansive portico wrapped around the building on three sides, with clustered Ionic columns spanning the two stories to terminate in a pedimented gable front. A traditional dentiled molding was carried along the perimeter to embellish the entablature. The appearance of the mansion was heavy, grounded, and imposing.

The Browards hosted their first reception in the twenty-room mansion in May 1907, though it was not yet completely finished. The scene must have been one of awe, as the sheer volume of the residence was impressive. Klutho's interior featured a wide central hallway leading to an imposing central staircase, with public rooms off the hall on either side, where a profusion of windows brought in ample light and air. The family's private bedrooms were on the second floor.

PERSPECTIVE (AND POPULATION) CHANGES

As imposing as the mansion was, over time its scale no longer awed. Just as Florida's growth expanded exponentially—with surges following World War I, leading to the 1920s real estate boom, and then after World War II the influx of returning servicemen—even the governor's mansion needed more room. The dining room was just a bit larger than the kitchen and could only seat twelve, and the parlor and sitting room had serious space limitations as the number of guests continued to increase.

By the time that Fuller Warren was elected governor in 1949, the mansion's physical limitations and the grumbling about them had reached a flashpoint. Its physical deterioration added to the zeal for replacement. Today, it is distressing to think that this venerable building, not yet fifty years old, was demolished without some other alternative considered. However, a different mindset existed in the 1950s, as the nation was in the midst of urban renewal. "Old" was not so much a distinction as a liability. The nation's preservation ethic was not yet universally acknowledged (only in 1966 was the National Historic Preservation Act passed).

Some legislators did champion the preservation and repair of the governor's mansion, as did the local United Daughters of the Confederacy, who sought to adapt the building for a museum. Other legislators thought that the continuing growth of Tallahassee was squeezing the mansion and that a suburban location was more appropriate.

As these points were argued, Governor Warren remained steadfastly determined to construct a new mansion. He once referred to the 1907 mansion as the "State Shack" and told the legislature: "I've had to move my bed two or three times to keep plaster from falling on the occupant."

In 1952 Warren made this plea to the state legislature:

> I further recommend a sum of money to be appropriated sufficient to build an adequate residence for Florida's Chief Executive. The Executive Mansion is nearly fifty years old and in dilapidated condition. Its chimneys have been condemned as unsafe for use. . . . It is not believed that repairs can put the Mansion in a condition adequate and safe for human habitation.

Governor Fuller Warren is helped by his sister Alma to prepare for his inaugural day in 1949.

The die was cast. In the next few years came the funding, design, and construction of a new governor's mansion, one reflecting the vision of a contemporary Florida but constructed to stand the test of ages.

The *Tallahassee True Democrat* reported on August 10, 1906: "The building is as yet incomplete. From what stands there—its broad front and many windows—it is to be undoubtedly a noble structure, fitted exactly for this clime and purpose." Less than fifty years later, demolition befell the original mansion.

CHAPTER THREE

A MID-CENTURY MASTERPIECE

The Present Governor's Mansion

s we reflect on the decade of the 1950s, we remember a relatively quiet time in American history—at least domestically. Television was supplanting the radio as America's favorite pastime, and television programming was mild, with many shows like *Ozzie and Harriet, Father Knows Best*, and *The Lone Ranger* celebrating the nuclear family and the virtues of unselfish heroism. Our thirty-fourth president Dwight David Eisenhower, elected in 1952 (himself a hero of World War II), led his administration with concentration on domestic policy and the watchwords "Peace and Prosperity." During his administration Eisenhower created two new agencies: the Department of Health, Education and Welfare (HEW) and the National Aeronautics and Space Administration (NASA), the latter to have a

STUDY "C-2" EAST ELEVATI
EXECUTIVE MANSION FOR T
TALLAHASSEE, FLA.

WYETH, KING & JOHNSON
ARCHITECTS
WYETH BUILDING·PALM BEACH, FLORIDA
MARCH 18 55

transformational effect on Florida. Americans enjoyed a strong economy with little inflation and very low unemployment. ¶ In Florida, Governor Warren's term ended in 1952. Though he had spurred the legislature to replace the existing mansion, he did not participate in the design and construction phase of the project. The 1953 legislature appropriated $250,000 (the average single family home sold for about $30,000) to build the new quarters of the governor, and Warren's successor, Daniel Thomas McCarty (a citrus grower and cattleman from Fort Pierce), was left in the middle of the sometimes contentious debates about what form it would take, and where it would be built.

Top: Finishing touches to the new governor's mansion included planting young water oak trees on mansion grounds.

Botttom left: Florida Senate president Charley Johns shares a laugh with Governor McCarty on their way to McCarty's inauguration.

Bottom right: Wilton Carlile, son of building contractor J.O. Carlile, stands upon a capital during the construction process.

CONTROVERSY CONTINUES

Tragically, on February 25, 1953, a little over a month after his inauguration, McCarty suffered a debilitating heart attack. Six months later, the governor was admitted to the hospital with a terrible cold that developed into pneumonia. A heart specialist flew in to treat his already weakened heart, but to no avail. Governor Dan McCarty died on September 28, 1953. Even so, during his brief term of office, Governor McCarty influenced the future of a new governor's mansion. In a press conference held in January, newly elected McCarty said that he was well pleased with Florida's huge white executive mansion. "I am impressed with its fine Southern atmosphere," McCarty said, "and do not believe it should be junked." He went on to say: "I much prefer seeing it put in tiptop shape and kept that way. It looks wonderful and I'm delighted to be in it."

His remarks prompted the eighty-year-old Henry John Klutho, the architect of the original mansion, to write and thank him.

> Your statement shows that you have an appreciation of the beauty of our traditional architectural designs—but this appreciation was evidently lacking in our former governor. I feel sure that 90% of our citizens will agree with you. To me it is easily the most impressive old mansion in Tallahassee and one of the most outstanding in all the southern states. You see I am the architect of the "shack" as the former governor calls it.

In June 1953, Governor McCarty appointed a Special Committee on the Governor's Mansion to work with him on recommendations for the new mansion's location, design, and construction. The committee consisted of Secretary of State R.A. Gray (chairman), Attorney General Richard Ervin, State School Superintendent Thomas A. Bailey, State Senator LeRoy Collins, and State Representative Davis Atkinson. Almost immediately the committee was flooded with letters offering residential real estate outside the capital area as a new home for a new mansion. Brinkley Brothers Realtors wrote a particularly thoughtful letter pointing out why the mansion should be relocated: the vicinity of the current mansion had changed from a strictly residential area to a commercial one; the mansion's present site lacked adequate acreage around it;

and the land and mansion could be sold to help fund a new mansion located within a five-mile radius of the city of Tallahassee.

The site of the new mansion caused quite a stir around the state. On July 22 John D. Pennekamp, associate editor of the *Miami Herald*, wrote to Senator Collins asking him for his thoughts on the matter. Collins was somewhat circumspect in his reply, acknowledging that because his own home, the Grove, was directly north of the present mansion site, some might perceive a conflict of interest. He made it clear that his response was purely his personal point of view.

Senator Collins was strongly in favor of a location that provided public access. "The social entertaining facilities should be open to the public frequently." Collins wrote, "and also should be a tourist attraction for people to ride by, look at, and take pictures of." He continued, "If I were governor I believe that I would want to take care of the big bulk of my administrative work right at the mansion, and go down to the Capitol to see visitors, attend Board meetings, make inspections, etc." He summarized his opinion in this way: "It is obvious that a mansion to serve these purposes should be downtown and near the Capitol, and regardless of where the mansion is located within town, I personally don't feel that it should be out in the country. While the Governor is in Tallahassee I think he should expect to be somewhat in the center of things." Senator Collins added as an afterthought: "This would not preclude him from running out to a fishing camp from time to time when he had the need for getting away from it all."

On July 30 Senator Collins wrote to Governor McCarty asking to be relieved of his mansion committee duties, putting to rest any perception of his own self-interests. The very next day, the governor reluctantly accepted his resignation.

Former governor Millard F. Caldwell (1945–1949) also weighed in on the issue. He was unequivocally *against* building a new mansion on the same site. While he favored keeping the old mansion for a museum or university purpose, he ended his letter: "Although I am confident that the present site will never be accepted, the bare suggestion shocks and impels me, as one privileged to know the facts first hand."

Just two days before Governor McCarty's death, Walter E. Keyes, the director of the Florida State Improvement Commission, completed an engineering survey of the old mansion and provided the governor with estimates for its rehabilitation. Keyes wrote that it would cost $135,784 "to put the Governor's Mansion in a safe and more permanent condition." He recommended that the budget be increased an additional $15,000 for contingencies. "It has been my experience," Keyes wrote, "that when you open up an old structure for the purpose of repair you find obstacles to overcome that are unknown in the original estimate." For many, his remark was the understatement of the year.

Looking at more than $150,000 in repair costs, the ardor of those who wished to keep the old mansion was dampened to the point where it was deemed fiscally irresponsible to look into the matter any further. After McCarty's death on September 28, Charley E. Johns, president of the Florida Senate, became the acting governor. Although in 1954 Johns ran to complete the last two years of Governor McCarty's term, Tallahassee native LeRoy Collins defeated him, and Johns returned to the senate where he continued to serve until 1966.

Governor Charley Johns

DECISION TIME: LEROY COLLINS LEADS

Governor and Mrs. Mary Call Darby Collins (the great-granddaughter of Florida's territorial governor Richard Keith Call) moved the short distance from the Grove, built by Call in 1825, to the 1907 mansion. It was time to resolve the conflicts about the new mansion, and Governor Collins was more than up to the task. The governor and his cabinet made the final decision to demolish the old mansion and to build on the same site. A majority of legislators approved, and it was now time to select the architect and the mansion's form.

Governor Collins began by appointing an architect selection committee that included Robert H. Brown, the architect-engineer for the Board of Commissioners of State Institutions, the agency charged with executing public works projects. He then gathered some of the most influential architects from around the state, including Gustav Maas and John Volk from Palm Beach; Marion Sims Wyeth, with the firm of Wyeth, King and Johnson from Palm Beach and New York; James Gamble Rogers from Winter Park; and Earnest Stidolf from Tallahassee. They collectively selected sixty-seven-year-old Marion Sims Wyeth, whose achievements in designing magnificent homes spanned a lifetime, as the lead designer for the new mansion.

Following a ruling by the Florida Supreme Court allowing Collins to pursue another four-year term, he would face an election in 1956, so there were no guarantees that the Collins family would ever occupy the new edifice.[‡] Mary Call Collins had no illusions about their status, but took on the job with intensity and single-mindedness. In an April 1956 interview with the *Winter Haven Daily News Chief*, she said: "Of course it would be fun to be the first woman to live in it, but that isn't my primary concern. I want it to be a house that the whole state is proud of, whether I ever live in it or not. . . I don't see it as just any beautiful house. It can't be any particular person's house, mine, or anyone else's. It belongs to every citizen in Florida."

Opposite: Governor and Mrs. Daniel McCarty with their young family.

[‡] The Florida Constitution at that time prohibited a governor from serving two successive four-year terms. The court ruled favorably for Collins because he had served only two years of Governor McCarty's term. The Florida Constitution was amended in 1968 to allow two four-year terms.

WYETH HONORS THE HERMITAGE

Architect Wyeth was instructed to model the new mansion after President Andrew Jackson's Hermitage, an early-nineteenth-century Greek Revival home on his plantation in Tennessee. Florida's connection to Andrew Jackson was a strong one, as he had been appointed its first territorial governor and was the prime mover in its statehood.

The Collins family had an even greater connection with the man dubbed "Old Hickory." Not only had Richard Keith Call been Jackson's chief military aide, but the men's friendship was so great that Richard married Mary Kirkman at the Hermitage on July 15, 1824. Then United States Senator Andrew Jackson gave the bride away. Consequently, it seemed more than fitting to honor that nineteenth-century leader by constructing a visual memorial to him. After all, the home of the state's chief executive needed to be timeless, looking back to Florida's achievements and forward to its aspirations. Governor Collins wrote to the Hermitage requesting a set of plans to ensure that his architect had the means to truly understand President Jackson's magnificent estate.

In August 1955, architect Wyeth personally visited the Hermitage to experience the place. His ultimate objective was not to create an imitation of the Hermitage, but to extrapolate from its form and create a mansion that truly belonged to Florida.

ANDREW JACKSON'S HERMITAGE

While always looking forward to progress, newly independent Americans looked back to antiquity, toward the ideals embodied in Greek and Roman design. During the mid-eighteenth century, Greek art was rediscovered with the excavations at Pompeii and Herculaneum. Books illustrating the richness of the art and architecture were published in France and England, capturing the popular imagination of a world hungry for pedigree.

In 1770, Thomas Jefferson designed his own residence, Monticello, in Charlottesville, Virginia, capturing the quintessential details of Greek architecture in the prominent portico, symmetry of massing, and avoidance of applied ornament. In the next century, President Andrew Jackson would build a home whose timeless classical architecture greatly influenced the character of the present Florida Governor's Mansion.

Andrew Jackson was one of America's most flamboyant figures, earning his reputation for unrelenting ambition, excesses, and tireless enthusiasm for life and its possibilities. Born in South Carolina in 1767, Jackson spent much of his lifetime against a backdrop of armed conflict. At just thirteen, he volunteered for the Revolutionary War and ultimately rose to major general in the War of 1812. He studied law in North Carolina and was licensed by 1787. Jackson's enduring link to Florida is his appointment as its first territorial governor in 1821.

In 1804 Jackson purchased land in east Georgia (presently just outside of downtown Nashville) and moved into a log farmhouse on the plantation. His home would undergo several incarnations,

growing in stature as he assumed more important roles in the state and nation. Between 1819 and 1821, Jackson built a two-story Federal Style residence for his family on his thriving plantation of over one thousand acres. The brick home featured a front-facing side-gabled roof, a prominent doorway with sidelights, and the regular spacing of equally sized rectangular windows across the façade on both stories, creating a series of five bays. Jackson initially called his estate Rural Retreat but later changed the name to the Hermitage, meaning roughly the same thing.

Jackson was elected president in 1828. In 1831, while living in Washington, he hired Nashville architect David Morrison to remodel the home. A portico, confined to the center bay, extended the original home outward, and one-story hipped-roof pavilions were added on either end of this main block. The portico's Doric columns supported a second-story balcony.

In 1834, a devastating chimney fire damaged the mansion. Jackson employed master builders and architects Joseph Reiff and William C. Hume to rebuild. While the mansion's basic symmetry was retained—a central entrance flanked by two equal bays—the changes

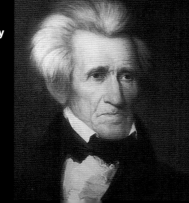

Governor Collins was quite clear in his charge to the architect concerning the interior spaces. They were to serve three basic purposes: (1) to provide spacious areas for state receptions, dinners, and other public functions; (2) to provide independent family living quarters so that more elegant state function areas could be spared the wear and tear of family use; and (3) to provide some office accommodations, so that business conferences and other work could be conducted without interfering with family uses. To accomplish this, the mansion was designed with twenty rooms, including five bedrooms.

The site itself allowed for some manipulation of the space. The mansion faces east and is located on the rise of a steep hill. Behind it, to the west, the ground steeply drops off. A view of the mansion's two-story front is deceiving, as there are three stories to the central block: a ground story is concealed in the hillside behind the mansion.

Wyeth developed several variations to his basic design. In the schemes *not* selected, he revealed a greater part of the roof and, while still using the one-story pavilions on either side of the central block, varied the roof designs by pitching them steeper as well. The connecting wings were also made more prominent in the alternative designs. In a 2005 interview former first lady Mary Call Collins explained that she preferred the hipped roof design for the pavilions, but that it was Captain Gray (Secretary of

represented a dramatic departure from the earlier look.

In the 1831 building, the side-gabled roof was most prominent. The new design all but obliterated the roofline in favor of a two-story portico that ended in a flat entablature carried across the entire width of the façade. Rather than focusing the center pedimented bay as in the earlier design, the two-story colossal portico distributed the focus equally throughout the façade, producing an even grander look. The

side pavilion roofs were also flattened. The remodeling was completed in 1836, and it was here that Jackson retired after leaving the presidency in 1837. The Florida Governor's Mansion is patterned after the home's final realization.

Jackson died on June 8, 1845, just seventeen days before the inauguration of Florida's first elected governor, William Moseley. At the inaugural celebration, many wore black armbands in Jackson's memory, a very personal tribute to the man who did so much to see that Florida became a state.

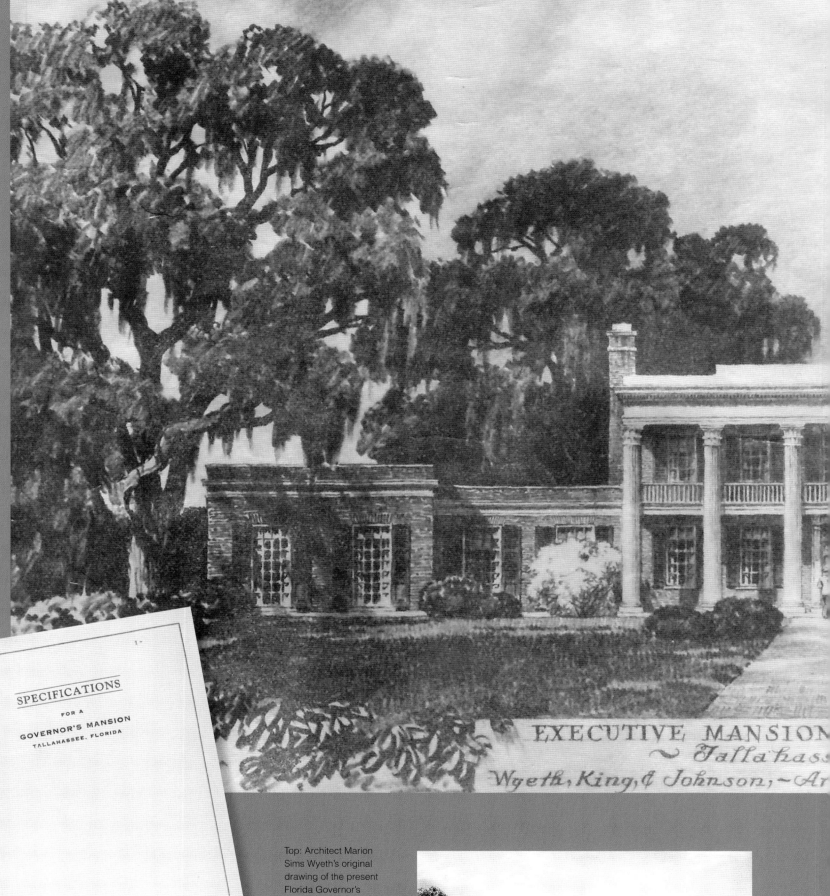

SPECIFICATIONS

FOR A

GOVERNOR'S MANSION

TALLAHASSEE, FLORIDA

WYETH, KING & JOHNSON

ARCHITECTS
PALM BEACH, FLORIDA

EXECUTIVE MANSION
~ Tallahass
Wyeth, King, & Johnson, - Ar

Top: Architect Marion Sims Wyeth's original drawing of the present Florida Governor's Mansion.

Bottom: Two potential design schemes (left and center) with pitched roofs were ultimately rejected due to cost, and the final design (right) was constructed.

the STATE of FLORIDA

Florida ~

tects – Palm Beach, Florida

SCHELL LEWIS
1 9 5 5

EXECUTIVE MANSION FOR THE STATE OF FLORIDA
TALLAHASSEE, FLORIDA
WYETH, KING & JOHNSON – ARCHITECTS
PALM BEACH, FLORIDA

State Robert A. Gray) who insisted that the roofs be flat to avoid what he considered too great an expense. (Robert Gray held considerable influence. He eventually served an unprecedented thirty-one-year term as secretary of state, from 1930 to 1961. The Tallahassee building named for him now houses the state history museum and archives and its historic and archaeological preservation staff.)

Wyeth arranged the interior of the mansion so that guests entered into a commodious entrance hall. Beyond that were the formal state rooms: the reception room (the largest room in the house), reached through a doorway at the north end of the hall, and the formal dining room, designed to seat twenty-four, reached through a doorway on axis with the main entranceway. The huge kitchen and pantry, adjacent to the dining room on the south, was designed to handle preparations for elaborate state functions. Adjoining it was the family kitchen and the governor's living quarters, which included a dining room and sitting/ living room. The north wing was reserved for the guest bedroom with its own private bath.

The second floor contained the private bedrooms and included a master bedroom suite with adjoining bath and three other bedrooms, each with private bath. The basement floor was designed to include the governor's office (approached through an adjacent room for his secretary), a laundry, rooms to accommodate the mechanical equipment for the heating and air conditioning systems, storage space, and offices and restrooms for the staff.

In mid-May and in early June, the state ran two separate advertisements soliciting bids in major newspapers across the state. One was for the demolition and the other for construction. Architect Wyeth completed the final plans, and the state cabinet unsealed the bids received for construction in June 1955. The contract for construction was awarded to J.O. Carlile, a Tallahassee builder, and the demolition duties were assigned to the P.L. Burkhalter Wrecking Company of Jacksonville. The local architectural firm of Prentiss, Huddleston and Associates was also hired to serve as Wyeth's on-site representative.

In December 1955, a little less than a year after Governor Collins's inauguration, the original 1907 mansion was razed and most of the furnishings sold at auction. Governor Collins and his family moved temporarily back into the Grove and could watch as progress was made on the new structure.

A COMMISSION, SERENDIPITY, AND COGAR

Prior to the creation of the Governor's Mansion Commission by the 1957 legislature, Governor Collins received permission from the cabinet to appoint a Mansion Advisory Commission (sometimes referred to as a "Committee"). On July 15, 1955, the governor appointed a distinguished group of Tallahassee citizens, with Mr. Frank Moor, a real estate executive, to serve as chairman, and Mrs. Thomas D. Bailey, Mrs. John H. Phipps, Mrs. Rod K. Shaw, Mrs. J. Edwin White, and Mr. William Watson, as members. The Mansion Advisory Committee assumed a great role in the mansion's construction and became the conduit for the daily decisions required as the building took shape.

One wonders whether the commission members were fully aware of the demands on their time that this appointment would make. In particular, Chairman Moor served as the go-between with the governor and cabinet and the architects and engineers. The commission was especially vigilant in its duties, as Governor Collins was busy running a reelection campaign. In fact, this all-volunteer committee met five times in July 1955 and *fifteen* times in 1956. Mary Call Collins and the mansion commission were left to make the myriad decisions that went with the building's construction, along with furnishing the rooms and landscaping the grounds for this, the most important commission in the state.

After the original mansion was demolished in December 1955, preparation of the construction site began. Details were still being worked out to determine the materials and finishes for the mansion. The choice of brick over hollow clay tiles for the basic building materials spoke to the permanence meant to be conveyed. By January 1956, building could begin in earnest. Construction proceeded at a frantic pace as the walls of the mansion grew from the ground. The target date for its completion was early 1957.

With the building well underway, the next most urgent matter was to determine how it would be furnished, the color schemes, and the fixtures which would complement the whole. The Mansion Advisory Commission

> "I just learned from Nelson that the best decorator at Williamsburg was James Cogar, who now has a gallery in Williamsburg and can be reached there. . . . Nelson said this man was really the one who had the best ideas and fine taste."

MARY ROCKEFELLER IN A LETTER TO MRS. JOHN H. PHIPPS

Top left: Letter written by Mrs. Mary Rockefeller to Governor's Mansion Commission member Mrs. John H. (Clippy) Phipps, recommending James Cogar.

Top right: Mrs. John H. Phipps seated in the state entrance hall, many years later.

Bottom: Mr. and Mrs. Frank Moor who chaired the Governor's Mansion Commission during its infancy.

The Chronology of Construction

1953
Legislature appropriates $250,000 for construction of new governor's mansion.

January 1953
Governor Daniel McCarty's inauguration.

June 1953
Governor McCarty appoints a committee to select site for the mansion.

July 1953
State Senator LeRoy Collins resigns from committee, observing that his participation could be perceived as a conflict of interest because his home, the Grove, is just north of existing mansion.

September 17, 1953
Site committee unanimously recommends grounds of Florida State University, a location the Board of Commissioners soon rejects.

September 28, 1953
Governor McCarty dies while in office; Charley Johns becomes acting governor.

January 1955
LeRoy Collins inaugurated governor after beating Johns in an election to fill McCarty's unfinished term; Governor Collins and cabinet decide not to change mansion site.

February 1955
Palm Beach architect Marion Sims Wyeth commissioned to design the mansion. Wyeth agrees to work for a fee that represents "no more than cost."

March 1955
Wyeth sends plans for new mansion to governor for approval.

May/June 1955
Advertisements for bids from building contractors and from demolition companies appear in newspapers statewide.

Mid-June 1955
Wyeth plans completed.

Late June 1955
Bids opened. J.O. Carlile (Tallahassee) selected as building contractor, P.L. Burkhalter Wrecking Company (Jacksonville) for demolition.

July 1955
Governor Collins appoints Mansion Advisory Committee.

August 1955
Wyeth visits Andrew Jackson's Hermitage outside of Nashville, the residence he is instructed to emulate.

December 1955
Demolition of 1907 mansion completed.

January 1956
Building begins on new mansion.

May 1956
Interior plastering completed.

June 1956
James Cogar, the first curator of Colonial Williamsburg, completes three-day interview for position of decorator.

August 1956
Contract between Cogar and state executed. Cogar, assigned to furnish mansion with eighteenth- and nineteenth-century period pieces, leaves on buying trip to British Isles.

January 8, 1957
Governor Collins's second inauguration. Mansion completed, though still unfurnished; public gets first view during open house.

February 1957
Florida Nurserymen and Growers Association agrees to contribute shrubbery for mansion grounds.

April 18, 1957
Governor and Mrs. Collins conduct preview of new mansion for Florida Society of Editors.

April 25, 1957
First official social event at mansion: the traditional governor's reception honoring legislators.

1957
Legislature formally establishes Governor's Mansion Commission, "charged with preserving the style and character of the original plan of construction and furnishing."

May 1957
Governor Collins moves his family from the Grove into new mansion.

began a search to find the right decorator to fulfill their collective vision. One of those under consideration was James L. Cogar.

As so often happens, the consideration of Cogar was a consequence of serendipity. Mrs. John H. Phipps was a friend of Mary French Rockefeller, who was married to Laurance S. Rockefeller (1910–2004), financier, philanthropist, and conservationist. Laurance was the son of John D. Rockefeller, Jr., and brother to Nelson. John D. Rockefeller, Jr., was the man who almost single-handedly financed and directed the restoration of Colonial Williamsburg, Virginia's eighteenth-century capital, beginning in the late 1920s.

In a letter to Mrs. Phipps, Mary Rockefeller wrote: "I just learned from Nelson that the best decorator at Williamsburg was James Cogar, who now has a gallery in Williamsburg and can be reached there. . . . Nelson said this man was really the one who had the best ideas and fine taste." Mrs. Phipps personally contacted Cogar in Williamsburg and began the chain of events that led to securing his services for the mansion.

In a letter to Cogar in May 1956, Frank Moor estimated there would be approximately $100,000 for the mansion's decoration and furnishings. "It is the belief of the committee as well as the Architect for the Mansion," Moor wrote, "that the décor of all the State rooms should be in keeping with the period (circa 1812) of the Hermitage."

Cogar was asked to come to Tallahassee for an extended interview with the committee in June 1956. In accepting the invitation, Cogar wrote: "I should like to explain that I do not consider that I am a decorator in the strict sense of the word. For seventeen years I was Curator of Colonial Williamsburg which included not only work of a decorating nature, but considerable research on the projects which were undertaken and intensive study of period decoration."

"A GRACIOUS HOME"

In response to Moor's letter, Cogar explained his approach to the mansion's decoration: "My overall plan for the Governor's Mansion would be to have it a dignified interior, painted in a harmonious color scheme, furnished in good taste with pieces of character, and although an official residence, give to it the feeling of a

Opposite: The *Tallahassee Democrat* announced the first Mansion Open House on January 8, 1957. Governor and Mrs. Collins and their daughters in front of the new mansion.

Top: The address is 700 North Adams Street, an empty lot once again in 1955, when the original mansion was razed.

JAMES L. COGAR
139 YORK STREET
WILLIAMSBURG, VIRGINIA

June 18, 1956

Mr. Frank D. Moor, Chairman
Governor's Mansion Advisory Committee
Post Office Box 749
Tallahassee, Florida

Dear Mr. Moor:

Allow me first to say how much I enjoyed meeting with you and your committee in Tallahassee and I did appreciate your many courtesies during my stay.

I have given a great deal of thought to the furnishing of the new Governor's Mansion, in fact I have thought of little else since my return. I honestly feel that you have a real opportunity to do something very special and to have a mansion that will be outstanding in every way. As it is a new building I believe that you will create an interior of distinction by using as many antique pieces as may be practical and come within the limit of your budget. Such pieces give real atmosphere and a subtle grandeur and are doubly effective in a building which is of entirely new construction. I further believe that by careful buying and a knowledge of good antiques and where to find them this can be accomplished. Having been in this field since my college days I do not think that I am speaking without authority when I say that it is perfectly possible.

Should you decide that I am the person to do this I will begin to line up all possible antique pieces

(5)

JAMES L. COGAR
139 YORK STREET
WILLIAMSBURG, VIRGINIA

s I told the Committee when I met with them
eaving August 9 for Great Britain and will
around the middle of November. On this
could be on the lookout for suitable pieces
Mansion. As I will not teach at the College
am and Mary the fall semester I will be free
turn to give my undivided attention to the
n of the Governor's Mansion. The final
could be easily completed by January 1 and
n shown without furnishings at that time.
two months the furniture and furnishings
place and the building ready for occupancy.
in like to stress the advisability of not
job but doing it with great care and at-
rder to produce satisfactory results.
this pertains to the paint schedule also.
sonally like to see the walls have the
properly before paint is applied. It
submit a paint schedule before 1 leave
since the responsibility will be mine
appearance I should like to be on hand
ng is being done and not have it com-
in advance of the actual furnishing

am retained to do the furnishing of
mansion or not I wish for you and your
e Committee the very best success possible which I
know you will have because of the care and attention
you are giving to this worthwhile project.

Yours very sincerely,

James L. Cogar

James L. Cogar

"The jumble of furniture styles and the constantly changing wallpaper and color schemes which shifted with every change of administration in the old Mansion that was torn down was a lesson in the need for a good plan. The home of the state's chief executive needed to be timeless, representing both its aspirations and accomplishments. What better way to embody those noble ideals than to look back to the time of Florida's statehood? Nineteenth century America was a time of expansionism, a time of fearless exploration, a time of industrialization, a time of explosive unrest and wrenching separation. In the end, the ideals and philosophical bedrock of the American people was firmly implanted."

THE *TALLAHASSEE DEMOCRAT* IN AN EDITORIAL

PUBLISHED IMMEDIATELY FOLLOWING COGAR'S SELECTION

gracious home of quiet beauty that would please but not overpower those that were entertained there."

His ideas were clearly consistent with those of the commission and the governor, and in August 1956, Cogar's contract was signed. The contract obligated him to decorate the entire mansion, with the exception of the kitchen, service areas, and pantries. "Decoration" included all the choices of rugs, carpeting, draperies, furniture, upholstery, accessories, and colors, including colors for walls and ceilings.

In an editorial published immediately following Cogar's selection, the *Tallahassee Democrat* had this to say: "The jumble of furniture styles and the constantly changing wallpaper and color schemes which shifted with every change of administration in the old Mansion that was torn down was a lesson in the need for a good plan. The home of the state's chief executive needed to be timeless, representing both its aspirations and accomplishments. What better way to embody those noble ideals than to look back to the time of Florida's statehood?" The editors categorically agreed with the period chosen to best represent the state: "Nineteenth century America was a time of expansionism, a time of fearless exploration, a time of industrialization, a time of explosive unrest and wrenching separation. In the end, the ideals and philosophical bedrock of the American people was firmly implanted."

Even with a limited budget, Cogar recognized that the mansion should be furnished with fine antiques. By doing so, the newly constructed building would benefit from the pedigree of its furnishings. He told the committee that, "As a new building, I believe that you will create an interior of distinction by using as many antique pieces as may be practical and within the limit of your budget. Such pieces give real atmosphere and a subtle grandeur and are doubly effective in a building which is entirely of new construction."

In August 1956, Cogar left for a buying trip to the British Isles. His journey took him to England, Scotland, and Ireland, where he personally selected many of the pieces that were to grace the mansion. The inventory of his purchases evidences the depth of Cogar's insights into eighteenth- and early-nineteenth-century America. For example, for the state dining room Cogar purchased a set of nine mahogany Chippendale chairs (c. 1770) in Belfast, Ireland ($1,326); a late-eighteenth-century (c. 1780) inlaid mahogany English sideboard in Malmesbury, Wiltshire ($1,500); and a Chippendale-style mahogany tier table in Stirling, Scotland ($270). One of Cogar's favorite pieces was the grandfather's clock for the entry hall. He purchased the Chippendale-style mahogany piece in Dundee, Scotland, for $600.

Cogar greatly valued antique pieces for the mansion, but he was also a pragmatist. For that reason he called for a number of reproduction pieces to be used for the furnishings receiving the greatest wear and tear, like the sofas and chairs. Cogar's experience in the field would once again bear on the quality of the reproductions used in the mansion. While serving as Colonial Williamsburg's curator, Cogar was involved in a craft program begun in 1937. Largely because of public demand, Colonial Williamsburg sought out manufacturers who could reproduce the original furniture for sale. The Kittinger Furniture Company of Buffalo, New York, was selected as the exclusive licensee. Kittinger was selected because of its fine craftsmanship, producing pieces within the highest standards and exactitude demanded. For many years Kittinger artisans, dressed in eighteenth-century garb, demonstrated their craft at the Ayscough House at Colonial Williamsburg. Cogar purchased the governor's mansion reproduction pieces from the Kittinger

Opposite: James L. Cogar was eminently qualified to provide decorative arts expertise to the members of the Governor's Mansion Commission. His notes reveal a painstaking penchant for detail which was evident throughout his presentation materials.

"With a view toward getting the best possible job, the Road Department has made arrangements with a contractor from Tampa to furnish several experienced paving brick men to do the work in accordance with the best established practices in that area. It was in the Tampa area that Mrs. Collins saw several brick drives that appealed to her very much."

ROBERT BROWN, ARCHITECT-ENGINEER

Company, demonstrating his rigorously high standards in everything installed at the mansion. Today reproductions by the Kittinger Company, no longer in business, are themselves highly sought after.

FINISHING TOUCHES

Meanwhile Governor Collins was soundly reelected. He made political history in Florida when he defeated five Democratic candidates (including former governor Fuller Warren) and became the first Florida governor to win a first primary victory. He ran against Republican William A. Washburne, Jr., in the general election, winning by an almost 3–1 margin. The newly reelected governor attended his second inauguration ceremony on January 8, 1957. Although still unfurnished, the mansion was opened to the public for the very first time that day.

Now that the interior of the mansion and its furnishings were under control, the final details could be considered. Those details included the landscaping, driveways, and other site improvements. The iron fence that had surrounded the original 1907 mansion was removed, and the choice was made to pave the drives and walkways with brick. The selection of contractors to lay the brick was problematic, as a relatively small number of contractors had experience with the special nature of the material. In a letter dated December 7, 1956, architect-engineer Robert Brown told the mansion committee that it was nigh impossible to lay the brick for the curving driveway with the patterns usually laid for rectangular patios or terraces.

To secure the best possible artisans, Brown took charge. He said: "With a view toward getting the best possible job, the Road Department has made arrangements with a contractor from Tampa to furnish several experienced paving brick men to do the work in accordance with the best established practices in that area. It was in the Tampa area that Mrs. Collins saw several brick drives that appealed to her very much." The brick came from the streets of Tampa, salvaged when the old trolley tracks were removed. Mrs. Collins later said she was so impressed with Tampa's contribution of the bricks and labor that she did not think there was any way to adequately thank those whose largesse made the brickwork happen.

To assist with the beautification of the grounds, advisory committee members Mrs. Phipps and Mrs. Shaw persuaded landscape architect Henry Shaw from Florida State University to donate his time to the mansion project. They further convinced the Florida Nurserymen and Growers Association to donate untold numbers of plant materials, trees, and shrubs for the beautification of the grounds.

On April 18, 1957, Governor and Mrs. Collins held a special preview for the Florida Society of Editors, headed by James Clendinen of the *Tampa Tribune*. A Mount Dora newspaper covering the story characterized the visit in this way:

> Expressing the enthusiasm of children showing off a fabulous doll house, the Collinses took their guests over the entire mansion, showing its formal drawing room, its state guest room and the state dining room now big enough for a dinner party that could include the Cabinet and the Supreme Court justices. Mrs. Collins acknowledged that she was apprehensive with the great length of the dining table, fearing that she might not be able to see who was at the opposite end.

The first official social event took place one week later, when the state's legislators were honored at the traditional governor's reception. Governor and Mrs. Collins made the move to their new home in May.

The governor's mansion, completed by the end of December 1956, and occupied by the spring of 1957, is now at the threshold of the half-century mark. Residents, guests, and visitors who have been a part of its fifty-year history bear testament not only to the changes that have occurred, but also to the permanence of tradition and the great role that the mansion continues to play in the lives of all Floridians.

Opposite: Detail of the semi-circular driveway's bricks, embossed with the names of the companies which made them. The bricks provide a warm accent to the current mansion grounds. First Lady Mary Call Collins felt that the bricklayers were never adequately thanked for the beauty which their work added to the mansion landscaping.

CHAPTER FOUR

DESIGN AND DÉCOR
A Perfect Meld

he new governor's mansion was envisioned after Americans emerged from the trials of World War II into a new world where optimism reigned, personal wealth skyrocketed, and federal laws helped returning servicemen and women buy homes and go to college. After President Roosevelt signed the GI Bill into law in 1944, hundreds of thousands of veterans enrolled in college, creating a boom in campus building. A Veterans Administration loan allowed veterans to purchase a home with as little as one dollar down and a low monthly mortgage. ¶ Socially this meant the abandonment of the city center for the suburbs, where land was still inexpensive and development was rampant. The quintessential suburb Levittown, in Long Island, New York, established trends emulated throughout the United States. Beginning in 1947, thousands of "cookie-cutter" houses were constructed on former potato fields. Levittown, masterminded by William Levitt, established a basic but eminently versatile house type that lent itself to expansion. The affordable average cost of $8,000 enabled thousands of families to own houses for the first time. By 1951, Levitt and Sons had built 17,477 homes that ranged from their initial two-story Cape Cod version to the top-selling ranch house. Suburbia and its architecture are important to our story because of the governor's mansion's connection with the ranch style, which reached its apogee of popularity during the 1950s. ¶ When architect Marion Sims Wyeth (1889–1982) was directed to model the mansion after Andrew Jackson's Hermitage, Wyeth had no issue with that choice. He wrote about his design: "As Tallahassee is a part of the 'Deep South' it was only proper that the building be traditional in Southern Colonial style, and in view of the fact that Andrew Jackson was the first Territorial Governor of Florida, the mansion has been inspired by Jackson's famous house." ¶ A comparison of the Hermitage and the Florida Governor's Mansion quickly reveals differences attributable to their periods of building. The Southern Colonial style of the Hermitage leans heavily on classical precedents and bears a strict formality. In contrast, the governor's mansion has a decidedly horizontal emphasis created by the one-story wings that extend out from the central two-story block, ending in pavilions. The plan allowed the building to follow the contours of the land, expressing an organic relationship with the grounds that the Hermitage lacks. The one-story pavilions at the Hermitage connect directly to the central block, creating a more monolithic and formal look. In its more rambling, longitudinal emphasis, the Florida Governor's Mansion reflects the architectural trends of contemporary times.

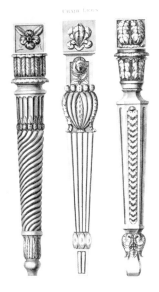

CHAIR LEGS

Left: Detail art from James Cogar's design presentation for the governor's mansion.

Right: Detail of the pelican-shaped handle of the USS *Florida* silver punch bowl.

Opposite top: The state reception room as it originally looked in the late 1950s.

Opposite bottom: A packing label from a British antique company, addressed to James Cogar's design firm, indicating that it was meant for shipment to America and earmarked for the Florida Governor's Mansion.

The Mansion Advisory Commision chose James Lowry Cogar as interior designer for the mansion. With Cogar's infinite knowledge of antiques and dealers, he explained to the mansion commission that antiques purchased in England actually cost less than reproductions from American manufacturers.

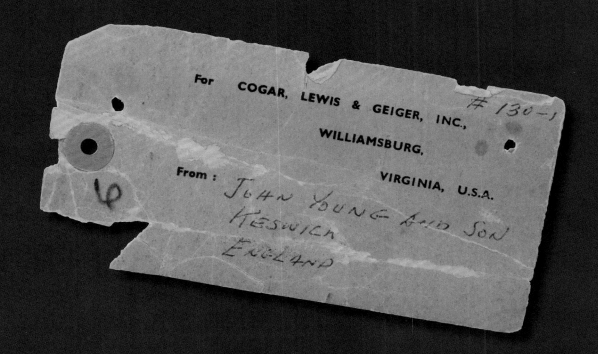

MARION SIMS WYETH: AN ARCHITECT FOR THE AGES

Wyeth's architecture evolved over a long period from his earliest practice in Palm Beach to the mansion project at age sixty-seven. The commission was special to the architect, as he told the *Palm Beach Daily News* in a March 1981 interview: "It was the best job I ever did. It served a dual purpose. It had to be formal and livable too. It was the hardest job to conceive." Wyeth brought to bear all of his previous training and knowledge of classical architecture. His appreciation for rich finishes, decorative touches, and the formality necessary for ceremonial functions melded seamlessly with his understanding that the mansion was a home and sanctuary for the families of the state's chief executive.

Marion Sims Wyeth lived during an age that allowed his prodigious skills and imagination full expression and brought him continuous commissions. He was born into a highly successful and educated family. His grandfather, J. Marion Sims, founded New York's Women's Hospital, and his father, John Wyeth, founded New York's Polyclinic Hospital. Before coming to Florida to design the palatial mansions of the wealthy, Wyeth had an enviable education and apprenticeships with some of the most influential and successful architects practicing during the early twentieth century.

Wyeth graduated from Princeton University in 1910 and went immediately to Paris where he studied at the École des Beaux-Arts until 1914. He was one of the few Americans studying there who was awarded a diploma. Paris was the center of the art world, and the École, founded in the seventeenth century, was the preeminent seat of learning for any who called themselves artists or architects. (The school comprised an Academy of Painting and Sculpture and an Academy of Architecture.) The École stressed classical art and architecture, with study of Greek and Roman precedents paramount in its disciplined approach. The bombastic Beaux-Arts style of architecture, named for the school, perfectly suited the rising kings of turn-of-the-century industrial America.

Following his return to New York, Wyeth worked briefly for Bertram Grosvenor Goodhue. Particularly adept at Gothic Revival designs, Goodhue is credited with the U.S. Military Academy at West Point and the Nebraska state capitol in Lincoln. Wyeth's next assignment surely influenced his decision to work in Florida. He apprenticed with the firm of John M. Carrere and Thomas Hastings in 1916. (Carrere and Hastings had themselves been apprenticed to the firm of McKim, Mead and White, the nation's most influential architectural firm at the end of the nineteenth century). Henry Flagler, the Standard Oil partner of John D. Rockefeller and Florida East Coast Railway baron, hired Carrere and Hastings to design his magnificent Ponce de Leon Hotel in St. Augustine, completed in 1888. As evidence of his esteem for them, in 1901 Flagler hired the firm to design his own residence, Whitehall, in Palm Beach.

Wyeth moved to Palm Beach in 1919, when the town was just beginning its ascendancy as *the* winter capital of America's wealthy and influential. Only one architect was in practice, the legendary Addison Mizner. Although Mizner invited the young Wyeth to work with him, Wyeth chose to go it alone and formed his own company and was commissioned to design a host of mansions in Palm Beach for clients that included Edward F. Hutton, Clarence Geist, and Jay F. Carlisle.

Author Dr. Donald Curl in *Mizner's Florida* explains the friendship and close association that Wyeth and Mizner shared as the leading society architects of the day, as well as Wyeth's immense popularity: "In a career that spanned over fifty years, Wyeth designed houses for practically every street in Palm Beach." Among his major commissions outside of Palm Beach are the J.R. Parrot residence in Jacksonville (1923) and Los Cedros, the Colonel Raymond C. Turck residence in Ortega (1924).

Although Florida's real estate boom collapsed by 1927, this did not substantially affect Wyeth, who was licensed to practice in New York, New Jersey, Massachusetts, Illinois, and Pennsylvania. His wideranging commissions included the Church of the Epiphany, New York City (1926); the plantation for Walker P. Inman in Georgetown, South Carolina (1935); the Worthington Scranton residence in Scranton, Pennsylvania (1940); and the Doris Duke residence Shangri La (a *tour de force* of Islamic inspiration) in Honolulu, Hawaii (1936). In 1934 Wyeth formed a partnership with his lifelong friend Frederic Rhinelander King; William Johnson joined them in 1944. The firm maintained offices in both New York and Palm Beach.

Marion Sims Wyeth, architect of the present governor's mansion.

Opposite top: Detail of a Wyeth drawing of the columns of the entrance portico, juxtaposed against the actual columns (bottom).

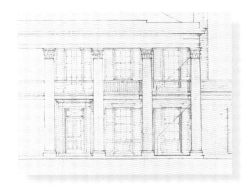

Over the course of his long career, Wyeth is credited with over 700 commissions. In 1954 he was the first Palm Beach architect elected a fellow of the American Institute of Architects, for his "notable contribution in the field of design." (He was elected the same year as Mies Van der Rohe, renowned as a creator of International Style.) It was suitable that this master of design was selected for Florida's most important residential commission: the new governor's mansion in Tallahassee.

JAMES LOWRY COGAR:
FROM A COLONIAL CAPITAL TO FLORIDA'S CAPITAL

In its search for an interior designer, the Mansion Advisory Commission would have preferred a Florida native, yet finding James Lowry Cogar proved a destined match. Cogar as designer was another masterstroke of the commission. James Lowry Cogar (1907–1987) was a 1927 graduate of the University of Kentucky, where his studies included courses in art. In 1929, he received his master's degree from Harvard University in American social history. He later attended Yale for a year, taking courses at the School of Architecture. He became the first curator of Williamsburg in 1931 and held that post until 1948.

Williamsburg, Virginia, was the nation's *first* large-scale outdoor museum project. England had established a colony there as early as 1633. In 1693 King William III and Queen Mary II granted a charter for the College of William and Mary. In 1699, the colonial capital was moved from Jamestown to Williamsburg. The city not only richly represents life in an eighteenth-century British colony but is also inextricably linked to the first stirrings of American independence. In 1765 Patrick Henry delivered his Stamp Act Speech in the House of Burgesses, and in 1774 it was the meeting place for the First Continental Congress. Following the American Revolution, Thomas Jefferson moved the capital to Richmond for better security. As Williamsburg changed with the times, new buildings were constructed and many original British colonial buildings were lost.

In 1924 the Reverend Dr. W.A.R. Goodwin, rector of Williamsburg's Episcopal Bruton Parish Church (established at the colony's founding), met with John D. Rockefeller, Jr., and enlisted his support to restore the colonial capital. During the restoration, almost 600 nonperiod buildings were demolished, 88 original

Top: James Cogar's expertise as the first curator at Colonial Williamsburg was especially fortuitous for Florida.

Bottom: Cogar chose furniture design styles that lent themselves to a dignified, traditional, 18th-century interior.

Opposite: Copious lists made by Cogar reveal his expertise and attention to detail.

eighteenth-century buildings were restored, and an additional 500 buildings were reconstructed using the exacting measurements and details gleaned from historical records and archaeological evidence. The level of detail and obsession with exactitude called for a man like James Lowry Cogar, who was asked to recreate furnishings, colors, and décor for the buildings. While at Williamsburg, Cogar was greatly involved in the work on the Wythe House, the Governor's Palace, the capitol, and the Raleigh Tavern. With this background, Cogar was considered the nation's leading expert on colonial interiors.

After leaving Colonial Williamsburg, he became a partner in the firm of Cogar, Lewis, and Geiger in Williamsburg, operating an antique gallery specializing in eighteenth-century English furniture and furnishings. While there, he also lectured on period social history at the College of William and Mary. It was here that Cogar received the call that set him on a path to the union's southernmost state.

With his infinite knowledge of antiques and dealers, Cogar was well placed to select the furnishings. He explained to the mansion commission that antiques purchased in England actually cost less than reproductions from American manufacturers. Cogar was given a budget of $100,000 for interior painting, draperies, furnishings, light fixtures, venetian blinds, kitchen cabinets, and equipment.

Cogar's list of some furnishings offers insight not only into costs, but also into his characteristic depth of detail.

Antiques	$35,315.00
Fabrication of Drapes	$4,000
Freight (Antiques)	$1,098.66
Curtain Materials	$4,050.54
Upholstering Antiques and Materials	$753.55
Hardware for Installation: Curtains	$339.27
Labor and Materials: Bed Drapery	$1,200.00
Venetian Blinds: Upstairs, Guest Bath, Kitchen	$620.00
Broadloom Rugs: Hovater Bid	$2,861.00
Lighting Fixtures: Halls, Dining Room	$750.00
Rugs for Reception Room (3)	$1,386.00
Rug for Dining Room (18' x 26')	$1,835.20
Reproduction Chairs (Dining Room)	$1,240.00
2 Biggs Reproduction Sofas	$725.00
Reproduction Furniture: Kittinger	$5,765.00
Office Furniture: Kittinger-Shaw	$3,025.00
Lantern for Stair Hall and Mirror for Stair Hall	$530.00
Hauling-Insurance: Antiques	$1,200.00
Lamp Shades	$300.00
Mattresses: Special Size Springs	$300.00
Prints: Stair Hall Passage	$800.00
Reproductions-Antiques: Upstairs	
To Complete Bedrooms	$3,000
Return Rugs: Schumacher	$68.00
Telephone	$16.62

In all, fifty-six chairs and one settee were *bona fide* antiques. The Kittinger Company supplied most of the reproduction pieces, including six wingchairs, six open-arm chairs, three sofas, two "King of Ease" chairs and ottomans, and twelve dining room chairs. The total cost for upholstering these pieces was a little over two thousand dollars. In April 1957 at the request of Mrs. Collins, six Windsor chairs were ordered for the porch. Cogar remains highly regarded for the initial work he performed at the mansion, and ever since, it is his vision that is most closely adhered to.

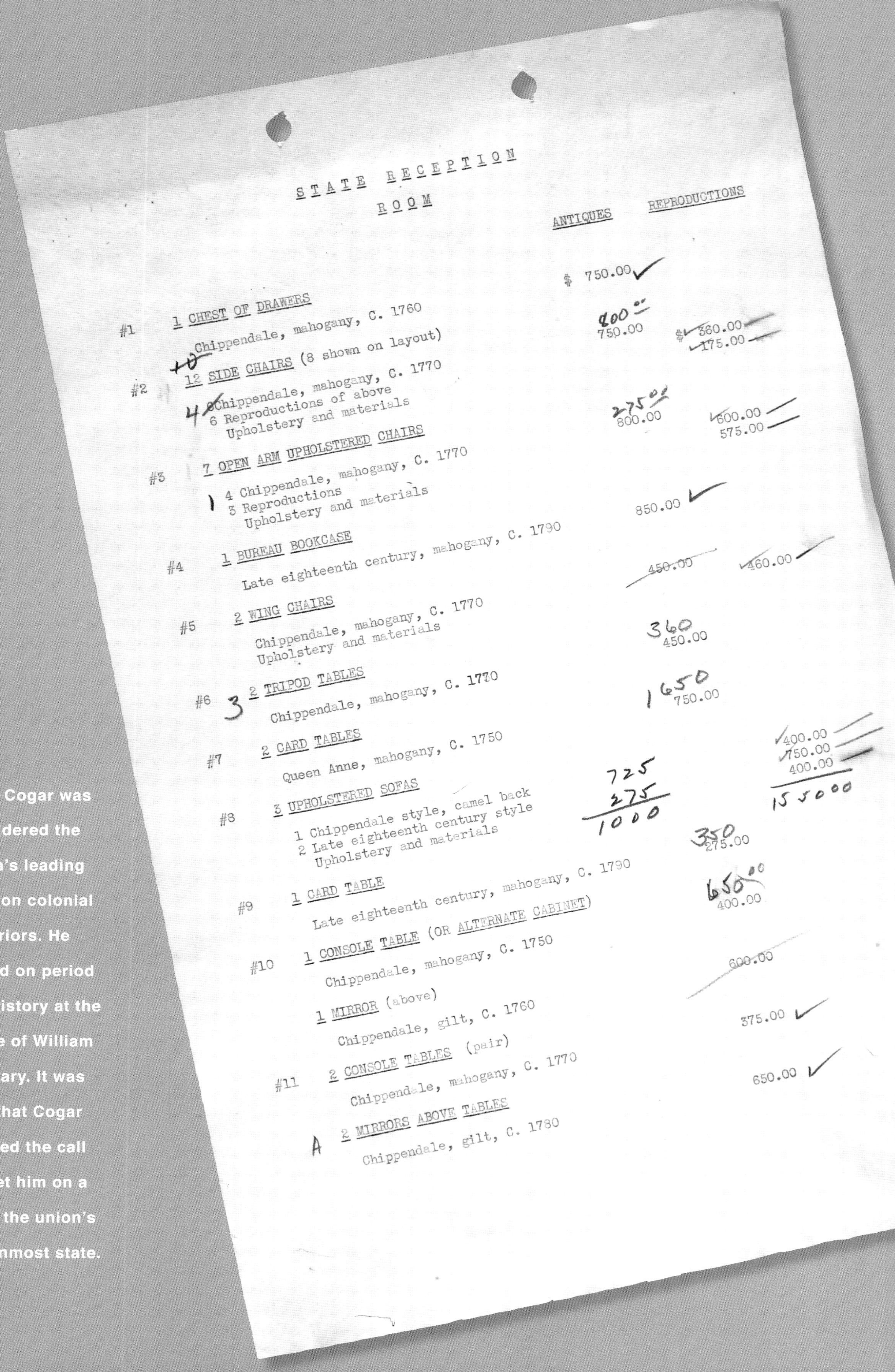

James Cogar was considered the nation's leading expert on colonial interiors. He lectured on period social history at the College of William and Mary. It was here that Cogar received the call that set him on a path to the union's southernmost state.

STATE RECEPTION
ROOM

ANTIQUES   REPRODUCTIONS

$ 750.00 ✓

#1   1 CHEST OF DRAWERS
          Chippendale, mahogany, C. 1760   800.00
      +0   750.00 $ 360.00
#2   12 SIDE CHAIRS (8 shown on layout)   175.00
          Chippendale, mahogany, C. 1770
      48 6 Reproductions of above   275.00
          Upholstery and materials   800.00   600.00
                                                                575.00
#3   7 OPEN ARM UPHOLSTERED CHAIRS
          4 Chippendale, mahogany, C. 1770
      1   3 Reproductions
          Upholstery and materials   850.00 ✓

#4   1 BUREAU BOOKCASE
          Late eighteenth century, mahogany, C. 1790
                                                 450.00   460.00

#5   2 WING CHAIRS
          Chippendale, mahogany, C. 1770   360
          Upholstery and materials   450.00

#6   3 2 TRIPOD TABLES   1650
          Chippendale, mahogany, C. 1770   750.00

#7   2 CARD TABLES   400.00
          Queen Anne, mahogany, C. 1750   725   750.00
                                                  275   400.00
#8   3 UPHOLSTERED SOFAS   1000
          1 Chippendale style, camel back   155000
          2 Late eighteenth century style   350
          Upholstery and materials   275.00

#9   1 CARD TABLE   650 00
          Late eighteenth century, mahogany, C. 1790 400.00

#10   1 CONSOLE TABLE (OR ALTERNATE CABINET)
          Chippendale, mahogany, C. 1750   600.00

      1 MIRROR (above)
          Chippendale, gilt, C. 1760   375.00 ✓

#11   2 CONSOLE TABLES (pair)
          Chippendale, mahogany, C. 1770   650.00 ✓

A   2 MIRRORS ABOVE TABLES
          Chippendale, gilt, C. 1780

The state reception room, as originally envisioned by decorative arts expert James Cogar. His original plan, dating from 1956–57, included color and fabric swatches, as well as a detailed furniture placement guide that is still utilized, to a large degree, even today.

BEFORE AND AFTER

The state dining room glitters with formality when set for twenty-four.

Top: The state dining room prior to the addition of the 18th-century chandelier in 1962 and the 19th-century Zuber wallpaper in 1985.

Bottom: The inlaid, 18th-century Hepplewhite sideboard and knifeboxes as they looked in an English gallery, prior to purchase by James Cogar for the state dining room.

INTERIOR VIEWS OF PRIVATE AREAS OF THE MANSION

Top and right: The state guest bedroom as it looked from the late 1950s to the mid-1980s and as it looks today.

Archival photos from 1957 of the private den, governor's mansion office, and private dining room.

Jonathan Lees's hand-painted lunar dial continues to herald the arrival of a full moon each month at the Florida Governor's Mansion. Created ca. 1790, this grandfather (long-case) clock maintains its accuracy despite the passage of two centuries since its creation.

The state entrance hall as it looked in 1957 (bottom) and as it looks today (top).

TALE OF A CHANDELIER

Visitors to the state dining room are immediately struck with the beauty of gleaming faceted crystal, dripping down in sumptuous tiers from the centerpiece of the room, an elegant chandelier. When the mansion was constructed, architect Marion Sims Wyeth ensured that electric wires were strung into the middle of the dining room in anticipation of a grand lighting fixture. That fixture was installed in the summer of 1961, during Farris Bryant's term of office, but its origins were debated as late as 2005.

In his book *Time for Florida*, author John E. Evans explained that Mrs. Bryant found chandeliers in the old garage, which was afterward demolished:

> She [Julia Bryant] found that the crystal chandeliers from the old state mansion had been ingloriously packed away when it was torn down, and retrieved and renovated them. One was hung in the family dining room of the new Residence, another in the vestibule of the formal guest room. Two others, not suitable for the Residence, found new life in the dining room of the President's Home and at West Hall at Florida State University.

FAST FORWARD

In a November 2005 interview with this author, Bryant daughters Cecilia and Adair began an animated and good-natured debate about the origin of the chandelier in the state dining room. Each defended her recollection with a fiery determination, insisting that her childhood memories were the gospel truth.

Cecilia (fourteen when she moved into the mansion) remembered that the chandelier had been purchased by her mother in an antiques shop in New Orleans. Equally certain, Adair (four years younger) explained in great detail that the chandelier was found in the old garage, and lovingly restored to hang in its place today. Mansion docents have for many years informed visitors that the chandelier is French and originally hung in a castle there. Mansion curator Carol Graham Beck, whose professionalism ensures that the mansion's docents are provided with correct information about the furnishings, was perplexed.

REWIND

Biographer Evans continued the chandelier tale, explaining, "To enhance the beauty of the State Dining Room of the Residence, Mrs. Bryant sought out a large French crystal chandelier, hand-made in the late 1800s for a French castle. The occasion of its installation was noted with a chandelier hanging party, for the wives of the Cabinet and Supreme Court and the members of the Mansion Advisory Commission who had aided in its acquisition."

Following the conversation with the Bryant daughters, Mrs. Beck went back to her research on the provenance of the mansion's furnishings. Evidence revealed that the chandelier was purchased in an Atlanta antique boutique for $2,500. In a March 1966 letter to Mrs. Haydon Burns (Mrs. Bryant's successor as first lady), G. Warren Sanchez, then chairman of the Governor's Mansion Commission, clarified the source of the dining room chandelier.

Mr. Sanchez explained that while the original memorandum delivered to Mrs. Bryant had been lost, he could verify that the chandelier had come from Atlanta and that the $2,500 included the cost of its rewiring, cleaning, and installation. He included an endorsement from the insurance policy carried on the fixture, which described it as a "French chandelier of finest French crystal, the chandelier has four graduated tier of lights mirrored by baccarat pendants and prisms cut from ground glass, finely polished to reflect light. The cut glass bowl centerpiece has a lid that can be lifted. The extended cuppings beneath the lights are known as 'bobeches' and were originally used to catch wax drippings."

With the mystery solved, the chandelier continues to occupy a special place in the hearts of all the mansion's resident stewards. As Evans put it in 1966, "There are all these memories and more, of a stately residence that was a home."

THE USS *FLORIDA* SILVER SERVICE

Not everything in the new governor's mansion was selected by a consultant. The collection of silver pieces is a visitor favorite, not only because of its intrinsic artistry, but also because of its venerable history.

It is through traditions and ceremonies that each new generation learns to appreciate those who came before. Traditions define who we are, what we value, and how we came to those ideals. The United States Navy has cherished traditions that unify those whose lives are too frequently imperiled. Uniforms, rank insignia, the flag, and the salute are such traditions, but another long-standing one is featured at the Florida Governor's Mansion, the silver service from the USS *Florida*.

A Navy directive explains the purpose of naval presentation silver:

> A gift of presentation silver in conjunction with the commissioning of a naval vessel is a long-standing tradition in the U.S. Navy. The silver forges a symbolic and historical link between the military crew of the vessel it is aboard and the civilian community from whence it came. . . . The term 'presentation silver' refers to gifts to U.S. Navy vessels which are made of silver (a single item or a group of items) such as punch bowl sets, tea sets, coffee sets, trays, candelabras, and related hollowware or flatware. Presentation silver is typically engraved with the names of the vessel, donor, occasion of the presentation, and emblems or symbols of the Navy or the donating organization.

Interesting background comes from Kenneth Trapp, curator-in-charge for the Renwick Gallery of American Art in Washington, D.C., which mounted an exhibit in 2000 entitled "Silver on the High Seas: U.S. Navy Presentation Silver Services." Trapp was interviewed by Will Chandler, an editor with *Silver Magazine*. Trapp explained that the silver service tradition began in the 1880s. In 1883, Admiral David Dixon Porter changed the way ships were named. Formerly, ships bore Indian tribal names, but difficulties with pronunciation led the admiral to name the ships after American cities and states. (Trapp notes the irony that many state and city names — such as Arkansas, Kansas, and Illinois — are derived from indigenous peoples.) For the most part, cruisers were named for cities and battleships for states.

At first, it seems incongruous that a naval ship outfitted for battle, prepared for deprivation, would have a silver service on board. The explanation is that the silver serves an important peacetime function. The Navy has always provided a demonstration of national strength to impress foreign governments and to instill patriotic pride at home. When a U.S. ship enters a friendly foreign port, it is greeted with much fanfare. Frequently, the captain entertains dignitaries in the ward room, with the silver service a centerpiece.

Trapp explained that patrician silver on naval ships comes directly from a British tradition: "The services were a means of planting on a ship vivid images and symbols of cultivation and culture. The officers were meant to live up to their silver services. The officers were meant to be cultivated and they were meant to be gentlemen."

The purchase of naval silver was a grassroots movement. Donations came from individual citizens of the state whose name the ship would bear, often only pennies and nickels. In 1900, though, when a laborer's salary might be $5.00 a week, a nickel was a sincere contribution. Trapp relates that the silver bought for the USS *Nevada* made a whistle-stop tour, enabling the citizens of that sparsely populated state to take pride in the magnificent pieces they had helped purchase.

Presentation silver was highly ornate and crafted by the finest silversmiths in the nation. Embellished with ornaments of each state's unique history, characteristics, and emblems, every service was a signature set. As an example, for the USS *Pennsylvania*, commissioned in 1905, the soup tureen depicted some of Pennsylvania's most notable leaders. The loving cup was decorated with eagles and nautical motifs, as well as the state seal, a locomotive, an observation car, and a forest.

The story of the USS *Florida* silver is especially noteworthy, as it was truly a gift of the people. The Florida Legislature appropriated the initial part of the $10,000 needed to craft the pieces, with the balance raised principally through donations from school children and the Florida Silver Service Commission, chaired by William A. Bours.

Opposite top: The crew of the USS *Florida*.

Opposite bottom: The San Carlos Hotel in Pensacola, Florida, as it looked on December 18, 1911, when the Navy acquired the USS *Florida* Presentation Silver Collection. An original invitation to the dedication ceremony aboard the ship is addressed to Mrs. T. E. Taylor.

The USS *Florida* was the fifth naval vessel named for the state. It was launched at the New York Navy Yard on May 12, 1910, and on December 18, 1911, in Pensacola, Governor Albert W. Gilchrist presented the silver. The ship was dispatched in 1914 to protect American lives and property at Vera Cruz, Mexico. The ship was later stationed in the Chesapeake Bay and was used as a convoy during World War I, protecting shipping in the North Atlantic. When the ship was decommissioned in April 1931, former first lady May Mann Jennings (1901–1904) was one of many who asked for the silver's return to the state. Governor Doyle Carlton persevered, obtaining the silver service for display at the governor's mansion rather than at the state museum in Gainesville.

When originally presented, the collection included forty-seven pieces crafted by the Gorham Company of Providence, Rhode Island. Over the years at least two of the punch cups featuring alligator handles and two goblets with the state seal were lost. Mary Call Collins speculated that some of the ship's officers may have collected their own souvenirs. In 1995 during Governor Chiles's administration, Mr. and Mrs. William Bours Bond of Jacksonville donated a punch cup owned by Mrs. Bond's great-grandfather, who had chaired the Florida Silver Service Commission. The cup was presented to Mr. Bours in 1911 as a token of appreciation for his work. The cup made up for at least one of the alligator-handled vessels that had been lost.

The service includes a magnificent twelve-gallon punchbowl and matching punch ladle, the punch cups and goblets, a coffee urn, a fruit dish, several sizes of serving trays, and a large flower bowl. The largest serving tray is inscribed *Presented to the USS Florida by the People of Florida*. The pieces are profusely decorated with symbols of Florida's uniqueness. The alligator motif is most popular, appearing not only as cup handles, but at the base of the punch bowl. Their powerful tails also support the fruit dish. The dolphin comes in a close second, providing the *leitmotif* for the elegant coffee urn.

The emblems go beyond the state's flora and fauna to include cultural and historical references. On the punch bowl appear beautifully incised vignettes of Seminole Indians poling a canoe; on the centerpiece is a depiction of the Castillo de San Marcos in St. Augustine, referring to Florida's Spanish period.

Along with long-standing traditions come long-standing superstitions. One side of the punch bowl illustrates Juan Ponce de Leon's discovery of Florida and gives the date as March 27, 1512. In fact, the year was *1513* when Ponce de Leon discovered what we now know as the state of Florida. Mansion curators speculate that the date was knowingly changed to avoid the use of the dreaded number 13.

In 1982, during Governor and Mrs. Bob Graham's residence at the mansion, the Navy asked that two pieces of the silver be given to a new submarine named *Florida*. Mrs. Graham and the Florida Governor's Mansion Commission said no, digging in their heels, even though the state cabinet had voted to return the silver. The silver stayed.

While beautiful and historic in its own right, the USS *Florida* silver service is much more than a group of decorative pieces. The silver is emblematic of Florida's sacrifices as well as its contributions to the nation. Its commanding presence in the state dining room has and will continue to fascinate and inspire visitors as it embodies both beauty and high principles.

U. S. S. "FLORIDA"

Length, 521 feet 6 inches.
Beam, 88 feet 2 5-8 inches.
Draught, 28 feet 6 inches.
Complement, 1002 officers and men.

Displacement, 21,825 tons.
Indicated Horse-power, 28,000.
Speed, 20.75 knots.

ARMAMENT

MAIN BATTERY

Ten 12-inch Breech Loading Rifles in five turrets
Two 21-inch Torpedo Tubes.

SECONDARY BATTERY

Sixteen 5-inch Rapid Fire Guns.   Four 3-pounders (for saluting)

Presented to the U. S. S. FLORIDA
BY THE
PEOPLE OF FLORIDA

"The silver forges a symbolic and historical link between the military crew of the vessel it is aboard and the civilian community from whence it came."

A NAVAL DIRECTIVE EXPLAINING THE PURPOSE OF NAVAL PRESENTATION SILVER

The USS *Florida* Presentation Silver Collection is among the most important historic objects on display in the mansion.

Opposite bottom: The largest silver tray is inscribed, "Presented to the USS *Florida* by the People of Florida." These words represent the spirit in which Governor Albert W. Gilchrist gave the 47-piece collection to Captain H.S. Knapp during the 1911 ceremonies in Pensacola.

A HIGHER AUTHORITY

The decisions about changes to the mansion structure and furnishings are not left to the preferences of successive governors and their spouses. Governor and First Lady Collins, the mansion's first residents, understood the need for continuity.

Governor Collins created a Mansion Advisory Committee of private citizens to advise on building and furnishing. The committee, chaired by Frank Moor, performed an invaluable service to the state, meeting frequently to determine the eighteenth-century décor for the mansion.

In 1957, after the mansion was completed, the legislature officially established the Governor's

Over the years, the Governor's Mansion Commission has recognized the need to consider the Florida Governor's Mansion as a museum, open to Florida's citizens and to visitors.

Mansion Commission with this specific charge: "To maintain the style, structure, and character of the Governor's Mansion consistent with the original plan of construction."

The commission was composed of five citizens along with state officials whose responsibilities related to the mansion's upkeep and authenticity. Their authority extended only to the public rooms, although they were always available to advise on the governor's private quarters if asked.

Over the years, the commission has recognized the need to consider the Florida Governor's Mansion as a museum, open to Florida's citizens and to visitors. For that reason, the mansion now employs a full-time curator, whose expert guidance ensures that the People's House will forever retain the eighteenth-century vision of its original creators.

The first ladies of Florida were honored by their husbands, children, grandchildren and mansion docents on November 2, 2005, at the residence which each of them once called home. Together they celebrated the eleven first ladies whose daily accomplishments made the mansion's fifty-year history so memorable. Seated from left to right: First Lady Mary Call Collins, First Lady Columba Bush, First Lady Mary Jane Martinez, First Lady Margie Mixson, First Lady Donna Lou Askew, Kevin Askew. Standing from left to right: Cecilia Bryant Lipsey, Mary Call Collins Proctor, Jane Collins Aurell, Darby Collins, Gwen Graham, Lydia Keen, Kristen and Erik Kirk, Adair Bryant Simon.

Part Two

THE PEOPLE

Reunions of governors and first ladies are always cause for celebration. An air of elegant formality is lent to the occasion when formal invitations and menu programs are created.

Top: An invitation from the Annual Docent Luncheon, which gives each first lady an opportunity to thank the volunteer docent corps who present guided tours to the public each year. In recent years, the number of annual visitors to the mansion has reached 20,000 guests.

Bottom left: The governors of Florida reunite in the 1970s in the state entrance hall. Standing left to right: Governor Farris Bryant, Governor LeRoy Collins, Governor Charley Johns, Governor Reubin Askew, Governor Fuller Warren, Governor Haydon Burns.

Bottom right: The first ladies of Florida have a 1980s reunion during the Graham years. Standing left to right: First Lady Adele Graham, First Lady Julia Bryant, First Lady Mildred Burns, First Lady Mary Call Collins, First Lady Donna Lou Askew.

Governor and Mrs. Jeb Bush
request the pleasure of your company
as we welcome back the
First Ladies of Florida

Governor's Mansion Docent Luncheon
Wednesday, November 2, 2005
12:00 o'clock noon until 1:30 pm

The Governor's Mansion
Tallahassee, Florida

Florida governors and first ladies step out front for an official group photograph before assembling on the private side of the mansion to sign books and celebrate the publication of *700 North Adams Street* in 1977.

Back row, left to right: Governor Farris Bryant, Governor Bob Graham, Governor Lawton Chiles, Governor Reubin Askew, Governor Wayne Mixson. Front row, left to right: First Lady Adele Graham, First Lady Rhea Chiles, First Lady Donna Lou Askew, First Lady Mary Call Collins, First Lady Margie Mixson.

CHAPTER FIVE

THE FIFTIES
Florida Enters the Modern Age

ust five years before the decade of the fifties began, Florida celebrated one hundred years of statehood. Still young by comparison to other states in the union, Florida possessed a unique history that defied comparisons. ¶ On August 14, 1945, news of the Japanese surrender ending World War II reached the state, and Floridians took to the streets in celebration. The war, fought on the battlegrounds of Europe and the South Pacific, would have lasting consequences for America's southernmost state. Thousands of GIs, many of them trained in Florida, would return *en masse*, finding the state the perfect place to start a new life. Florida's future governors Daniel McCarty, LeRoy Collins, Farris Bryant, Haydon Burns, Claude Kirk, and Reubin Askew all served gallantly in the war. ¶ Florida's economy greatly benefited through the federal government's investments during the war. Over two million men and women were sent to Florida for training, and major military bases sprang up across the state. In turn, tens of thousands of laborers migrated to Florida to work on military base

A light blanket of snow covers the grounds of the governor's mansion on one rare morning in Tallahassee in February of 1958.

construction and at shipyards in Jacksonville and Tampa. The arrival of so many led to the dramatic growth of cities from Miami to Jacksonville to Pensacola. Federal funds were also available to build modern transportation facilities and improved roadways that connected the major metropolitan cities, once impossibly far apart. Technological advances that introduced air conditioning and more effective mosquito control affected Florida's growth inestimably. Unlike the boom of the 1920s, when men and women made their way to Florida as temporary guests, this time they stayed.

Unlike the boom of the 1920s, when men and women made their way to Florida as transient guests, this time the post-war arrivals stayed.

Governor and Mrs. Leroy Collins enjoy an outdoor barbecue on the grounds of the new mansion.

GOVERNOR FULLER WARREN
1949–1953

With Florida poised on the brink of its transition from an agricultural to a modern state with a multifaceted economic base, Governor Fuller Warren was plagued with the incongruities of tradition and progress meeting face to face. One of his most remembered initiatives is the end of free-range policies across the state. In 1950 Florida was ranked twelfth in the nation as a producer of beef cattle. As more and more people entered the state, a head-on collision loomed between the ever-increasing automobiles and the herds of cattle and horses that roamed freely over the terrain.

Between the illustrations of STOP and YIELD signs, the 1950 edition of the "Florida Driver's Handbook" included another that every driver was required to know: OPEN RANGE BEWARE OF CATTLE. At this time, public lands and the right-of-way were open to grazing, and an inordinate number of accidents occurred when an unsuspecting driver was suddenly confronted with a cow in the road. In 1949, Governor Warren saw to it that all grazing lands along state roads were fenced, eliminating the potential confrontation but making him unpopular with many of the state's farming interests.

In many ways, the end of the free-range cattle era signaled the beginning of a new perception of Florida, moving it away from its long-associated "cracker" image. Florida was after all in the Deep South, even though its allegiance with the Confederacy was now a dim memory. Cultural traditions, however, were alive and well and in the very near future would create a crisis in the ongoing battle for civil rights.

Florida began with its population concentrated in the north, bordering Alabama and Georgia. Hundreds of miles south, in Dade County, a different culture would emerge, generously influenced by immigrants from Cuba and the Caribbean. Florida would grow exponentially at mid-century, and those who made their way here from so many diverse cultures influence Florida's politics to this very day.

FROM LABORER TO ORATOR

Left: Governor Fuller Warren

Right: Governor Warren's new bride, Barbara, posing on the lawn beside the original governor's mansion.

Fuller Warren was born in Blountstown, Calhoun County, Florida, in 1905 into a family of seven children. Even as a young child Warren worked to help support his family, becoming a farm laborer at the age of eight, working for seventy-five cents a week and board. As a youth he held jobs in grocery stores and sawmills and worked as a peddler, seaman, salesman, surveyor, and auctioneer. Later in life, those humble beginnings led Warren to a deep commitment to laborers and the impoverished, expressed in his personal political agenda.

In 1927, at the age of twenty-one and still a student at the University of Florida, Warren was elected to the Florida Legislature as the representative from Calhoun County. In 1929 he began the practice of law in Jacksonville, soon becoming a leading criminal attorney. Warren was elected to the Jacksonville City Council for three terms between 1931 and 1937. During the 1940 gubernatorial race, Warren was a candidate on the Democratic ticket. Although losing to Spessard L. Holland, Warren received the third highest number of votes in the Democratic primary, an impressive show in his first attempt at the state's highest office. When WW II began, Warren enlisted and served in the Navy as a gunnery officer. During his tour of duty he crossed the Atlantic not less than twenty-three times. His gallantry in combat earned him a special naval citation.

After the war Warren returned to Jacksonville to practice law. Warren is often referred to as an eloquent orator, which no doubt enhanced his success in the courtroom. He shared his gifts of elocution in two books, *Eruptions of Eloquence* (1938) and *Speaking of Speaking* (1944). Warren served as a state representative from Duval County for two terms before he won the Democratic nomination for governor in the spring of 1948. He was forty-three when he was elected the thirtieth governor of Florida.

THE PEOPLE'S INAUGURATION

Warren was one of the few to reach the high office of governor not to have the backing of the "establishment," and some newspapers characterized his inaugural celebration as the "People's Inauguration." In a piece for the *Tallahassee Democrat*, Howard Jay Friedman referred to Warren's supporters across the state as the "little people" on the political "outs," excited about now being "in."

On inauguration day, January 4, 1949, those faithful little people flocked to Tallahassee to witness the ceremony for one of their own. They came by car and bus and special train to cheer and revel in their great victory. Many of them sported yellow-gold armbands designating them as "colonels" on the governor's staff, a time-honored tradition in the southern states. Friedman went on to describe the day: "The sky was cloudy but the weather warm and between ten thousand and forty thousand people turned out to watch the parade and gorge themselves [on barbecue] at picnic tables set up in an unpaved dirt parking area where the Senate Office Building now stands."

A parade wound its way around the vicinity of the capitol, with floats from each of the sixty-seven counties and bands from all over. When it came time to take the oath of office Warren, bedecked in a top hat and tails, listened while Wah Nese Red Rock (an Alaskan Indian and wife of an Air Force veteran) sang "The Star Spangled Banner." Traditionally, the oath of office was administered precisely at noon, but Warren cut into Governor Caldwell's time in office by eight minutes, in order to speed up the ceremony to get out of the drizzling rain. After a night of dancing at the Capital City Club (since demolished) the governor would begin to take care of business. Early in Warren's administration, he married Californian Barbara Jean Manning, giving the state and mansion a first lady.

The state coffers were nearly empty when Governor Warren assumed office. His predecessor, Millard F. Caldwell, had left a $500,000 deficit in the State Road Department and $9,000,000 in contracts yet to be awarded. The state could not meet its operating budget, and despite reducing each agency's share of the pie, was still without a means to balance the budget. The legislature mounted a strong push to institute a sales tax, even though Warren strongly opposed it. Following a special session in September, a 3% limited sales tax was enacted. Governor Warren did not veto the bill but insisted that food and clothing purchases under $10 be exempt.

During his term, the governor was successful in seeing legislation passed that included a citrus bill elevating the standards for the sale of fresh and canned fruit, a reforestation program for planting over 65 million pine seedlings (pine being a source for the turpentine industry), a water control program by the Army Corps of Engineers, and a coordinated year-round advertising program promoting tourism. Governor Warren can also be credited with the initial planning for the Florida State Turnpike, seeing that the Jacksonville Expressway was begun, and arranging for the financing and construction of the Sunshine State Parkway.

THE INFAMOUS "STATE SHACK"

Governor Warren is remembered for his remark referring to the 1907 governor's mansion as the state shack and lobbying the legislature for funds to build a suitable residence for the state's chief executive. Coming at a time when the first state sales tax was enacted, many considered his remark bad form. The Florida State Archives contains one letter that sums up those feelings, sent with no return address or date. That letter foreshadowed the controversy during the next two administrations about where the governor should live.

Dear Governor Warren,

I noticed an article appearing in the *St. Petersburg Times*. . . . In this article the associated press quotes you as stating that the executive mansion is a State shack. As a citizen, taxpayer and resident of the State of Florida I feel that this is a very unbecoming statement to be made by the chief executive of our state.

You certainly worked hard enough to become governor, knew what the executive mansion was like before you were elected and if you are dissatisfied with it, and think it is a shack and don't want to reside in it, I would suggest that you resign and remove yourself therefrom and allow someone who is proud to reside in the executive mansion to occupy it. I believe that if you would follow this suggestion you would do the people of Florida a great service.

David R. Gallagher

As the decade of the fifties began in earnest, Florida would experience its share of turbulence. The state would undergo a sea change and the world of its chief executive would become an ever more demanding one. On the national scene, in 1950 Senator Joseph McCarthy began a campaign of intimidation, alleging that the government had been infiltrated by Communists and that the intellectual elite—which included writers, actors, university professors and broadcasters—had a secret agenda to overthrow our democratic government.

In other unease, Florida experienced racial tension in every part of the state. A rash of terrorist bombings struck at synagogues and the homes of African-Americans who were registering blacks to vote. In a particularly heinous crime, Harry T. Moore, a state leader in the NAACP, and his wife were murdered in Orange County on December 25, 1951. The Ku Klux Klan was thought responsible for this act, which was compounded by the seeming indifference of law enforcement officials in bringing the guilty parties to justice. Governor Warren responded by banning the Klan from public places and publicly denouncing their racist activities.

GOVERNOR DANIEL (DAN) T. McCARTY
January 6, 1953–September 28, 1953

Dan McCarty served the state of Florida as its governor for barely eight months, but he is warmly remembered. A Democrat, McCarty ran on a platform that included promises to veto new taxes, to build a four-lane highway from Tallahassee down the east coast, and to create a state Department of Labor of cabinet rank. McCarty played a substantial role in building a new governor's mansion.

THE YOUNGEST SPEAKER

Daniel Thomas McCarty was born on January 18, 1912, in Fort Pierce, Florida. McCarty's family had settled in the area in 1896 and begun farming citrus and pineapple, eventually acquiring substantial acreage. In 1934 he graduated from the University of Florida's College of Agriculture. When he returned to Ft. Pierce he organized a cooperative of citrus farmers as the Indian River Citrus Association. McCarty was one of the few elected governors who did *not* practice law. He became a highly successful cattle rancher and citrus

The five McCartys must have made for a tight fit in the station wagon, as they also brought their Boston terrier and the children's toys.

grower in St. Lucie County before he entered the political arena. He was elected to the Florida House of Representatives in 1937, becoming the youngest, at twenty-nine, to be selected by his colleagues as speaker.

When the United States entered World War II, McCarty enlisted in the army. Before leaving, he married Olie Brown, also from St. Lucie County. His tour of duty with the field artillery frequently placed him in peril, and he was among those who landed with the Seventh Army in the south of France on D-Day. McCarty rose to the rank of colonel and earned the Legion of Merit, Bronze Star, Purple Heart (for wounds he received), and Croix de Guerre.

McCarty returned to his civilian life and started a family. His political ambitions were still strong, and in 1948 he made an unsuccessful bid for the Democratic nomination for governor, running a close second to Fuller Warren. That year Harry S. Truman, a Democrat, narrowly won a victory over his Republican rival Thomas Dewey. In 1952, Daniel McCarty successfully won the Democratic nomination for governor and

"He hasn't changed a bit. He still brings guests home to dinner at a moment's notice, still can't find the right shirt without help, and still spoils our young daughter Markleyann."

FIRST LADY THELMA JOHNS

easily defeated Republican Harry S. Swan. On the morning of McCarty's inauguration, Governor Warren was cleaning out his desk and came upon a half-empty bottle of aspirin. About to put it in his pocket, Warren thought twice and, perhaps reflecting on the tenor of the times, left it for his successor.

GRAND PLANS CUT SHORT

The newly elected governor left Ft. Pierce for Tallahassee with a station wagon packed with his family: wife Olie, daughter Frances Lela, and sons Danny and Mike. They must have made for a tight fit, as the McCartys also brought their Boston terrier and the children's toys. Mrs. McCarty also packed her husband's hunting and fishing equipment, no doubt hoping the new governor would find some respite from the demands of his office.

January 6, 1953, inauguration day, was warm and sunny as Daniel T. McCarty succeeded Governor Warren. It was the first time the ceremony was held on the west side of the capitol, in Waller Park. Named for Judge Curtis Waller of the U.S. Circuit Court of Appeals, the area today contains the fountain and steps west of the new capitol. The program for the state's youngest chief executive (at forty) featured photos of him tending his citrus and cattle farm: a trim, energetic man who was seemingly in the very best of health. That same January, Dwight D. Eisenhower, a Republican, was inaugurated as the president of the United States.

Governor McCarty inherited a state in a strong financial position, with $20 million in the general fund. Early on, the governor expressed his concern for Florida's environmental causes when he came out against oil exploration in the newly created Everglades National Park. As he prepared to address the legislature at their biennial session, the governor's agenda held a series of initiatives, but he was felled by a minor heart attack (at first thought to be the flu) on February 25. Secretary of State R.A. Gray delivered the governor's message, which included an increase in the state's advertising budget, an increase in teachers' salaries, the creation of a turnpike commission to build and operate the lower 110 miles of a toll highway from Miami to Ft. Pierce, and the outlawing of the Communist party in the state. By June of that year Governor McCarty was able to carry on the business of his office, usually from the governor's mansion but occasionally making trips to the capitol. It was during this time that he appointed a committee to select the site for the new executive mansion.

On September 23, Governor McCarty was admitted to Tallahassee Memorial Hospital suffering from a cold. The governor developed pneumonia and died on September 28, 1953, at the age of forty-one. Many were dumbstruck that this young, vital man could so quickly perish, and the tributes poured in.

Many were dumbstruck that this young, vital man, Daniel T. McCarty, could so quickly perish, and the tributes poured in.

GOVERNOR CHARLEY EUGENE JOHNS
September 28, 1953–January 4, 1955

When Dan McCarty passed on, the Florida Constitution of 1885 still dictated laws of succession. There was no lieutenant governor, and the governor's seat fell to the president of the state senate. The position of acting governor was temporary, with the office officially filled upon the next general election.

Charley Eugene Johns had been elected senate president on April 6, 1953, and to him the mantle of leadership fell. Governor Johns had a long history of service to the state, having been elected to the house of representatives in 1935, representing Bradford County. The following year he was elected to the senate as the representative from the fifteenth district, which included Bradford and Union counties. He served in the senate during the 1937 and 1939 sessions and then again in 1945 (until 1966).

Johns was born in Starke on February 27, 1905, to Everett E. and Annie Johns. His father was once the sheriff of Bradford County and was killed in the line of duty while serving as a deputy sheriff of Nassau County. Johns attended public schools and the University of Florida. He spent some thirty years as a conductor for the Seaboard Airline Railway, was also employed as an insurance broker, and at one time owned an ice company. Johns's wife was the former Thelma Brinson of Starke, and they had two children, Charley Jerome (twenty-five at the time of his father's succession) and daughter Markleyann, who was eleven. After her husband's elevation to the office of governor, Mrs. Johns said: "He hasn't changed a bit. He still brings guests home to dinner at a moment's notice, still can't find the right shirt without help, and still spoils our young daughter Markleyann."

Although only briefly in office, the Johns administration was instrumental in removing the tolls from the Overseas Highway between Miami and Key West and in encouraging road construction throughout the state. Mrs. Johns summarized the family's experience when she said: "It was a rich and rewarding experience living in the Governor's Mansion, and I shall treasure the friendships made in Tallahassee for the rest of my life."

GOVERNOR THOMAS LEROY COLLINS
1955–1957 & 1957–1961

Governor LeRoy Collins is remembered as one of the state's most extraordinary statesmen, leading during an era that was fraught with the chaos of civil unrest. Thomas LeRoy Collins (or Roy to his friends) was born in Tallahassee on March 10, 1909, to Marvin and Mattie Brandon Collins. Mr. Collins ran a successful grocery store to support his family of four sons and two daughters.

LeRoy Collins was an honor graduate and president of the senior class at Leon High School. In 1927 he left Tallahassee to study at the Eastman College of Business Administration in New York for a year, where he earned a business certificate. When he returned home he worked as a shipping clerk for a wholesale grocer and as a bank teller at the Exchange Bank. To earn enough money to attend law school, his father agreed to match the money LeRoy earned dollar for dollar. As a result of his constancy, LeRoy Collins attended Cumberland University in Lebanon, Tennessee, where he received his law degree in 1931.

TYING TWO POLITICAL LINES

Collins married the beautiful Mary Call Darby, daughter of a former state senator and the great-granddaughter of two-time territorial governor Richard Keith Call. They married in 1932, at a time when Collins first sought public office as the Leon County prosecutor. His plans to wed were at least partially dependent on his success-ful election, as it would provide sufficient income to properly support his new wife. Collins lost the election by fewer than 200 votes, but they married anyway. In 1934, when Collins was just twenty-five, he was elected to the Florida House of Representatives as a Democrat. He was then reelected in 1936 and 1938 and elected to the Florida Senate in 1940 to complete an unexpired term of William C. Hodges, who had died in office. Collins was reelected in 1942, but his political career was interrupted by the worldwide conflagration of World War II. Senator Collins resigned his seat in 1944 to join the United States Navy. Lieutenant Collins's family temporarily moved to Princeton, New Jersey; Seattle, Washington; and Carmel, California as Lieutenant Collins trained in his military specialty.

When Collins returned from the war, he was reelected to the Florida Senate in 1946 and 1950. Collins was well into his term when Governor McCarty died and acting governor Charley Johns assumed office. The November 1954 gubernatorial election pitted Governor Johns against Collins in two Democratic primaries. Governor Collins bested Johns and became the Democratic nominee. His Republican opponent, Tom Watson, died before the general election, and Collins won by default. LeRoy Collins assumed office as the thirty-third governor of Florida on January 4, 1955. Dan McCarty had been a close personal friend, so undoubtedly Collins's victory was even more meaningful to him. The newly elected governor would not have far to move when he began his term of office.

Around 1825 Richard Keith Call had begun building an imposing Greek Revival–style home for his family on a 640-acre tract of land that was then just outside Tallahassee's boundaries. Governor Call's magnificent home, the Grove, still stands today, one block north of the governor's mansion, an imposing example of Florida's antebellum plantation period. Following Governor Call's death in 1862, the mansion was owned by a series of heirs but by 1940 had suffered from the family's economic downturn and the consequences of the Great Depression. In 1941 the property was offered for sale and LeRoy and Mary Call Collins made an offer which, to their surprise, was accepted. In 1942 the family moved in and proceeded to restore the house as they were able. (The colorful and fascinating history of the mansion and its residents is recounted in *The Grove: A Florida Home Through Seven Generations*, written by Jane Aurell Menton, grand-daughter of Governor and Mrs. Collins. Mary Call Collins encouraged her granddaughter in this effort and was a primary source of information.)

The election of LeRoy Collins enabled a remarkable historical continuity. The Call-Collins ties to the land and to the governance of the state now extended from Florida's territorial days through to the modern age. The

Opposite: Governor and Mrs. LeRoy Collins and their family, the first residents of the present governor's mansion in spring of 1957.

Top: An animated and dignified former first lady, Mrs. Mary Call Collins, photographed during a 2005 interview at her home, the Grove, located across the street from the mansion. Governor LeRoy Collins spoke lovingly of her and his family at his inauguration: ". . . only one who has actually served in this position can understand how much a Governor's family is called upon in the overall job . . . I want to say publicly that, while I am conscious of my own deficiencies, you could not have a better First Lady."

Bottom: The notebook that Mrs. Collins left behind for future first ladies, hoping that their tenures would proceed as smoothly as possible.

Opposite: First Lady Mary Call Collins in the early years of the new mansion at 700 North Adams Street.

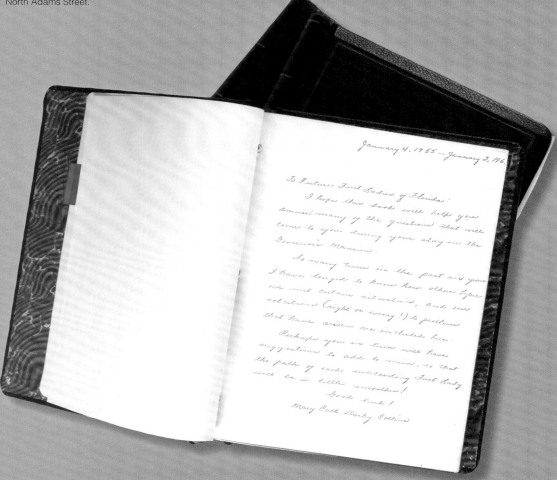

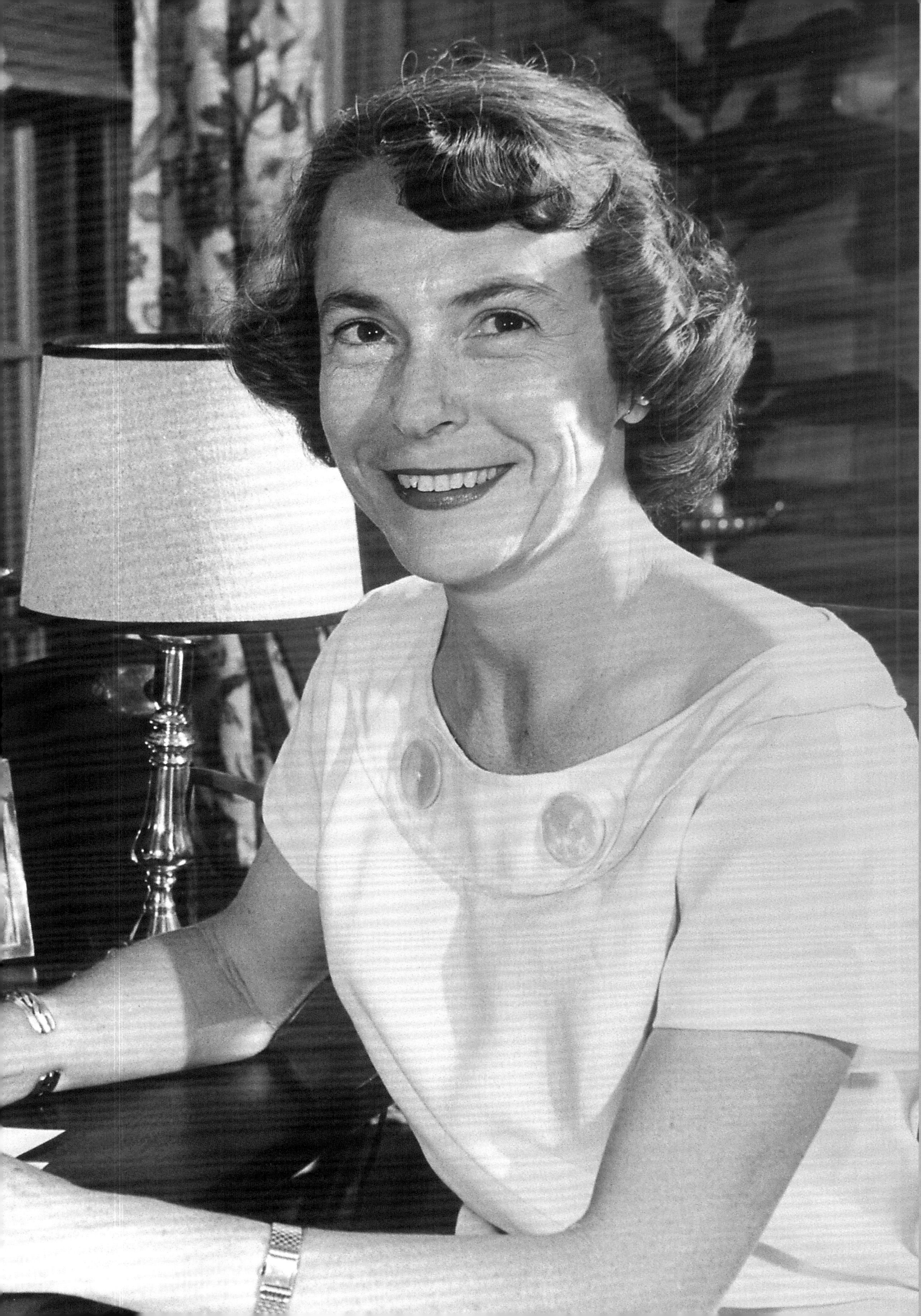

Opposite: The Collins family pose on the balcony of the new mansion for their family holiday card.

Top: Darby Collins with Thanksgiving turkey at the mansion, November 1959.

Center: The Collins family with the Thanksgiving turkey in their private dining room, November 1959.

Bottom: Mrs. Collins's cookbook.

Collinses easily made the move from their ancestral home to the home of the state's chief executive, amidst towering magnolias and live oaks.

His second inauguration was January 8, 1957. By that time the Collins family included LeRoy, Jr. (born in 1934), Jane (1938), Mary Call (1942), and Darby (1950). The six Collinses would have the distinction of being the only governor's family to occupy two different mansions.

A Family Inauguration and Reunion

The day of the inauguration dawned sunny and bright. The oath of office was administered by Justice Campbell Thornal of Orlando, a close friend of the governor's. Thousands attended the inauguration, but the surprise arrival of LeRoy, Jr., made it even more perfect. Ensign Collins had graduated from the United States Naval Academy at Annapolis and at the time was stationed aboard a ship at Yokosuka, Japan. His trip home took five days aboard a number of different conveyances, but LeRoy made it to the inauguration, much to the delight of his family, especially his younger sisters.

Governor Collins took the oath of office with his hand firmly planted on the same Bible used by territorial governor Richard Keith Call upon his swearing in. Fittingly, he acknowledged the vital role his family played in his life:

> . . . only one who has actually served in this position can understand how much a Governor's family is called upon in the overall job, I do not mean simply in the ways you are probably thinking about, but perhaps the biggest chore of all is having to live with the Governor and endure all his shortcomings as a husband and father, distracted as he is almost invariably by the duties of his office.

> I want to say publicly that, while I am conscious of my own deficiencies, you could not have a better First Lady. I am indeed proud of, and grateful to, Mary Call and the children, my mother and father and the others. And I cannot resist the impulse to express my sentiments here.

Mary Call Collins had impressed many with her devotion to family and her own remarkable talents. Journalist Eloise N. Cozens, in Florida Women of Distinction (vol. 5), characterized Mrs. Collins in this way: "With an easy grace that comes from gracious living and years in public life, this charming lady takes life 'straight.' The lack of any kind of artificiality is evident in her conversation. She speaks frankly in a friendly and warm manner, as if you were long-time friends, which indeed, you can easily be—even through correspondence with her."

The governor was not the only one to speak about the remarkable contributions of Mrs. Collins the day of the inauguration. Secretary of State Robert A. Gray introduced Mrs. Collins and said: "This sagacious little lady had the wisdom to select for a great-grandfather, a man who was twice Governor of Florida, and then to select for a husband, a man who is twice Governor of Florida."

Governor Collins summarized the accomplishments of his previous two years in office, pointing out the efficiency and honesty in state government; the increased support to public education; the planning for nuclear energy for industry, medicine, agriculture, and education; and the state's greatest road building program of all time. The Sunshine State Parkway, the first section of the Florida State Turnpike, opened to traffic on January 26, 1957. The whole turnpike was estimated to cost $74 million, funded by bonds sold on June 7, 1955.

Yet Governor Collins was about to take up a subject of compelling importance to the state, that of civil rights and court-ordered desegregation. He concluded his speech with these inspiring words: "This is the call of history—a history which grows impatient. Ours is the generation in which great decisions can no longer be passed to the next. We have a State to build—a South to save—a Nation to convince—and a God to serve."

Governor Collins took the oath of office with his hand firmly planted on the
same Bible used by territorial governor Richard Keith Call upon his swearing in.
Fittingly, he acknowledged the vital role his family played in his life.

Top: The inaugural gown worn by
First Lady Mary Call Collins.

Bottom: Inauguration day for
Governor LeRoy Collins (left)
standing with outgoing Governor
Charley Johns (right).

CHAPTER SIX

THE SIXTIES
Turmoil and Transitions

n 1960, Florida ranked as the tenth largest state in the union with a population of almost five million. During the 1960s the baby boomers, born to returning World War II soldiers, were becoming teenagers and young adults. An estimated 850,000 "war baby" freshmen entered college at the beginning of the decade, and their coming of age led them to challenge a multitude of values from the conservative era of the fifties. ¶ The United States became increasingly involved in the conflict in Southeast Asia. As more and more young men became eligible for the draft, scenes of protest on college campuses became ever more

frequent. Respect for authority declined, and the hippie movement embraced drug use, rock music, alternative religions, and sexual freedom. At the end of the decade, the legendary Woodstock festival in upper New York state brought 400,000 together for a mega-rock concert soon characterized as the pinnacle of excess. ¶ The Civil Rights Movement made great strides in the 1960s, but not without a corresponding backlash of violence, particularly in southern states. The Reverend Martin Luther King, Jr., led peaceful protests, making his landmark "I Have a Dream" speech in 1963. At the same time Malcolm X preached the superiority of blacks and advocated black separatism. ¶ The Presidential Commission on the Status of Women in 1963 concluded that there was a pervasive inequality in our society's treatment of women. Betty Friedan, Pauli Murray and Gloria Steinem were instrumental in creating the National Organization of Women. The women's liberation movement was the result. ¶ The cold war escalated, with our distrust in the Soviet Union coming to a head with the Cuban Missile Crisis during August through November of 1962. The threat of cataclysmic global war was on Florida's doorstep.

Top: Governor Haydon Burns.

Bottom: Governor Claude Kirk dances with his new bride, First Lady Erika Mattfeld Kirk, on their wedding day.

Opposite: Governor Collins and Governor Bryant leave the mansion in top hats on their way to Governor Bryant's inauguration in 1961.

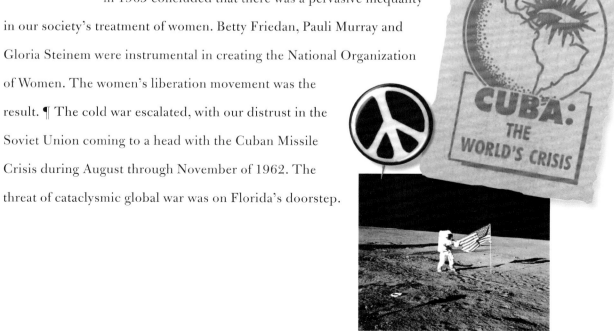

GOVERNOR CECIL FARRIS BRYANT
1961–1965

Against this global backdrop Florida's thirty-fourth governor, Cecil Farris Bryant, was elected. Bryant was born on July 26, 1914, one of the three children of Cecil and Lela Farris Bryant, third-generation Floridians. The Bryants operated a farm in Marion County, just outside of Ocala. In addition to his farming, Cecil Bryant was a professional accountant and one of the first members of the State Board of Accountancy. His brother Ion Farris was twice speaker of the Florida House of Representatives.

As a youth, Farris Bryant attended public schools and earned his "O" as a member of the Ocala High School football team. After a year at Emory University, Bryant attended the University of Florida, earning his bachelor of science degree in business administration in 1935. Bryant went on to Harvard Law School and earned his law degree in 1938. Bryant then found employment in the Office of the State Comptroller in Tallahassee.

It was in Tallahassee that Bryant met his future wife. Julia Burnett was the daughter of Mr. and Mrs. D.F. Burnett of Madison. As Julia was growing up, her father served as a circuit court clerk. Julia attended Florida State College for Women (the predecessor to Florida State University). After her graduation in 1939, Miss Burnett began teaching at Leon High School in Tallahassee.

According to daughter Adair in a November 2005 interview, Farris Bryant swept Julia Burnett off her feet, even though she had plans to go to New York and pursue a career in theater. The story goes that Farris saw Julia on the tennis courts of FSCW and called that evening for a date. After three dates, Farris proposed marriage. Although young Julia asked her fiancé if they could wait until she lived in New York for a year, Farris slyly replied, "This is a one-time offer." The future Mrs. Bryant stayed put. The couple was married in 1940 and moved back to Ocala, the county seat of Marion County, where Farris Bryant took up the practice of law.

A MOST-HONORED COLLEAGUE

In 1942 Bryant ran successfully for a seat in the Florida house. By 1943, however, Bryant resigned and entered the Navy as an ensign, where he served for three and a half years as a gunnery officer. Bryant's assignments took him into the heart of the conflict, with service in the Atlantic, the Pacific, and the Mediterranean. By the end of the war, Farris Bryant had been promoted to lieutenant (equivalent to captain in the other armed services).

Bryant was again elected to the Florida House of Representatives in 1946 and was reelected for a total of five terms. In his last four terms, Bryant ran without opposition. In 1947, Bryant's colleagues voted him the "Most Outstanding First-Term Member of the House" in the Allen Morris Poll. During the years 1949, 1951, and 1953 he was voted "Most Valuable Member." In 1953 Bryant was elected speaker. A culminating achievement was Bryant's selection as the "Most Valuable Member of the Legislature" by the members of both the house and senate in 1955. Allen Morris, whose on-going series *The Florida Handbook* catalogued the political, social, and economic history of the state, said: "As a legislator, he was one of those unique lawmakers who excel as a debater, as a parliamentarian, as a draftsman and as a behind-scenes strategist and persuader."

When Bryant turned his attention to the office of governor, he first ran unsuccessfully for the Democratic nomination against Governor LeRoy Collins. By 1960, the previous experience paid off, as Bryant had achieved recognition within the party. The major issues in the campaign were segregation, sit-down strikes, reapportionment, taxes, and economic development. In the first primary, Bryant received the most votes within a field of ten candidates and in the second won a substantial majority. During the general election Bryant ran against Republican George C. Peterson. Bryant carried 59.8% of the popular vote and won the privilege of succeeding LeRoy Collins.

When the Bryant family moved into the "new" governor's mansion, they had three daughters: Julie Lovett (nineteen), Cecilia Ann (fourteen), and Allison Adair (ten). Julia Bryant was an elegant and articulate first

Governor Bryant was the first to invite the members of his cabinet to share the
inauguration spotlight and also be sworn in that day.

In the days before the mansion gates were built, the Bryants' German shepherd Vic was faithful as a playmate as well as a watchdog.

A down-to-earth man, Governor Bryant even asked that the mansion be referred to as the "executive residence." Traditions die hard, though, and the new name never really caught on.

lady who brought great joy to the governor's mansion. Eloise Cozens, in Florida Women of Distinction (vol. 1), writes: "When we asked friends of Julia Bryant to describe her personality they were unanimous in the words 'charming' and 'well-poised.'" About Mrs. Bryant *before* she became first lady, Cozens wrote:

> Attending to her lovely garden around her hill-top home is time-consuming for the petite blonde mother of three, but she has also found time to travel extensively with her husband, to play an occasional game of golf, and to act currently as landscape design chairman of the Ocala Garden Club. She is also an organizer of the Ocala Junior Woman's Club, she has been vice-president of the Woman's Club, she is a member of the Garden Club, she has been Sunday School teacher and the superintendent of Junior Sunday School in the Ocala First Methodist Church and is an ex-high school teacher. Asked about her aspirations, she says simply: "I'd like to make my deeds as great as my dreams."

FLORIDA FIRSTS

Governor C. Farris Bryant was inaugurated on January 3, 1961. Julie, who had been attending Mary Washington College, moved to Tallahassee to join her family and attend Florida State University. Governor Bryant was the first to invite the members of his cabinet to share the spotlight and also be sworn in that day (their swearing in was purely ceremonial, as the cabinet members actually sign their oaths when they receive their commissions).

Governor Bryant was responsible for a number of Florida firsts, but perhaps a lesser-known fact about the governor is that he was an accomplished pilot. Bryant introduced extensive travel by plane, reaching out to Floridians both north and south in a fraction of the time it took traveling by car. Farris Bryant took advantage of modern conveniences and stressed the need for an educational system that enabled Floridians to keep up with the times.

When the Russians launched the first orbiting satellite *Sputnik* in 1957, the space age had begun, and Florida figured prominently in the subsequent space race. Along with President Kennedy, Governor Bryant pledged his support of this new industry for Florida, centered at Cape Canaveral. In one speech the governor jokingly said: "Florida is thinking about making the moon its next county."

In keeping with his long-held emphasis on education, Governor Bryant's efforts led to FICUS (Florida Institute for Continuing University Studies), GENESYS (Graduate Engineering Education System), the trimester (year-round academic sessions), and a constitutional amendment that authorized bond sales to construct institutions of higher learning, leading to a $1 billion investment in new campus buildings.

In a 2005 interview, Governor Bryant's daughters Cecilia Bryant Lipsey and Adair Bryant Simon explained that, early on, Walt Disney Productions discussed with their father a Disney park in Florida. The perfect location was a nexus of major roadways. Governor Bryant's aggressive campaign to build new roads led to major improvements across the state. When he took office, Florida was forty-ninth in the use of federal highway funds, but by the end of his term, Florida was number one. His road building program included completing I-10 from Jacksonville to Lake City, four-laning SR 60 from Tampa to tie in with east coast roads, and bringing I-75 from the Georgia line to the juncture of the new turnpike and I-4. If you plot the course of the new roads and extensions, their path creates a "golden triangle" with Orlando in its heart. What better place to build a theme park in Florida? As Disney began its purchase of 27,000 acres of land, the governor was sworn to secrecy. When the purchase was revealed (during the Burns administration), the price per acre rose from $183 to $1,000.

The governor, himself an athlete and outdoorsman, was critically aware of the special Florida environment. He led a successful campaign for another constitutional amendment that allowed the sale of bonds to acquire land for conservation and recreation.

After the Russians launched Sputnik, Governor Bryant pledged his support to the space industry, joking, "Florida is thinking about making the moon its next county."

Governor Bryant was responsible for a number of Florida firsts, but perhaps a lesser-known fact is that he was an accomplished pilot.

LIFE IN A FISHBOWL:
CECILIA AND ADAIR BRYANT

On November 2, 2005, Governor Jeb Bush and First Lady Columba Bush hosted a luncheon at the governor's mansion to honor the docent corps and to welcome back former governors, first ladies, and their children. Cecilia Bryant Lipsey and Adair Bryant Simon graciously spoke to the author about their experiences at the mansion.

Leaving Ocala for their trip to Tallahassee in January 1960, fourteen-year-old Cecilia Bryant did not find it strange that her father was leaving for a new job in a new city; she was more anxious about the newness of it all. From her adult perspective, she explained that anxiety was minimal because of the strength of the family's relationship. Her father and mother had always protected their children, and the importance of family was overarching and inviolate, no matter where they were headed.

Julie (the oldest sister), Cecilia, and Adair were coming from their home in Ocala, population 11,000. With one high school, it truly was a town in which every one knew one another. Tallahassee was not much bigger, and for the girls their world became much smaller. Unlike in Ocala, they were not in a neighborhood with other families and young children. Their closest neighbors were Governor and Mrs. Collins, whose children were already grown.

As only the second family to occupy the mansion, the Bryants found it basically a shell. The lovely window treatments and rugs, as well as the crown moldings, were all added later. Cecilia explained her dual perspective as a young child and as a returning adult. In the mid-1950s, the mansion was a big house perfectly suited to the Florida of the day. In fifty years, Florida has grown exponentially, making the mansion modest by today's standards. Cecilia noted its significance as an historic building that has been maintained while the world around it has moved meteorically fast.

In 1960 Governor Bryant's salary was a mere $22,500 a year, and the first lady had a $50,000 budget with which to maintain the mansion and pay the salaries of at least five staff members. With fewer staff members compared to today, Julia Bryant relied on her good friends, who were always willing to assist. One such lady was Marge Schmit, very active back home in the Ocala Garden Club. Mrs. Schmit made sure of fresh floral arrangements around the mansion, much to the delight of Mrs. Bryant, who added a number of additional flower beds during her tenure. Cecilia and Adair explained that Mrs. Schmit had only one request as repayment for her services—that the Sabal palm be named the state tree. This most appropriate and selfless request was granted.

Cecilia and Adair Bryant command attention—they are spontaneous, articulate, and beautiful women with a profound perspective of days spent in their youth. Both girls speak about their mother Julia with great affection and marvel at the relationsh of their mother and father. Cecilia dubbed her "a true Steel Magnolia." As Adair put it: "It was a love affair for fifty-six years. [Mother] knew that she was appreciated and that father relied on h advice." Cecilia added that throughout their long journey in politic her mother and father had a unity of purpose and vision that made their connection to one another even more vital. The sisters' love and admiration for their parents (both of whom have passed away) is evident in the energy and enthusiasm they radiate when speakir about them.

The family shared regular meals, and at the dinner table the governor talked about the issues of the day. Cecilia remembers her father's weighty concerns, among them how the state would accommodate the baby boom generation's need of higher learning and the imperative to find housing and jobs for the Cuban émigrés fleeing from the Castro government. Cecilia (who chose a career in law and was one of only six women in her 1970 class) explained th these discussions taught her critical thinking at an early age, a sk she has put to great use all her life. Cecilia noted that at sixteen, when she was with a group of friends talking about a movie, she was probably thinking about foreign policy.

Adair, a flamboyant and candid woman, went into film producti and carried her mother's theatrical ambitions to fruition. The siste described the movie room downstairs at the mansion where they would have "popcorn nights" with their friends. Different film companies allowed the governor to screen their films at home, a favorite pastime of the children. Cecilia remembers ordering classics with stars like Nelson Eddy and Jeannette MacDonald. Cecilia was the projectionist, and when at times the film broke, she quickly repaired it with her handy splicer. Even today she worries about the possibility of a missing frame or two.

While both Adair and Cecilia admit that their lives at the governor's mansion were different from their peers, neither one would give up the experience for anything. They had opportunities others could only dream about. Adair remembers attending a state dinner in Washington at the age of twelve, when her father was being honored by President Lyndon Johnson. Even among the highest dignitaries in the land, there is no doubt that the precociou girl held up her end of the conversations.

When asked if they ever ventured from their private quarters to the state reception and dining rooms, they both responded: "Who would want to play in the state dining room?!" Each had her own

bedroom at the top of the stairs, sharing a bath. The only time they spent in the state rooms, apart from functions, was at the piano practicing their lessons. Both girls studied, and one would use the mansion's spinet while the other played the family's grand piano. One of their favorite "playmates" was their German shepherd Vic. Almost inseparable from the girls, Vic served an important role as security in the days before fences and gates.

Before the interview was over, Cecilia and Adair spoke about Bryant initiatives they are particularly proud of and which continued to have a positive impact on life in Florida. During the Bryant administration a new constitutional amendment allowed the state to purchase environmentally sensitive land. The John Pennekamp State Park in Key Largo was the first such land to be dedicated for public use. The governor also saw to it that state lands were not carelessly sold to the highest bidder. Prior to his action, any state land could be bought for its appraised value. There was no process to determine whether the sale was

in the best interests of Florida's citizens. Governor Bryant initiated legislation whereby any state-owned land sought for purchase was formally evaluated to determine if the land could serve a higher purpose for the people.

Following through on his concerns about educational opportunities, Governor Bryant invested further in the junior college system created during the Collins administration, as well as in additional universities. In 1960 only three universities existed in Florida. While the junior colleges provided the first two years in a four-year degree, there was a shortfall in completing the last two years. The governor was instrumental in obtaining funding for an expanded state university system.

One can describe first-hand that Cecilia Bryant Lipsey and Adair Bryant Simon are two perfectly poised, articulate, concerned, and energetic people. The same was said about both Farris and Julia Bryant. The family's legacy indeed lives on.

Top: Governor and Mrs. Bryant's daughters Cecilia and Adair during an interview with the author at the governor's mansion, November 2, 2005.

Bottom: Governor and Mrs. Bryant with daughters at family dinner in the private dining room, where important topics were discussed daily.

Opposite: Cecilia Bryant serenaded by the boys. In January 1962 the Bryant family welcomed 49 teenagers from Peru, the visit a program of Operation Amigo, for which Governor Bryant was honorary chairman. The program sought to educate Latin American youth who were subjected to propaganda from their Communist leaders claiming that American officials were "Imperialist Dictators." After touring the Capital City and Florida State University, the teens were treated to a "Coke and Cookies" party, hosted by the lovely teenaged Cecilia. The rugs in the state reception room were rolled back as they danced to twist tunes played on the grand piano by one of the Peruvian students. The bus taking the students back to their plane was delayed for at least 20 minutes as the admiring boys surrounded Cecilia, anxious for an autograph to memorialize their exposure to the real American way of life.

President Lyndon Johnson shares a dance with a poised Cecilia Bryant during her parents' tenure as governor and first lady of Florida.

Daughter Adair especially loved acting. Imagine her thrill when Helen Hayes, the grand dame of theater, came to the mansion as a houseguest.

Farris Bryant was once a member of the Tallahassee Little Theater, and Julia Bryant had chosen marriage and family over a career as an actress.

Farris Bryant swept Julia Burnett off her feet,
even though she had plans to go to New York and
pursue a career in theater. The story goes that
Farris saw Julia on the tennis courts of FSCW and
called that evening for a date. After three dates,
Farris proposed marriage.

Mrs. Bryant's hat was a gift to the
Museum of Florida History.

"It was a love affair for fifty-six years. [Mother] knew that she was appreciated and that father relied on her advice."

ADAIR BRYANT SIMON

Opposite: First Lady Julia Bryant in her inaugural ball gown on January 3, 1961.

First Lady Julia Bryant helps pin a corsage on the shoulder of First Lady Lady Bird Johnson, visiting the mansion with her daughter, Luci Baines Johnson. They were the Bryants' houseguests that evening and spent the night in the state guest bedroom.

At Home with the Bryants

Governor Bryant relied on his wife Julia's perceptions and advice and supported her belief in family. Though certainly his life as governor was more than hectic, he made it a point to be home for dinner with his family, who remained a priority in his life. In an interview given to reporter Hettie Cobb in February 1961, Mrs. Bryant shared some of her philosophy about juggling the duties of the first lady and raising three daughters: "We pass this way but once, no matter who you are, if you neglect your family . . . these are the things that can never be recaptured . . . there is a void that can never be filled . . . these are the lasting values."

She explained that life with a husband in public office is not the easiest. When the governor was a legislator, Mrs. Bryant would spend two or three days in Tallahassee "because Farris needed me" and then make the 176-mile trip back to Ocala to be with the children "because they needed me too."

As the governor's wife she expressed confidence that the family was more than up to the tasks at hand: "Now we must rearrange our thinking, our goals, and our lives to meet the challenges of our new way of life . . . the children are prepared for a gold fish bowl existence for the next four years." Her trust and affection for her husband are evident in these words: "Farris is so self-confident that he gives us confidence in ourselves. We always talk things over together and he encourages the children and me to lean on him." Daughters Adair and Cecilia recalled that their father also spoke to them about the issues and concerns of the day. Although so young, their lives were inestimably enriched by the world view offered by their father.

The family's time together was inviolate, but Mrs. Bryant also loved to entertain. She solved the dilemma by instituting "at homes," so that friends could come at a time when they were expected rather than dropping by. Despite their high standing in state government, the Bryants were unpretentious and down to earth. Governor Bryant even asked that the mansion be referred to as the "executive residence." While the change was well intentioned, traditions die hard, and the new name never really caught on.

The Bryants were all musically inclined, with theater another of their passions. Farris Bryant was once a member of the Tallahassee Little Theater, and Julia Bryant had chosen marriage and family over a career as an actress. Daughters Cecilia and Adair were equally fascinated by stagecraft, and both appeared in Little Theater productions in Tallahassee.

It was Adair who found her greatest joy in the theater. Imagine her thrill when Helen Hayes, the grande dame of theater, came to Tallahassee in November 1964. A houseguest at the mansion, Miss Hayes discussed with thirteen-year-old Adair their own special muse. Miss Hayes helped the Bryants welcome first lady Mrs. Lyndon B. Johnson, who was aboard a special campaign train stopped for the evening in Tallahassee. Adair showed Luci, the Johnson's youngest daughter, through the mansion.

Mansion Enhancements

During Bryant's term of office, several changes were made to the mansion. In October 1962, with relations between the United States and the Soviet Union continuing to degrade, the Governor's Mansion Commission strongly recommended that the unused area in the basement of the mansion be converted into a fallout shelter. Commission Chairman G. Warren Sanchez said: "We feel that it makes good sense to have a designated area from which the governor and his assistants can direct the vital affairs of our state in time of emergency. The available space at the residence provides a well-suited location for this purpose."

Just before Thanksgiving in 1962, a heated pool, a gift from the Florida Swimming Pool Industry Association, was completed. Although the air was a bit chilly, the governor took advantage of the gift that very day. In March 1962 the mansion commission passed a resolution to build a four-car garage, with an efficiency apartment, to replace the dilapidated garage, and to build a cabana with baths and a fireplace, a screened recreation area, and storage areas adjacent to the new swimming pool. With the old garage replaced, Mrs. Bryant in consultation with the commission planned brick walkways and steps that led from the front down into a grass terrace on the southwest side of the mansion. With a love of gardening so evident back in Ocala, Julia Bryant took on the task of beautifying the mansion's grounds. She planted hydrangeas on the south side of the grounds, daylilies in the northwest area, and calendulas in the front of the mansion. She supervised repairs to the greenhouse and employed a plot of land directly south of the mansion as a cutting garden, where seasonal flowers and herbs could beautify the mansion year-round.

As state functions required additional parking, a paved parking area was added on the east side of the grounds, directly across from Adams Street. The lot was screened with landscaping, and Mrs. Bryant supervised the planting of additional seasonal flowers. To tend to all of the new plantings and greenhouse production, a full-time gardener was employed.

After leaving office, Governor Bryant returned to law in Jacksonville. Just one year later President Johnson appointed him to his cabinet as the director of the Office of Emergency Planning, as a representative to NATO, and as a member of the National Security Council. Farris Bryant ran for the U.S. Senate in 1970 but was defeated by Lawton Chiles.

As only the second residents of the mansion, the Bryants left their legacy for all. The governor's eloquent words, given in a January 1961 speech, illumine the character of the man who gave his best to the state of Florida: "Let us come again to this historic ground we reach, at the end of our appointed time, confident in the verdict of history that we, as a people, have highly resolved to do the best of which we could conceive—that each failure has been a source of learning, each success a new inspiration."

With her love of gardening, so evident at home in Ocala, Julia Bryant took on the task of beautifying the mansion's grounds.

GOVERNOR WILLIAM HAYDON BURNS
1965–1967

Governor Haydon Burns's two-year term of office resulted from a constitutional amendment that changed the election schedule to ensure presidential and gubernatorial elections were not held the same year. Nevertheless, the governor made full use of his tenure, making progress on constitutional revision, outdoor recreation, industrial development, and tax reform.

William Haydon Burns was born in Chicago in 1912 to Harry Haydon and Ethel Burnett Burns. The Burns family moved to Jacksonville in 1922 where the boy attended public schools. Burns then enrolled at Babson College in Massachusetts and earned his degree.

When he returned to Jacksonville, Burns earned his pilot's license and operated a flying school. In 1934 he married Mildred Carlyon. Burns enlisted in the Navy during World War II, serving as an aeronautical salvage specialist, and was assigned to the Office of the Secretary of the Navy. When the war ended Burns returned to Jacksonville where he owned an appliance business and developed a public relations and business consulting firm.

Burns first ran for mayor of Jacksonville in 1949; his four reelections earned him the distinction of the longest mayoral tenure in Jacksonville's history. In 1960 Burns was a candidate for governor, finishing third and surprisingly well in the Democratic primary. In the next election cycle, he was the high man in both the first and second Democratic primaries.

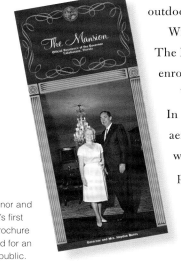

Top: Governor and Mrs. Burns's first mansion brochure was created for an interested public.

Bottom: Governor and Mrs. Burns pose with their children and grandchild.

"I would like to pay tribute to that group which blessed my life—leading always onward and upward—

that is my family—especially my wife, Mildred, who, along with our son Bill—our daughter, Eleanor,

her husband, Lloyd—and my mother—have consistently provided the kind of warm, sympathetic

understanding and devoted family relationships that make it possible for a man to enter and remain a part

of public life. They have truly been my beacon of light—my haven of stability and serenity."

GOVERNOR HAYDON BURNS, INAUGURATION DAY, JANUARY 5, 1965

Top: Mrs. Burns coordinates the menu for an upcoming event with her staff in the mansion kitchen.

Bottom: Invitation to a mansion dinner during the Burns tenure, honoring Dr. J. Broward Culpepper, chancellor of the State Universities, and Dr. John E. Champion, president of Florida State University.

Top: Mrs. Burns unpacking
a box with a toy car for her
grandchildren in the governor's
mansion office.

Bottom: Mrs. Burns stands in
the state entrance hall before
the mural that was installed
during her tenure.

With its year-round climate and growing

On his inauguration day, January 5, 1965, Burns inspired his audience with his speech about the progress and future of Florida, but he also made this poignant tribute to his family:

> I would like to pay tribute to that group which blessed my life—leading always onward and upward—that is my family—especially my wife, Mildred, who, along with our son Bill—our daughter, Eleanor, her husband, Lloyd—and my mother—have consistently provided the kind of warm, sympathetic understanding and devoted family relationships that make it possible for a man to enter and remain a part of public life. They have truly been my beacon of light—my haven of stability and serenity.

FIRST FAMILY INITIATIVES

Mrs. Burns, entering the furious pace of entertaining at the mansion, noted: "As soon as we came here in January and began having guests, I realized how often they asked if I didn't have something telling about the mansion, or a souvenir." Mrs. Burns set about designing a brochure entitled "The Mansion," which explained the building's history and its furnishings, illustrated with eighteen color photographs. In doing this Mrs. Burns recognized the mansion not only as the executive residence of the governor and his family, but also as an important "state museum." Governor and Mrs. Burns made few changes to the mansion except for adding wallpaper on one wall of the entrance hall. The paper was specially printed and featured birds and flowers in muted tones. While at the mansion Governor and Mrs. Burns saw to it that the abandoned houses across the street were demolished, and in their place planted gardens of roses, azaleas, and camellias.

In 1965 Governor Burns led a statewide initiative to bring Walt Disney Productions to Florida. Walt Disney and his brother Roy, who opened the ground-breaking California theme park Disneyland in 1955, decided to build a theme park in the East. With its year-round climate and growing tourist industry, Florida was the perfect place. The corporation had begun buying land in the Orlando area during Governor Bryant's term. The theme park industry was big business, and Governor Burns was also approached by Roy and Dale Evans with plans to build a park called West World, which did not materialize.

Years later, attending a reception at the mansion, the Burnses' son Bill shared some of his recollections. When his father was governor, Bill was attending the University of Florida, so he did not experience mansion life on a daily basis. He did remember that the state rooms were reserved for functions and that the family spent most of their time together in the family quarters, reading, playing cards, and watching television.

At the end of the fifties and into the sixties the nation was consumed by issues of civil rights, particularly the cause of African-Americans' rights to equal treatment under the law. Florida, a Confederate state, had a long history of segregation and was one of the last to fully embrace integration. Governor LeRoy Collins was the first to encounter civil rights uprisings and took a moderate approach, but as time passed too many (particularly in north Florida) still refused to accept the nation's mandates of the Civil Rights Act (1964) and Voting Rights Act (1965).

The issue of race factored greatly into the gubernatorial election in November 1966. By this time south Florida's population had exploded, particularly because of the influx of hundreds of thousands of exiles fleeing Castro's Cuba. South Florida's demographics became a force of reckoning in any election campaign.

In the 1964 election, newcomer Mayor Robert King High of Miami had run against Haydon Burns in the Democratic primary and carried the majority of the African-American voters. High's opponents characterized him as a liberal, and he vowed to support the Civil Rights Act, then pending in Congress. Burns, the "conservative," however, opposed the act. The number of votes each man garnered was close enough to require a runoff, which Burns won.

In 1966 Mayor High again squared off with Haydon Burns in the Democratic primary. Although Burns received the highest number of votes, the two candidates were forced into a *déjà vu* runoff. This time Mayor High was the victor. He would run against Republican Claude Kirk for governor of Florida.

After many visitors' requests, Mrs. Burns set about designing a brochure entitled "The Mansion," which explained the building's history and its furnishings, illustrated with eighteen color photographs.

GOVERNOR CLAUDE ROY KIRK, JR.

1967–1971

One definition of *flamboyant* in the 1963 edition of *Merriam-Webster's Dictionary* is "flashy display." Of all of Florida's governors, Claude R. Kirk earned the term's use most frequently. Claude Kirk was a man with great charisma, a huge personality, and a passion for living life to the fullest.

Claude Kirk was a virtual newcomer to the political scene. In 1960 he had headed Florida's "Democrats for Nixon" presidential campaign, and as a result changed his party affiliation from Democrat to Republican. His first political contest came in 1964 as the Republican candidate for the U.S. Senate. He ran against former Florida governor Spessard Holland, who won decisively. Kirk reentered the political arena in 1966, defeating Richard Muldrew of Melbourne by a 3-1 margin for the Republican nomination for governor.

In a 1967 *New York Times* article titled "Flamboyant Governor," a journalist described Claude Kirk's campaign style: "He courted Florida as he courted women, with a big smile, a wink and a kiss on the hands for female spectators. He told the men he would cut their taxes. To the surprise of everyone, including himself, he won the governorship race handily."

When Kirk won against Democrat Robert King High, it was the first time a Republican had held the office of governor since the 1870s. The scene was set for epic battles between the newly elected governor and the Democrat-controlled legislature.

VERSATILITY AND VIGOR

Claude Roy Kirk, Jr., was born to Claude R. and Sarah McClure Kirk in 1926 in San Bernardino, California. He spent his formative years in River Forest, Illinois (a Chicago suburb), and in Montgomery, Alabama, where he attended high school. Almost immediately after his graduation in 1943, Kirk enlisted in the United States Marine Corps, where he was accepted for officer's candidate school. At nineteen, during World War II, Kirk was commissioned a second lieutenant, one of the youngest ever to hold that rank in the Marine Corps.

Second Lieutenant Kirk completed a tour with the Marines in 1946 and then attended school at the University of Alabama College of Law, where he earned his degree in 1949. While at law school he married Sarah Stokes, a former classmate. The Kirks divorced in 1951 after the birth of two daughters, Sarah Stokes and Katherine (Kitty) Gilmer. They were later remarried and had twin boys, Franklin and William. Their second marriage, however, ended in divorce in 1966.

When the Korean War broke out the Marines called Kirk back to active duty. He served as both an infantry officer and a fire control officer aboard the battleship New Jersey. He served with great distinction, earning the Air Medal.

In 1956 following the war Kirk, at the youthful age of thirty, formed a partnership and founded the American Heritage Life Insurance Company, headquartered in Jacksonville, Florida. The firm was highly successful, but in 1962 Kirk became a vice-chairman of the board, and then left to accept a partnership in the firm of Haden Stone, Inc., Wall Street investment bankers. He worked for the firm for eighteen months and then resigned to run for the U.S. Senate.

Kirk's next adventure led him to Rio de Janeiro, Brazil, where he formed the Kirk Investment Company and toured every capital in South America. It was in Rio de Janeiro that Kirk would meet the love of his life, the beautiful Erika Mattfeld, born in Bremen, Germany. In a December 2005 interview Mrs. Kirk explained that her meeting with Claude was the result of happenstance. Kirk was asked by a business associate who had a date with Erika, to pick up her up for dinner that evening. Though they had never met before, the German-speaking Erika and the dashing future governor instantly found delight in each other's company. Although Kirk could speak no German, they both knew enough Portuguese to communicate. The future Mrs. Kirk had been previously married and had a young daughter named Adriana. On his style of courtship Mrs. Kirk said: "He knew how to get to me, he was always bringing presents to Adriana." His thoughtfulness extended to Erika as well, and after learning of her fondness for blueberries, which she could not get in Rio, Kirk brought them to her from New York.

The future Mrs. Kirk knew relatively little of her fiancé's political aspirations. Imagine what it must have

"[Claude Kirk] courted Florida as he courted women, with a big smile,

a wink and a kiss on the hands for female spectators.

He told the men he would cut their taxes."

NEW YORK TIMES, JANUARY 9, 1967

Top: Governor Claude Kirk with his new bride, Erika Mattfeld Kirk, blowing a kiss. The Breakers Hotel, Palm Beach, Florida, February 18, 1967.

Bottom: Mrs. Kirk poses with "The Governor's Orange Tree" in front of the mansion, April 19, 1967.

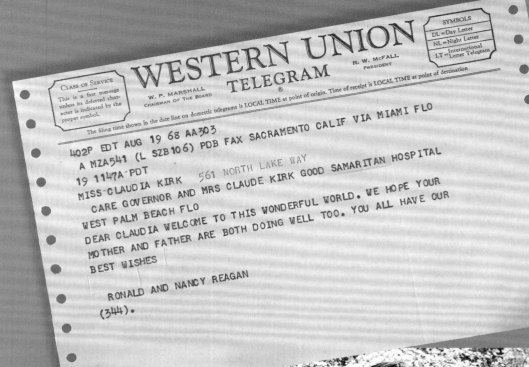

Top left: Ronald and Nancy Reagan's 1968 congratulatory telegram to Claudia Kirk, who was the first baby born to a family residing in the present governor's mansion.

Top right: Mrs. Kirk reading with her young daughters Adriana and Claudia (on her lap).

Bottom: Governor Kirk with young Adriana on the mansion grounds.

Opposite top: Two years later, a "Welcome Home" sign greets newborn boy Erik Kirk, the second baby born to the couple during their tenure at the mansion in 1970.

Opposite bottom left: Mrs. Kirk relaxes by the mansion swimming pool with her daughters Adriana and Claudia.

Opposite bottom right: Governor and Mrs. Kirk at Claudia Kirk's christening.

Claudia Kirk was the first child born to a presiding governor in fifty-two years.

been like: Erika, a thirty-two-year-old beauty with a young daughter coming to the United States knowing very little English, was about to be thrust into the spotlight. Not only would she begin a new marriage, but a new life in which she was called upon to host not only the leaders of Florida, but also Washington politicians and a host of celebrities. It must have been daunting.

IMMEDIATE ACTION

On Kirk's inauguration day Erika was present but not seated at the dais. Not until that evening during the inaugural ball would Governor Kirk introduce the press to his intended. There was much speculation about his lady friend, whom Kirk introduced as Madam X, setting the press into a frenzy of speculation. The Kirks were married little over a month later, on February 18, 1967, at the historic Breakers Hotel in Palm Beach. Governor Kirk's twin boys and two daughters were all in attendance. One of the many celebrity guests was Richard M. Nixon, who briefly danced with the bride. Erika Mattfeld Kirk would now attend to the governor's mansion officially as Florida's first lady.

In 1967 throughout the country, the establishment still operated under strict moral guidelines, and in Tallahassee the traditions handed down by the local gentry often caused Mrs. Kirk to be seen as an outsider and out of sync with images of a first lady. The language barrier aside, the stylish and fashionable Erika Mattfeld must have caused much consternation and perhaps just a hint of jealousy among the matrons of the Old South.

Governor Kirk scored a first when, during his inaugural address, he immediately called the legislature into special session to address his "war on crime." Governor Kirk founded the Florida Department of Law Enforcement in pursuit of those goals. That kind of intensity became the theme of the Kirk administration. During his first year of office the new governor was already primed for action, intending to focus on his campaign priorities, including a fight on air and water pollution, an anticrime program, and a plan to make Florida the "world capital" of oceanography.

During his first year in office, Kirk dove 2,000 feet to the ocean bottom, hired an army of detectives from the Wackenhut Corporation to fight crime, called for the resignation of Secretary of Defense Robert McNamara, and challenged Fidel Castro to a debate. Kirk was also instrumental in bringing the Republican National Convention to Miami in 1968. His energy seemed to have no limits. A *New York Times* story by Robert Sherill explained that Governor Kirk's normal workday began at 7:00 a.m. and ended around midnight.

A GROWING FAMILY

With her husband away on business so often, Mrs. Kirk had the pleasure of her daughter Adriana's company and that of her personal assistant, Mrs. Eleanor Ervin. Sarah Kirk, the teenaged daughter from Governor Kirk's first marriage, also lived at the mansion for a year while attending Florida State University.

Mrs. Kirk was enamored of fresh flowers, and she would arrange many of the pieces that were set about the mansion's state rooms and private gardens. She also spent a considerable amount of time around the pool, where daughter Adriana played. Mrs. Kirk tells the story of Adriana's breakneck runs on her Radio Flyer wagon from the crest of the hill in the front of the mansion, down the steep grade to the pool area. Adriana was a handful, a merry, delightful child. Frequent parties with her classmates usually centered on the pool. Mrs. Kirk recalls one of the more outlandish pranks Adriana played when she put their dog, a black poodle named Bizz, into the elevator and then ran upstairs to meet him. Neither the dog nor Mrs. Kirk was amused.

Young Adriana was soon joined by a sister, Claudia, born on August 14, 1968. She was the first child to be born to a presiding governor in fifty-two years, preceded by Elizabeth Hutchinson Broward, born in 1906 to Governor Napoleon Bonaparte Broward and his wife Annie. Claudia was delivered at the Good Samaritan Hospital in West Palm Beach, close to their family home, Duck's Nest, in Palm Beach.

The year 1970, ushering in a new decade, proved both politically challenging and personally enriching for Governor Kirk. His son Erik Henry was born in Tallahassee in April. That June his daughter Kitty married Alexander Mann (Ander) Crenshaw in Jacksonville. Ander Crenshaw would serve in both the Florida house and senate and go on to represent Florida's fourth district in the United States House of Representatives.

During his first year in office, Kirk dove 2,000 feet to the ocean bottom, hired an army of detectives from the Wackenhut Corporation to fight crime, called for the resignation of Secretary of Defense Robert McNamara, and challenged Fidel Castro to a debate.

Opposite: First Lady Erika Kirk photographed with her daughters Claudia Kirk Barto (left) and Adriana Dolabella (right) at the Breakers Hotel, December 2005.

Imagine what it must have been like: Erika, a thirty-two-year-old beauty with a young daughter coming to the United States knowing very little English, was about to be thrust into the spotlight. Not only would she begin a new marriage, but a new life in which she was called upon to host not only the leaders of Florida, but also Washington politicians and a host of celebrities. It must have been daunting.

MAJOR CONSTITUTIONAL CHANGES

Though Governor Kirk was constantly embattled in partisan politics, he was able to secure significant revisions to the state constitution of 1885, which actually resulted in a new constitution. The Florida Constitution as revised in 1968 recognized the court-ordered reapportionment (which significantly changed the number of Dade County legislators); strengthened the office of the governor by allowing two successive terms; recreated the office of lieutenant governor, running on the governor's ticket; consolidated executive departments; and granted the governor budgetary responsibilities. Although Governor Kirk and some public policy experts had recommended otherwise, the state kept its unique elected cabinet officers, who had no term limits and held primaries independent of the governor's race. The following year, the Legislative Reorganization Act changed the biennial meetings of the legislature to annual.

Governor Kirk championed environmental causes, leading an effort to stop construction of the Cross-Florida Barge Canal. Begun as a Works Progress Administration project in the 1930s, the canal was heavily promoted by Farris Bryant. Governor Bryant had argued the canal's east-west channel would make Florida

Governor Kirk championed environmental causes, leading an effort to stop construction of the Cross-Florida Barge Canal.

As the first Republican to win the office in almost a century, Governor Kirk would effectively reintroduce two-party politics to Florida.

the hub for sea traffic between the Gulf of Mexico and the Atlantic. The building of the canal lost citizens' support when they learned its potentially detrimental environmental effects.

In 1970 Kirk sought reelection, choosing as his running mate Ray C. Osborne (named his lieutenant governor in 1969). After a tough battle with Republican Jack Eckerd, who forced Kirk into a runoff, Governor Kirk won the party's endorsement. In the general election, Governor Kirk captured an amazing 43.1% of the votes considering his party affiliation, but lost to Pensacola Democrat Reubin O'D. Askew.

Kirk moved his family back to Palm Beach and assumed the presidency of Kirk and Company, merchant bankers. In 1978 he entered the eight-contender Democratic gubernatorial primary, won by Bob Graham of Miami Lakes.

Claude and Erika Kirk were among the most colorful residents of the Florida's Governor's Mansion. As the first Republican to win the office in almost a century, Governor Kirk effectively reintroduced two-party politics to Florida.

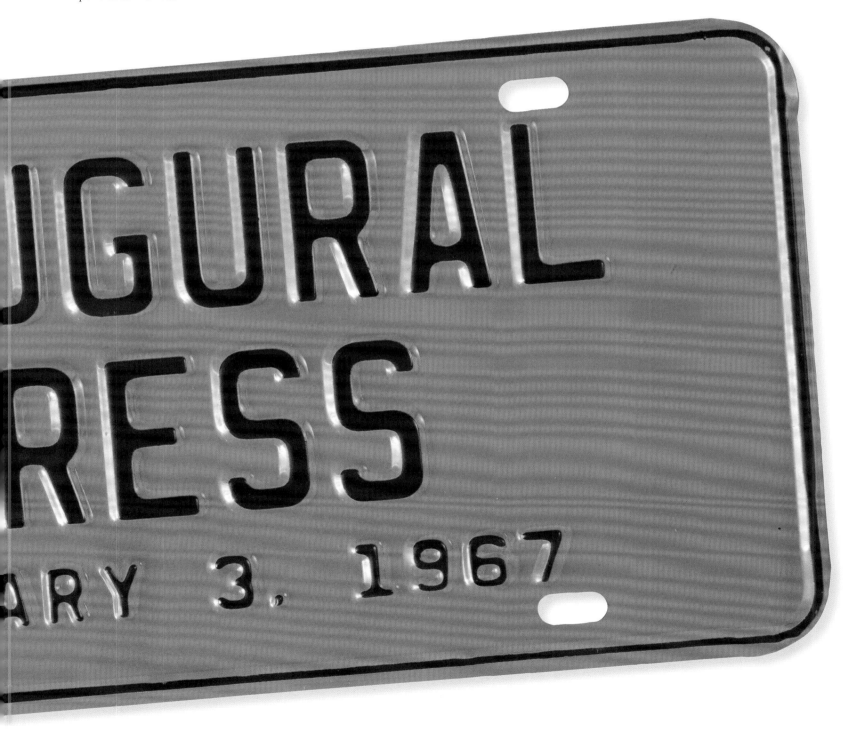

CHAPTER SEVEN

THE SEVENTIES
An Era of Profound Changes

Opposite: Governor and
Mrs. Reubin Askew with
Lt. Governor Jim Williams
and wife Louise during
a formal receiving line at
the mansion.

hen the decade of the seventies began, Americans were still caught up in the counterculture mood of the sixties. Escalating resistance to the Vietnam War caused great divisiveness, culminating in 1970 with the tragedy of Kent State. President Richard M. Nixon, elected in 1969, faced tumultuous unrest and ultimately ordered a cease-fire on the North Vietnamese, with U.S. involvement ending completely in 1973. ¶ Elected for two terms, President Nixon ushered in an era when environmental issues, so long disregarded, were thrust into the spotlight. Nixon signed into law the National Environmental Policy Act, and the Environmental Protection Agency began its operations. ¶ Momentous change reverberated throughout the country when the Supreme Court legalized abortion and declared capital punishment unconstitutional. The space program shifted from manned lunar landings to the space shuttle program. ¶ The first inklings of the explosive Watergate scandal were discovered in 1972 when White House operatives were caught burglarizing the offices of the Democratic National Committee. Vice-President Agnew resigned from office in 1973, charged with tax evasion. President Nixon recommended Gerald R. Ford from Michigan to replace Agnew, and after confirmation, Ford took the oath of office in December 1974. Ultimately President Nixon, facing impeachment for his role in Watergate, resigned in 1974, and Gerald Ford was president. ¶ Worldwide, tensions exploded when Egyptian and Syrian forces attacked Israel to start the 1973 Yom Kippur War. An Arabian oil embargo followed, punishing countries that aided Israel. The result at home was an unprecedented shortage of gasoline and necessity for rationing, not seen since World War II. ¶ In the world of technology, more and more computers appeared in the marketplace, and as the airline industry improved its trans-Atlantic flights, Americans increasingly traveled internationally. The United States celebrated its 200th birthday in 1976 with impressive displays and new monuments created nationwide. ¶ For the first time since the Civil War, a president was elected from the Deep South. Georgian Jimmy Carter sought to bring a peaceful prosperity and an end to the long-festering wounds of the Vietnam War. In Iran, Middle East conflict again erupted as the Ayatollah Khomeini's anti-American sentiment resulted in a hostage crisis lasting over a year, costing Carter his 1980 reelection bid. ¶ In Florida, the state's explosive growth demanded attention, especially government's role in addressing its permanent and potentially devastating effects. The stewardship of the environment was one of the top priorities on a growing list affecting Floridians for the long term.

GOVERNOR REUBIN O'DONOVAN ASKEW
1971–1975 & 1975–1979

The personalities and life style of the newest occupants of Florida's Governor's Mansion, Reubin and Donna Lou Askew, were in stark contrast to the flamboyance that characterized the Kirk administration. Mrs. Askew acknowledged that they were a close-knit family, and others described them as soft-spoken and unaffected. The Pensacola family (children Angela and Kevin were nine and seven) would adapt to life in the mansion, bringing their own special traditions to this highly visible and demanding new role.

Florida's thirty-seventh governor, Reubin O'Donovan Askew, was the first elected for two consecutive four-year terms, and he dominated Florida's leadership for almost the entire decade. Governor Askew presided over a number of firsts, not the least of which were the building of a new capitol complex (begun in 1972 and completed in 1977); instituting a corporate profits tax; naming the first African-American to the Florida Supreme Court (Joseph W. Hatchett of Pinellas County); appointing former Miami city commissioner Athalie Range as secretary of the Department of Community Affairs (the first woman and first African-American department head); creating the "Sunshine Amendment" requiring financial disclosure by all elected officials; and implementing environmental initiatives with long-term consequences.

In 1928 Reubin O'Donovan Askew was born to parents Leo G. and Alberta Askew in Muskogee, Oklahoma, the youngest of six children. When Reubin was just two, his parents divorced, and his mother was left to raise the children alone. In a 1998 interview with Jan Godown for Florida State University's *Research in Review*, Governor Askew recalled: "She was a wonderful, strong, Christian woman." He explained that when his father failed to make support payments, his mother, an excellent baker, sold pies for hard cash. That spirit of initiative and overarching concern for family continued when she moved the family to Pensacola, her hometown, in 1937. Mrs. Askew became an assistant housekeeper at the San Carlos Hotel, but the *entire* family helped to support the household, each taking on a certain responsibility. At age nine or ten, young Reubin had the largest magazine route in Pensacola. His responsibility was the water bill, which averaged about fifty cents a month, taken from his total earnings of around two dollars. The spirit of cooperation, teamwork, and loyalty were values that permeated Reubin Askew's personal and political life.

When he was just fifteen, Askew enlisted in the Florida State Home Guard. After graduation from high school at seventeen, he joined the U.S. Army and served from 1946 to 1948. He was selected to train as a paratrooper in the 82nd Airborne, hurtling from planes through the air, much to his mother's dismay.

Following his tour with the U.S. Army, Askew attended Florida State University using the GI Bill to help pay his tuition. As a member of the Air Force ROTC, Askew earned $28 a month and supplemented that income with additional part-time jobs. Even with this schedule Askew found the time to serve as student body president. Askew graduated with his bachelor of science degree and was named a distinguished military graduate. In 1951 during the Korean War, Lieutenant Askew began a two-year tour of duty in Europe with the U.S. Air Force. After active duty, Lt. Askew remained in the Air Force Reserve, earning the rank of captain.

Govenor and Mrs. Askew and their family at the 1971 Inaugural parade.

Upon his return to the states, the future governor enrolled at the University of Florida to earn his law degree. He was once again elected class president and served as executive editor of the *Law Review* and justice (president) of Phi Alpha Delta law fraternity.

A STATESMAN EMERGES

Askew's first role in the public sector was as the assistant county solicitor for Escambia County between 1956 and 1958. He married Donna Lou Harper, originally from Sanford, Florida, on August 11, 1956. In 1958, Reubin Askew ran for the Florida House of Representatives and so began a life of service in elected government.

In a February 2006 interview Governor and Mrs. Askew, nearing their fiftieth anniversary as husband and wife, displayed the easy comfort of a couple devoted to each other, as well as united over a lifetime in so many important matters. The governor's enormous breadth of experience makes it possible to cover only highlights. The governor illumines all events and encounters with a memory that covers every detail. Donna Lou Askew, attempting to hasten the governor and cover many important moments, chided her husband with affection: "I could tell you the same story, in half the time!"

Askew ran successfully for the Florida Senate in 1962 and served as president *pro tempore* from 1969 to 1970. As a freshman senator he was thrust into leading the heated debates about reapportionment. The governor later remarked: "I was placed in a position with the leadership on this issue I didn't want, and the responsibility I shouldn't have had." In 1970, Askew campaigned for the Democratic nomination for governor. In a runoff with Earl Faircloth of Miami, Senator Askew won the privilege of representing his party against incumbent Claude R. Kirk, Jr. Running with lieutenant-governor candidate Tom Adams of Orange Park, Askew won 56.9% of the vote.

Inaugural festivities began the day before the ceremony with a public fish fry at the Leon County fairgrounds. On January 5, 1971, the governor-elect began the day with a prayer breakfast before proceeding to the inaugural ceremonies at the capitol. Dressed in top hats and tails, Governor Claude Kirk accompanied his successor from the mansion to the dais, where Askew was sworn in and delivered his inaugural address.

In that address, now Governor Askew explained the priorities of his administration, which included tax reform, environmental protections, educational initiatives, transportation improvements, judicial and election reform, and improved economic opportunities for all people, rural and urban, black and white. Acknowledging the huge scope of these imperatives, Governor Askew said:

> The responsibilities before us are many—far too numerous to discuss each in detail here today. And we recognize that in meeting those responsibilities . . . in exercising the authority of the Chief Executive of this state . . . that we will make errors. But we are pledged to you today that our errors will not be those of unconcern. They will *not* be errors of inaction.

On that day he could not have known that, governing Florida for two terms, he would make significant strides toward all of his promises. The inaugural parade, its route covering 4.3 miles, was the longest in the city's history.

"FAIRYLAND" (WITH LIMITS)

From the start of his term of office Askew, who lived a disciplined life without alcohol or tobacco, was characterized as a "square" by some. Rather than taking offense at this, the new first lady underscored the importance the Askews placed on family and personal values. Donna Lou Harper was an only child, raised in a strict family with clearly defined ideas of right and wrong. In a 1972 newspaper interview she expressed appreciation for diverse lifestyles when she remarked: "And isn't that what America is all about—everyone living their own lifestyle, what's comfortable for them? Freedom with responsibility, not license."

In Pensacola the Askews lived in a modest three-bedroom home, and the governor's mansion was an elegant change for them. Mrs. Askew had taught elementary school until the arrival of the children. She

In Pensacola the Askews lived in a modest three-bedroom home, and the governor's mansion was an elegant change. The children were mesmerized. "They were in fairyland," said Mrs. Askew. "They had such a good time running the elevator up and down."

The 1975 inaugural parade covered 4.3 miles, the longest in Tallahassee's history.

HAPPINESS IS A NEW GOVERNOR

'GOODBYE' CLAU

"We have been apostles of abundance, a people of plenty. We have believed in the myth of inexhaustibility. But now we are learning that it was only that, a myth."

GOVERNOR REUBIN O'D. ASKEW, 1975 INAUGURAL ADDRESS

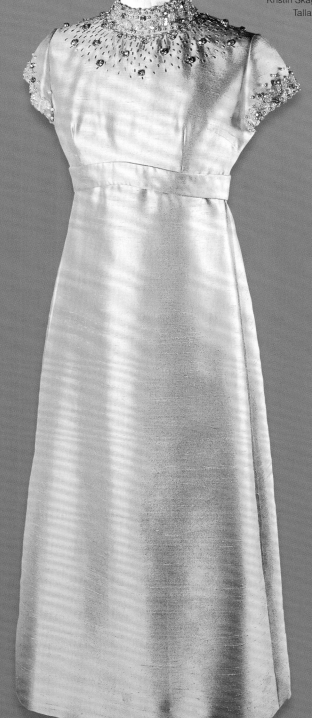

Top left: Governor and Mrs. Reubin Askew head to their inaugural ball.

Bottom left: Angela and Kevin Askew grew from youngsters to young teens during their eight years at the mansion.

Right: First Lady Donna Lou Askew's citrus lemon inaugural gown, designed by Icelandic designer Kristin Skagfield of Tallahassee.

noted that, "For the most part, for people like we were, we've adjusted pretty well. We were not used to living in this setting. There are people used to living it their whole life."

When the children first visited the mansion, they were mesmerized. "I wish you could have seen them," Mrs. Askew said, "They were in fairyland. They had such a good time running the elevator up and down." The children were grateful for another feature of the mansion. When they lived in Pensacola, they were required to double-up when their grandmother came for a visit. Now with all the extra room, that wouldn't be necessary.

With two young children and her husband the state's chief executive, Mrs. Askew found her life hectic but more than rose to the challenge. She said: "It's just the most natural thing in the world not to want conflict. That's human. But if we all lived for what's comfortable, nothing would be done in the world. If you're given certain responsibilities and talents, it's up to you to use them."

The Askews made every effort to see that their children weren't altered by their lofty position in the world, enrolling them in public schools. They were, of course, privileged and different in some respects, and Angela was embarrassed when driven to school in a security sedan. On the other hand, there were some great advantages, for example when the children received a visit from none other than Mickey Mouse, upon the opening of Disney World. Sundays were family days, and after church the family gathered at the dining table, with the talk usually revolving around the children. On one such Sunday, Angela proudly informed her father that with the new batch of guppies just born, a total of thirty-two live animals now lived at the mansion!

Angela also kept gerbils, and on one traumatic occasion, Smoky the family cat somehow got into the cage. Scores of gerbils ran down the stairs from the third floor with Smoky in close pursuit and Angela screaming. After finding half a gerbil tail under the bed, she was nearly inconsolable. The good news? All of the gerbils survived their harrowing ordeal.

One of the Askews' favorite games was marbles. The governor was especially fond of the game, played since his own childhood. In a 1973 interview, he revealed one of his concerns upon moving into the mansion: "When

we first moved here, I was worried we'd get in trouble if I took chalk and drew a circle on the rug. But then I walked in here, saw the rug and said, 'Lo and behold, we have been provided for.'" One of the loomed Indian rugs in the state dining room featured a circular pattern, immediately lending itself to marble play.

MOVING THE MANSION, REVISITED

Sadly, not all was fun and games in the real world, and as fears for the security of the first family grew, some modifications to the mansion grounds were made. The United States Secret Service had assessed the security of the mansion around 1972, when Vice-President Spiro Agnew was scheduled as an overnight guest. Because of the wide-open grounds, the secret service refused to allow his stay. Instead, Agnew spent the evening at the Downtown Holiday Inn where guards could monitor the elevators and fire escapes.

After the assassination of President Kennedy in 1963, security for all political leaders was reevaluated. Over the years the mansion received several telephoned bomb threats, and during the Kirk administration protesters gathered on the front lawn. A security fence was discussed as early as 1971, but not until December of 1975 was a metal picket fence installed around the perimeter of the property, with gates at the entry points. (On the rear side the fence is chain link.) The $101,839 project was built by the Bear Construction Company of Tallahassee. High-intensity light fixtures were also installed.

In what seems surprising just fifteen years after its construction, there was also a move afoot to relocate the mansion, if sufficient land around it could not be purchased. The heated conversations of 1953 (when the original 1907 mansion was considered for demolition) were revived. Ney Landrum, director of the Division of Recreation and Parks, Department of Natural Resources, was named chairman of the Governor's Park Committee in 1972.

The problems some saw in the present location were the lack of room for expansion and the increasingly commercial environment. General Services Director Chester Blakemore summed up the arguments in an

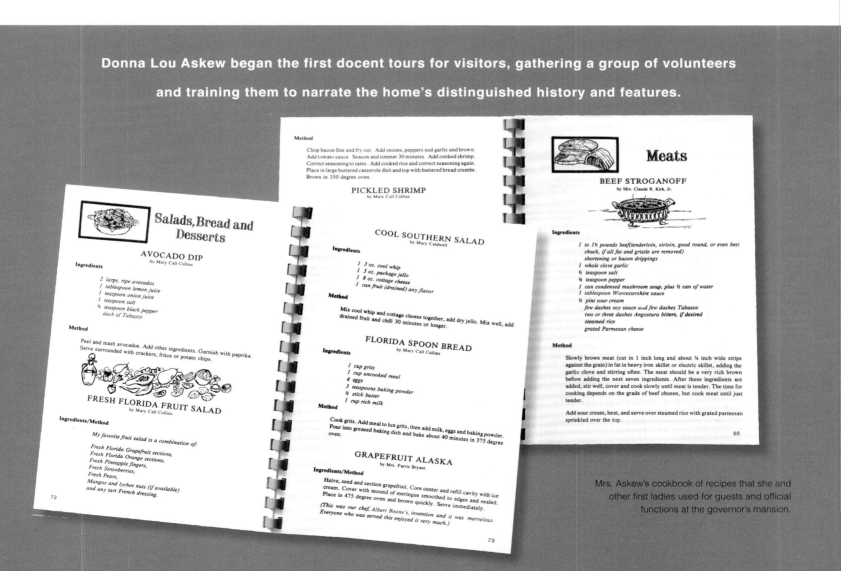

Donna Lou Askew began the first docent tours for visitors, gathering a group of volunteers and training them to narrate the home's distinguished history and features.

Mrs. Askew's cookbook of recipes that she and other first ladies used for guests and official functions at the governor's mansion.

interview: "[A]s a result of inadequate site and planning . . . the Mansion is poorly situated as an executive residence . . . its floor plan offers poor circulation patterns . . . and its mechanical core (heating and cooling) is outdated, inefficient and ineffective."

One proffered plan was to buy land around the residence to create a "Governor's Park." The committee would attempt to acquire a sixteen-block area surrounding the mansion and the Grove. Chairman Landrum explained a variety of ways to acquire and manage the land: by outright purchase; through zoning to increase compatibility of neighboring architecture; and by asking the voluntary cooperation of private property owners in developing their properties. The cost of this undertaking was estimated at $6 million. Barring the success of these measures, the committee was prepared to recommend that the mansion be relocated to Albert B. Maclay State Park, a 300-acre preserve with extensive gardens of azaleas, camellias, and oaks, some six miles north of Tallahassee.

Back in July 1953, then state senator LeRoy Collins resigned from a committee addressing a suitable location for the new governor's mansion. Mrs. Mary Call Darby Collins would resign her seat on the Governor's Mansion Advisory Council for the very same reason almost exactly nineteen years later. The words of her resignation letter to Governor Askew echo the sentiments of her husband years ago:

> I feel rather strongly in favor of an "in town" mansion. Easy and quick access to and from the mansion and the offices downtown for the Governor and those with whom he works and those he entertains, seems to us a great advantage. This, together with the value to the public of having a fairly central place to drive by and point out to visitors, will in my opinion outweigh any advantage to the Governor and his family of having a secluded place of residence. As we both know, a Governor simply does not have time to live the life of a country squire.

In her concluding remarks Mrs. Collins added: "To a degree, we went into this at the time the present mansion was built. So, I feel that you should replace me with a more 'open-minded' person and one whose background is not so rooted in public life as mine." Governor Askew reluctantly accepted Mrs. Collins's resignation by acknowledging: "We deeply regret that you cannot continue to serve, but I certainly understand your feelings about the matter. We would greatly appreciate your continued counsel and advice because your long service to the mansion is unparalleled by anyone."

The public took a particularly strong and perhaps emotional position on the issue of buying properties or relocating. A May 1972 editorial in the governor's hometown *Pensacola Journal* reflected general sentiments surrounding the plan.

> Certainly, we don't need to spend $6 million to create a park in the heart of downtown Tallahassee to provide a house for the governor, even if a few nuts make threats from time to time. . . . And while it might be nice to have a Governor's Mansion in Maclay Gardens, we think most taxpayers would think it would be even nicer to spend any extra state money on such things as schools. . . . The Mansion seems to us to be a pretty nice place. . . . Let's see if we can't make the current mansion last, like the last one, at least 50 years.

In August of 1972, an eighteen-page report summarized the findings of the Governor's Park Committee. While the state was able to purchase several lots, the grander Governor's Park plan and the idea of relocating the mansion were abandoned.

REFURBISHING FADED BEAUTY

Other opportunities arose to further develop the existing property, with one of the most popular improvements the tennis court built during the Askew administration. The Governor's Mansion Advisory Council approved the court's location, across Brevard Street just east of the existing greenhouse, at their meeting in September

1972. Governor Askew was particularly delighted, as the building funds were raised entirely through gifts from friends and colleagues.

In the meantime, Donna Lou Askew struggled to keep the mansion up to the high standards expected. In just fifteen years, some of the carpets had become threadbare, and in other cases the furniture was showing soiling and wear on the arms. Above all else, Mrs. Askew desired not to dilute the authenticity of the mansion. In September 1971, Mrs. Askew expressed her desire to create an overall plan to redecorate the public areas of the mansion and to make some minor improvements to the family living areas. The council suggested contacting three interior designers about their interest in creating such a plan. One of the three was James Cogar, the mansion's original decorator. Cogar was then managing the restoration of a historic community in Pleasantville, Kentucky. He agreed to meet with the advisory council, afterward concluding that the state areas had maintained "integrity through all administrations."

With the advisory council's assistance and approval, Mrs. Askew reupholstered some of the furniture, staying away from silks as they were less durable. She and the council were also successful in replacing some of the mansion's rugs, which had suffered the greatest disrepair as thousands had walked over them since 1957. The originals, pastel needlework rugs made in India, were now threadbare and in some places held together with masking tape.

The successful bidder for the new rugs was the Lacey Champion Company of Fairmount, Georgia, who along with the help of Sam Ewing, an interior designer from Winter Park, created the four 100% virgin wool rugs at a cost of $29,050. The largest rug, installed in the state dining room, measured seventeen by thirty feet and featured a design of orange blossoms and leaves, surrounded by a five-foot border design of seashells, palmetto fronds, and jumping dolphins. Mrs. Askew suggested the palmetto fronds, and the dolphin design matches the silver flatware used at the dining table and motifs from the USS *Florida* silver pieces. The three smaller rugs, measuring twelve by eighteen feet, and based on a Chinese Chippendale design, were installed in the state reception room.

Mrs. Askew also began a program to open the house to visitors. She gathered a group of volunteers and trained them to narrate the distinguished history of the home and its furnishings. Her initiative would greatly expand in the coming years as more and more guests came to tour the People's House.

Harsh Realities

Meanwhile, with his stature continuing to grow, Governor Askew was chosen as the keynote speaker at the 1972 Democratic National Convention in Miami Beach, when George McGovern won the party's nomination. Toward the end of Governor Askew's first term, Middle East events had disastrous consequences for Florida's economy. The Arab oil embargo in 1973 led not only to record prices but to a shortage of gasoline, the life-blood of Florida's tourist economy. In his book *Land of Sunshine, State of Dreams*, Gary Mormino recalls the widespread panic that the gas shortage brought. In Orlando, newly opened Disney World was faced with disaster as guests stopped coming. National newspapers foretold doom with headlines such as, "Disney, Trouble in Dreamland" and "Orlando's Hotel Boom Faces Bust." Plans for building an $11 million theme park called Bible World were abruptly canceled.

Following on the heels of the gas shortage, the Federal Reserve Board raised the prime lending rate, killing real estate transactions statewide. Mormino explains that new construction dropped from $7 billion in 1974 to just $2.8 billion in 1975. It seemed that the unlimited optimism associated with Florida's growth would suddenly end, just like the real estate boom of the 1920s almost a half-century earlier. Against this backdrop of a looming Armageddon, Governor Reubin Askew campaigned for his second term of office.

Governor Askew faced four opponents in the primary, one of whom was his own first-term lieutenant governor, Tom Adams. Askew easily won the primary and went on to face his Republican challenger, Jerry Thomas from Jupiter, and his running mate, Mike Thompson from Coral Gables. Governor Askew, who chose as his running mate Jim Williams, was reelected in a landslide victory, claiming 61.2% of the vote.

"We have been apostles of abundance, a people of plenty. We have believed in the myth of

After thousands of visitors since 1957, some rugs were threadbare and held together with masking tape. Mrs. Askew spearheaded a refurbishing plan that would not dilute the furnishings' authenticity.

inexhaustibility. But now we are learning that it was only that, a myth." The governor's inaugural address, on a bright and sunny January day, included those cautionary words. He pointed out that the state's revenues were almost $250 million short of projections. The state would make cuts in the budget with as little impact as possible to essential services.

While his second term started amid the harsh reality of economic downturn, Florida would once again prove its remarkable resiliency. The empty buildings weren't empty for long as, adjusting to the lower speed limits and higher gas prices, tourists and investors returned in record numbers.

A BELIEVER IN SUNSHINE

Askew inspired loyalty. Once in Pensacola in his early career, Trooper Casey Cason told him: "Boy, when you get to be governor, I'll be your driver."

This second term saw the governor's success with the constitutional amendment dubbed the "Sunshine Amendment," requiring financial disclosure for all public officials. It wasn't easy. After being rebuffed by the legislature, the governor took the issue to the people. For the first time, Governor Askew used the "initiative provision" of the Florida Constitution: an amendment could be placed on the ballot through a sufficient number of signatures. For four months, Governor Askew personally took his campaign to the people, and every weekend would find him at shopping centers soliciting signatures or at events sponsored by groups such as the League of Women Voters and Common Cause. *Two hundred and ten thousand* signatures later, the Sunshine Amendment was voted on by the people of Florida and passed with 80% in favor.

Governor Askew's personal integrity and courage to take on the issues he so strongly believed in certainly created some enmity from those who did not agree. The governor was not intimidated. His care, loyalty, and concern for those who earned his respect knew no limits, and they in turn respected him. Such was the case with Florida State Trooper Owen Thurmon (Casey) Cason.

Created in 1939, the Florida Highway Patrol had by 1952 established districts throughout Florida and called them "Troops." Trooper Casey Cason was stationed at Troop A in Pensacola when Reubin Askew was an Escambia County prosecutor. Governor Askew remembers Cason as one of the finest men he has known. During his lifetime Cason spent over forty-five years with Boys State, the American Legion's program to teach young people the ideals of American government. On one occasion in Pensacola, Trooper Cason told Askew: "Boy, when you get to be governor, I'll be your driver."

Captain Owen Cason's contributions are noted by this message on one of the bricks at the front gate where he welcomed many visitors over the years.

Fourteen years later when Askew was elected, he not only called upon Cason to serve as his driver, but also promoted him to captain. Captain Cason provided security at the governor's mansion during the administrations of Askew, Graham, Mixson, Martinez, and Chiles, long after his required retirement from the Highway Patrol at sixty-two. Captain Cason was representative of the many whose dedicated service at the governor's mansion caused them to be viewed more as family than as employees.

Governor Askew's work in protecting the environment and creating Florida's growth management legislation set the bar for all others who followed. As the capital city, Tallahassee reflected the state's burgeoning growth. In 1977, Governor Askew presided over the opening of a new capitol complex that included the restoration of the Old Capitol, the construction of new house and senate chambers and offices, and a twenty-two-story office building designed by famed architect Edward Durell Stone. Beginning in 1972, with an upturn in the state's economy, the governor had begun setting aside funds for the complex's construction. The center section of this massive public works project was paid for the day it opened.

DISTINGUISHED SERVICE TO NATION AND STATE

After leaving office in January 1979 following the election of D. Robert Graham from Miami Lakes, Governor Askew and the family moved to Miami where he once again practiced law. It was not long before he undertook a new public service role, this time in the national spotlight at President Jimmy Carter's personal request. The

Mrs. Askew poses with representatives of the Florida Forest Festival on the front lawn of the mansion.

governor's dedication, capability, personal integrity, and honesty led to his appointment as the United States Trade Representative, tasked with implementing the Trade Agreement Act as a member of President Carter's cabinet. Governor Askew left for Washington, D.C., and was sworn in on October 1, 1979.

After President Carter was defeated in his bid for reelection, Ambassador Askew returned to his family in Miami. With his now even more expansive experience, Askew began to consider seriously a bid for the 1984 Democratic nomination for president. The governor visited each of the fifty states during his campaign but was defeated in the New Hampshire primary in February 1984.

The governor continued to practice law in Miami until the family's move to Orlando in 1986 to open a branch office of his law firm. Askew briefly considered a run for the United States Senate, but ultimately withdrew in consideration of his family. The governor would realize one of his greatest joys and aptitudes when in 1989 he began to teach government, first at Florida International University and then at Florida Atlantic University, where he became a tenured professor in 1991.

The governor commuted by car between the two universities. The state university system recognized that the opportunity to learn from this selfless statesman should be shared, and although it meant a life of constant travel, Governor Askew (whose tenure was transferred to Florida State University in 1995) actually taught at all ten major public universities, logging over 115,000 miles on the road. Donna Lou Askew was with him for over 90,000 of those miles, and the governor acknowledged that those long commutes afforded him and his wife some of their best quality time.

The esteem in which he is held not only in Florida but throughout the nation is evidenced by the overwhelming number of awards, recognitions, and honorary degrees Reubin Askew has received over the years. In 1995, in a most fitting tribute, the University of Florida created the Askew Institute of Politics and Society, and Florida State University renamed its school of public administration the Askew School of Public Administration and Policy.

During the Askews' long residence at 700 North Adams Street, the governor's mansion became a cherished home. The mansion continues to bear the legacy of the family who lived their own comfortable lifestyle, made enormous contributions to the welfare of the state, and witnessed their children grow up within its walls.

Governor Askew personally took his Sunshine Amendment campaign to the people. Every weekend you could find him soliciting signatures at shopping centers or events sponsored by groups such as the League of Women Voters.

CHAPTER EIGHT

THE EIGHTIES

A World of Change

The eighties witnessed a decade of global conflict and reconciliation, of rampant consumerism and unimagined technological advances, of deadly disease and medical breakthroughs. It was the age of "Reaganomics," and Republican conservatism ruled the day. New words were coined almost daily; *technocrat* made its debut, along with *trickle-down economics.* The personal computer was now readily available to the public, and video-gaming would soon become one of America's favorite pastimes. ¶ In darker events, while we remembered some 58,000 soldiers lost in the Vietnam conflict—arguing about the appropriateness of that black granite gash on the Washington mall—other wars erupted

worldwide. The British invaded the Falkland Islands, the Israelis invaded Lebanon, and the Soviets invaded Afghanistan. ¶ The world was shocked and saddened by two inconceivable tragedies as the space shuttle *Challenger* exploded shortly after takeoff, and at Chernobyl the world's worst nuclear reactor accident sent clouds of radioactive material into the surrounding countryside. The eighties also gave us unprecedented achievement and hope for peace as Ronald Reagan and Mikhail Gorbachev of the Soviet Union agreed to a nuclear arms treaty. In Berlin, the wall that had so long separated East from West was completely dismantled. ¶ In Florida, the forces of change came from inside and out as devastating hurricanes pummeled the state, costing human lives and billions in property damage. Early in the decade, the acquittal of Miami police officers charged with murdering African-American Arthur McDuffie led to race riots that took the National Guard two days to control. Fidel Castro released over 125,000 Cubans at the port of Mariel who came to Miami, leaving the state to provide for their care and relocation and to maintain the peace. ¶ In 1978, D. Robert (Bob) Graham was elected governor. To him fell both the burden of leadership and the joys of accomplishment.

Top: One of Governor Bob Graham's "Work Day" hard hats worn while he was governor.

Center: License plate belonging to the governor of the state of Florida.

Bottom: The original patch flown aboard the Space Shuttle *Columbia* April 12–14, 1981. It was presented to the people of Florida from the National Aeronautics and Space Administration.

Opposite: The 1983 Mansion Foundation Ball, held on the mansion grounds, was a gala that is long remembered.

GOVERNOR DANIEL ROBERT (BOB) GRAHAM

1979–1983 & 1983–1987

"As we make a new beginning for Florida, we must be hopeful of our future and mindful of our past. For the past and the future are intertwined with the present. The past is shaping. The future is being shaped." In many respects, the Graham family put that noble sentiment from Governor Bob Graham into action as stewards of the environment and public education, and as residents of the Florida Governor's Mansion. The Graham family would complete a host of initiatives designed to protect and preserve those tangible and intangible assets that make Florida its own unique place.

Daniel Robert Graham was born in Dade County, Florida, on November 9, 1936, the son of Ernest and Hilda Simmons Graham. He was the only child of his widowed father's second marriage and was much younger than his two half-brothers and half-sister. Ernest Graham, a South Dakota mining engineer, came to Dade County in 1920 to manage the Pennsylvania Sugar Company's expanding sugar growing interests in South Florida. Although the sugar experiment was unsuccessful, Mr. Graham, who began dairy farming in 1932, would acquire the community bearing the name Pennsuco in northwest Dade County (consisting of some 3,000 acres). Ernest Graham (nicknamed Cap because of his service in World War I) sowed the seeds of interest in public service in his sons. In 1944, Cap Graham was a candidate in the Democratic race for governor, finishing third. Before that, the elder Graham had been a member of the State Road Board from 1933 to 1935 and Dade County's only state senator from 1937 to 1944.

From the beginning Bob Graham was a high achiever, and no stranger to physical labor. As a youth he spent time on the farm pitching hay, milking cows, building fences, and paving roads. Graham attended Miami Senior High and at sixteen was named "Dade County Best All 'Round Teenage Boy" by the *Miami Herald*. At seventeen, he was elected president of his junior class, was a champion debater, and was also president of the student council.

Bob Graham attended the University of Florida (where he was Phi Beta Kappa) along with his future wife, Adele Khoury, a native Floridian from Miami Shores. They were wed in February 1959 when Bob Graham was a senior and Adele a junior. Already interested in politics, Bob Graham interned with Florida Congressman Dante Fascell, before the Grahams moved to Cambridge, Massachusetts, after Bob's graduation. Mrs. Graham received her degree from Boston University and Bob his law degree from Harvard Law School in 1962. While her husband was busily studying, Mrs. Graham taught English and history at a public school in Wellesley, Massachusetts.

After returning to Florida, Bob joined his brother Bill in the development of the new town of Miami Lakes. In 1966, Graham was elected to the Florida House of Representatives and in 1970 to the Florida State Senate, where he served for eight years. He received the distinction of being named the Allen Morris "Most Valuable Senator" from his colleagues after the 1973 session.

The Graham family was growing, and by 1977—when Bob Graham decided to run for governor—they had four daughters, Gwendolyn Patricia (born in 1963), Glynn Adele ("Cissy," 1964), Arva Suzanne (1967), and Kendall Elizabeth (1969). With no incumbent, the field was wide open and held seven Democratic candidates, including former governor Claude Kirk. The primary ended with a runoff between Senator Graham and Attorney General Robert L. Shevin, both from south Florida. Bob Graham was the victor with a majority of sixty-four thousand votes.

Ever since the Civil War, rural north Florida had controlled the legislature, and distrust of south Florida's perceived liberalism and international demographics was deeply entrenched in the minds of Florida voters. Graham was the first candidate tied to south Florida ever to get this close to the state's seat of power. Graham chose as his running mate Wayne Mixson (Graham's colleague in the state legislature), who operated a 1,880-acre cattle ranch just north of Marianna in Jackson County. Mixson's long ties with north Florida would prove of invaluable assistance to Graham during his campaign. The Republican primary offered a choice of only two candidates and was easily won by Jack Eckerd (the drug store mogul) from Clearwater and his lieutenant governor running mate Paula Hawkins from Maitland (later a United States Senator).

Cap Graham sowed the seeds of public service in his son, but Bob was also no stranger to physical labor.

Opposite: Governor Bob Graham offers some advice to daughter Cissy as the two share some time in the evening walking on the grounds of the governor's mansion. (Special for the *Orlando Sentinel Star*/AP Laserphoto)

SPECIAL FOR THE ORLANDO SENTINEL STAR: ATTN LEE FIEDLER

(TD-4) TALLAHASSEE, Fla. Aug 6 -- FATHERLY ADVICE -- Governor Bob Graham offers
some advice to daughter Cissy as the two share some time in the evening walking
on the grounds of the Governor's Mansion. (AP LASERPHOTO) (dlp61240str-DIAZ)

The "down-home social" inauguration feast, open to all, featured home-made delicacies

from oysters to tamales to alligator tail to flan, reflecting not only Graham's statewide

support but Florida's increasingly international demographics.

Mrs. Bob Graham
The Governor's Mansion
Tallahassee, Florida 32303

French Silk Pie

Crust:
¾ Cup brown sugar
1½ Cups flour
½ Cup pecans, chopped
1½ sticks butter

Melt butter in a 9" x 13" pan in a 350 degree oven— Add the rest of the ingredients and stir every 5 minutes for 20 minutes till crumbly and crisp - do not pat down. Cool and add filling.

Filling
½ lb. butter
1½ Cups sugar
2 t. vanilla
3 oz. bitter chocolate, melted
4 eggs

Cream butter and sugar well, add vanilla and melted chocolate. Add 2 eggs, beat 3 minutes and 2 more eggs and beat 3 min. Pour in to pan and chill—when ready to serve, whip 2 cups heavy cream with 1 T. instant coffee and 1 T. powdered sugar added. Ice pie, then cover heavily with toasted, sliced almonds.

BREAKFAST MEETING
WRITERS FOR TIME MAGAZINE
SEPT. 19, 1979 - 8:00 A.M.

FRESH FRUIT WITH STRAWBERRY PUREE
CHEESE SOUFFLE
COUNTRY HAM
RED EYE GRAVY
GRITS
BLUEBERRY MUFFINS
FRESH FLORIDA ORANGE JUICE

During his months of campaigning, Bob Graham did more than talk about his vision for Florida's citizens; he attempted to personally understand their way of life. As he traveled across Florida, Graham conducted "work days" when he actually assumed the roles of his constituents. Graham had begun the practice in 1974 while still a state senator. His "temporary occupations" included teacher, police officer, railroad engineer, sponge fisherman, construction worker, factory worker, busboy, and logger. Mrs. Graham served as an elegant spokesperson for her husband, and tirelessly championed causes that included historic preservation, public education (increasing the number of senior volunteers in schools by 300%), mental health care, and services for the elderly. (After Governor Graham's election, Mrs. Graham became a registered lobbyist, the only first lady to do so, and continued her efforts on behalf of those causes, witnessing a string of successes including the first Hospice care program in Florida). In November 1978 Bob Graham's platform, sincerity, and talents led him to win the election, earning 55.6 % of the vote.

In one of her favorite stories, Mrs. Graham talks fondly about the governor's first inauguration ceremony. There was an often repeated political witticism, the origin of which has long been lost: "It'll be a cold day in hell when a candidate from Dade County becomes governor." At 11:00 A.M. that January morning, as outgoing governor Reubin Askew and governor-elect Bob Graham (dressed in business suits, rather than the traditional top hat and tails) arrived at the capitol for the inauguration ceremony, the temperature had dipped to 37 degrees. The strong wind made it feel more like 25 degrees. With the appearance of snow flurries that cold day, what was unimaginable in the past actually happened.

The master of ceremonies that day was former governor LeRoy Collins, who joined the other dignitaries shivering on the dais. Askew ended his farewell speech with the Irish blessing, "May the road rise up to meet you, may the wind be always at your back." Governor Collins came back to the podium and quipped, "Thank you, governor, but I think we could just as soon do without that wind right now!"

In October 2005, Adele Graham expressed her thoughts on the inauguration: "[We were] excited, filled with a sense of responsibility, proud of what our friends and family had accomplished, and ready to get to work. Our vivid memories of how cold it was—it snowed—and how pleased we were to have our 'workday coworkers' seated on the first several rows for the inauguration." Mrs. Graham recounted that following the rounds of receptions and parties, the family ordered out for pizza. They dined in the state dining room.

The Grahams' daughters were affected by their new life at the mansion to greater and lesser degrees. They were now in the spotlight full-time, surrounded by a staff of devoted professionals. Although they were required to pass through gates, coming and going from the mansion, those were only minor and inconsequential changes in their routine. It is clear that Adele Graham always made them her priority. Governor and Mrs. Graham's goal was to make the girls feel comfortable at the mansion, encouraging them to bring their many friends home and hosting innumerable events for the children throughout the years.

The Graham's daughters had their share of "perks" as well. They spent considerable time in the comfortable family room, and with no shortage of telephones, the girls kept the lines constantly blinking. Unlike their home in Miami Lakes (where Suzanne and Kendall were required to share a room), in Tallahassee they were delighted to have their own bedrooms which they personally decorated, while older sister Gwen enjoyed living in the mansion's guest apartment.

One of the first changes in the mansion itself was the conversion of part of the garage into a recreation room for the girls where they could be just that—girls. Years after their departure from the mansion, Mrs. Graham wrote: "Four of our daughters graduated from Leon High School. Our favorite memory is that our children felt comfortable to bring their friends home, that the mansion was not only filled with the official activities of government, but also with the laughter of happy teenagers and their friends."

The mansion's dual roles, as home to the first family and a place for the reception of dignitaries, required constant attention from a staff that became more like an extended family. Nella Schomburger, a personal friend of the Grahams, became mansion manager for what was to be a brief five weeks. She stayed for the duration of the Grahams' two terms, coordinating the staff and assisting the Grahams in the orderly and efficient operation of the mansion. In another vital role, Chef Art Smith, from Jasper, Florida, artfully prepared meals for the family and for hundreds during formal receptions. After leaving the governor's mansion, Smith became the personal chef to Oprah Winfrey.

As Governor Graham tackled matters of state, Adele Graham evaluated the condition of the mansion and, while making it their family home, was keenly aware of its role as the People's House. She began opening the mansion regularly, three days a week (as opposed to scheduling visits). Margie Mixson, wife of the lieutenant governor, took on the role of volunteer coordinator and established a fine docent program. Mrs. Mixson reported that in the month of May 1982, over 2,000 visitors were shown through the mansion.

The mansion had just about reached the quarter-century mark, and Mrs. Graham acknowledged that refurbishment was in order. She also recognized that the mansion's history reflected the accomplishments and evolution of the state itself and took steps to ensure that the history would be protected by hiring the mansion's first curator, Jerry Newell, in the fall of 1982, on a part-time basis.

In a 1982 interview with the *Tampa Tribune,* Mrs. Graham talked about her desire to feature more images, symbols, and décor that spoke directly to Florida. Of the paintings hanging upon their arrival, she said: "While they are quite good and on loan from the Ringling, paintings of a snow scene from Vermont on one wall and the King of Cyprus on another are just not the feeling I want at the governor's mansion." She introduced prints by John James Audubon and paintings of Florida landscapes by artist Albert Edward (Beanie) Backus, who was a favorite of Governor Graham's mother.

The quip "It'll be a cold day in hell when someone from Dade County is governor" came true on Bob Graham's inauguration day. It snowed.

Opposite top: First Lady Adele Graham's Silk Pie recipe.

Opposite middle: A mansion breakfast menu for writers from *Time Magazine*.

Opposite bottom: New acquisition being carefully inspected for suitability in the state reception room. The 19th-century Heriz rug does in fact find its place there, and sets the tone for colors that are used in the refurbishment of upholstery and draperies during the mid-1980s.

Top: Governor and Mrs. Graham step out of the front door of the mansion to greet guests and begin the festivities of the October 1983 Foundation Ball.

Bottom: Chandeliers illuminate the mansion grounds during that magical evening.

Opposite top: Lt. Governor Wayne Mixson dances with his wife Margie, who co-chaired the successful event with First Lady Adele Graham.

Opposite bottom: Governor and Mrs. LeRoy Collins (left) and Governor and Mrs. Farris Bryant (right) lent their support to their colleagues during the same evening. Fundraising efforts like these, sponsored by the Governor's Mansion Foundation, made future renovations and acquisitions for the residence possible, at no expense to the taxpayers of the state.

THE FLORIDA GOVERNOR'S MANSION FOUNDATION

As were all other first ladies before her, Mrs. Graham was subject to budgetary restrictions for the improvements she had in mind. Buoyed by the success of Jacqueline Kennedy's campaign to improve the White House by enlisting private donors, Mrs. Graham set about to create a foundation whose sole purpose would be to raise money for mansion improvements. "I feel during difficult times," Mrs. Graham said, "especially when there are very limited funds available—it's best to have the private sector support the state home and be proud of it."

The eloquently persuasive Mrs. Graham had no trouble finding supporters. In the fall of 1980 the Florida Governor's Mansion Foundation was formed as a private nonprofit organization led by president Mrs. Joseph Penner. Grace Penner and members of the foundation created fundraisers to begin to fill the coffers, first with the 1980 Governor's Ball co-chaired by Mrs. Penner and Bettie Bedell, next with a special 1981 Walt Disney World benefit, and then with a second Governor's Ball in 1983 co-chaired by Mrs. DuBose Ausley and Mrs. Steve Uhlfelder.

But the foundation's role was never just about raising money. By networking with friends, admirers, and acquaintances around the state, the members received donations of decorative arts and objects authentic to the period, some with a Florida pedigree. Those private gifts included a silver coffee urn from Mrs. John H. Phipps of Tallahassee, an eighteenth-century Chippendale desk from Mrs. Louis Hector, and an antique dictionary/reading stand from Mrs. Edward Swenson. The first gift to the mansion was a life-size painting of Andrew Jackson, which was prominently hung in the entrance hall, replacing the king of Cyprus. The painting is a copy of the portrait by celebrated nineteenth-century Hudson River School artist Asher B. Durand in the collection of the New York Historical Society. The donors were Mr. and Mrs. Joseph Penner from Sarasota. The painting currently hangs in the mansion's guest bedroom.

The role that the Florida Governor's Mansion Foundation served was made quite clear from its beginnings. What wasn't as clear was the role that the Governor's Mansion Advisory Council was to play in maintaining the highest standards and historical continuity. When LeRoy Collins pushed for the legislation that created the first Governor's Mansion Commission in 1957, he and wife Mary Call Collins had a prescient awareness that the mansion's original décor and furnishings might be changed in the future if no such external review body existed. The Collinses established a process whereby any changes would pass through the mansion commission to ensure authenticity and continuity. The need for review by an external body was not to everyone's liking. In fact, in 1969, under the Governmental Reorganization Act, the role and authority of the mansion commission was greatly reduced and the name changed to the Governor's Mansion Advisory Council, which was responsible to the Division of Building Construction in the Department of General Services.

When Governor Graham was elected to office, Mrs. Graham became an ex-officio member of the council. She was critically aware of the need for a group of sensitive, knowledgeable citizens who could objectively maintain the original mansion's legacy. One of Governor Graham's first appointments to the council was Mrs. Arva Moore Parks of Coral Gables.

Adele Khoury and Arva Moore were life-long friends, attending Miami Edison High School together. (Bob Graham attended Miami Senior, *the* main rival of Miami Edison.) By 1979, Mrs. Parks had earned the unofficial title of Miami's premier historian, having authored a series of illuminating and eminently readable books about Miami's history. At the very beginnings of the historic preservation movement in south Florida, it was Mrs. Parks who educated many and who became a prime mover in the constant battle to retain some of Dade County's most venerated buildings. She was the perfect choice as a guardian of the mansion's priceless historical treasures.

Buoyed by the success of Jacqueline Kennedy in enlisting private donors for White House improvements, Mrs. Graham set out to create a Governor's Mansion Foundation for gift-giving and fundraising.

Governor Graham framed a guest log with Jimmy Carter's signature. He gave his address as the White House.

Opposite: First Lady Adele Graham and Mrs. Arva Moore Parks McCabe (right) in December 2005.

Welcome Mrs. Graham

March 3, 1983

Dear Bob Graham,
Hi I like you, do you like me? I Really want to meet you, I don't know you It must be hard to be the governor of florida. I wish I could be a governor of a state. Do you like being a governor? I would like it. Well I have, I have to be going now.

Love,
Robert

Hi!

GRAHAM FOR GOVERNOR

Graham for Governor

GRAHAM FOR GOVERNOR

Graham for governor

Graham for governor

Graham for Governor

Graham for governor

GRAHAM for GOVERNOR

GRAHAM FOR GOVERNOR

Graham for governor

Opposite: Governor Bob Graham used this fire hose for one of his work days.

Top: Children always enjoy writing to their governor and first lady. Here are examples of endearing letters received by Governor and Mrs. Graham.

Bottom: First Lady Adele Graham's campaign dress is now part of the Museum of Florida History's First Ladies Collection.

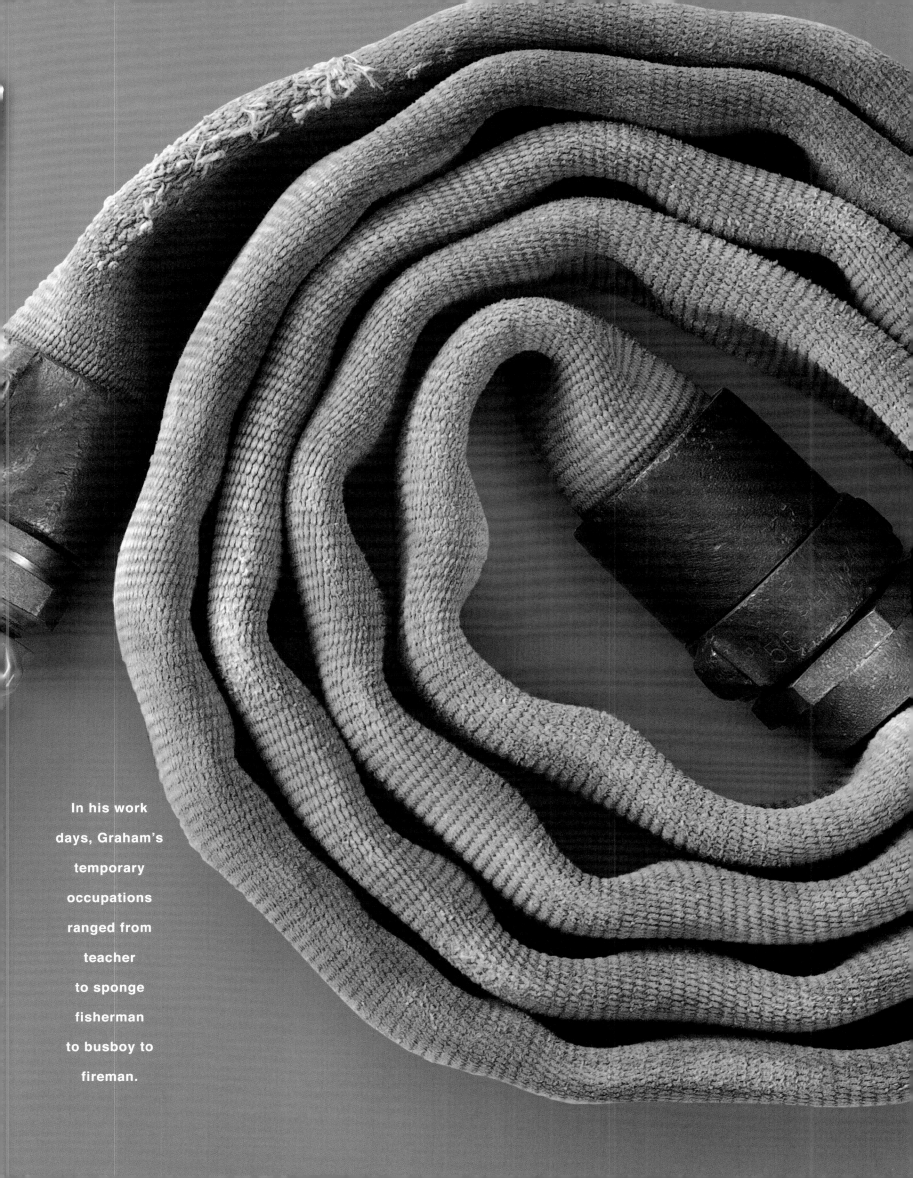

In his work days, Graham's temporary occupations ranged from teacher to sponge fisherman to busboy to fireman.

A Council or a Commission?

In 1981 the legislation that created the Governor's Mansion Advisory Council was set to be "sunsetted" (i.e., eliminated if no sufficient cause for its retention could be demonstrated). The stage was set for the first major conflict during the Grahams' stewardship of the People's House.

When a legislative committee asked the division director responsible for mansion oversight the consequences of abolishing the advisory council, he answered: "Although the Division [of Building Construction] might find it difficult to withstand the decorating whims of every new first lady, it would continue to maintain the grounds, insure the property, make inventories and prepare and submit budget requests." He added that the public would be affected to a "minor degree" if the advisory council were abolished.

For those who cherish history and acknowledge the special sensitivity and professionalism that produces "stewards" and not simply "caretakers," his words must have been anathema. Mrs. Graham and Mrs. Parks led the vanguard of those who believed that the mansion's advisory council was not simply a group of well-intentioned ladies, but a knowledgeable group of distinguished and responsible persons. Mrs. Graham addressed the legislative committee:

> The Governor's Mansion Advisory Council provides an important service to me and hopefully other First Ladies. The council serves in its advisory role as a positive, creative body, as well as a protection against dramatic change that would possibly change the character of the Governor's Mansion. The council, functioning properly, provides the continuity necessary to assure that our State home functions in its dual role as a private home and an important historical building.

Not only was the advisory council reinstated, it was elevated to its former role as the Governor's Mansion Commission with new rules, greater authority, and the responsibility for making its own budget requests.

Although the nine gubernatorial appointees of the Governor's Mansion Commission were themselves capable in a variety of fields, they brought with them the astute awareness that to arrive at the best possible solutions design professionals would add a dimension they themselves lacked. The call went out to such institutions as the Florida chapters of the American Society of Interior Designers (ASID), the American Institute of Architects (AIA), and the American Society of Landscape Architects (ASLA). Mrs. Graham noted: "The wealth of talent in the state is impressive and the word is spreading so that more organizations are offering their assistance whenever possible."

As a result, in 1981 a committee was appointed to advise the commission (all were members of the ASID and served without compensation). The design team included J. Emory Johnson (Tallahassee), chairman, Virginia Courtney (Delray Beach), Ed Heist (Jacksonville), and James Merrick Smith (Miami). When the designers first met, they agreed that the entrance hall should be given first priority. Mr. Johnson explained, "The first space one sees on entering the mansion should convey the best of Florida, its history, culture and people."

In 1982 the foundation made $50,000 available to refurbish the entrance hall. To add a feeling of warmth, and to relieve the discomfort of standing on a hard surface for periods of time, the designers selected a 1910 Heriz rug (from the northwestern corner of Persia near the border of Turkey) measuring 14.5 x 23.5 feet. The vegetable-dyed rug (donated by Mr. Ben Hill Griffin, Frostproof, Florida) enlivened the austere hall with colors of coral, blue, and cream. To complement these colors, new striped draperies were hung, and a Hepplewhite Martha Washington chair (c. 1790) was purchased to accompany a Chippendale reproduction already in the hall.

Because the room lacked light, a Williamsburg-style brass chandelier with leaded glass hurricane globes, from the Lester Barry reproduction lighting work room in Philadelphia (which had furnished pieces for the White House), was installed. At the cornice, a molding comprising tryglyphs and metopes (an ancient Greek motif), painted in a Wedgwood blue, was added to further complement the color scheme and add architectural interest. The motif was frequently used in Georgian and Greek Revival homes and is authentic to the nineteenth-century period. Other furnishings included a newly purchased antique George III mahogany display cabinet and the pieces already in use: a George III mahogany side table, a Queen Anne reproduction settee (reupholstered in a peach silk damask), and the grandfather's (long case) clock.

Another wise step was ongoing, organized assistance from Florida design professionals: interior designers, architects, and landscape architects.

Mrs. Graham wanted to feature more Floridiana in the mansion.
The Ringling art on loan was good, but "a snow scene from Vermont on one wall and
the King of Cyprus on another are just not the feeling I want."

THE SILVER BATTLE

In October 1982 the Governor's Mansion Commission would face its second skirmish, this time not with the legislature, but with the entire U.S. Navy. Assistant Secretary of the Navy George A. Sawyer wrote to Governor Graham, explaining that a new Trident submarine, the USS *Florida*, was to be commissioned in June 1983. He requested that pieces from the mansion's silver collection, given to the state in 1931, be made available to the captain of the new submarine. When the letter was received, Governor Graham was in the midst of his reelection campaign; in just a matter of months, the parties in the negotiations might have changed. Nonetheless, the seated members of the Florida Governor's Mansion Commission refused the Navy's request. Mrs. Graham emphasized that the silver belonged to the people of the state of Florida and that it would be kept forever in the mansion for all to appreciate.

In January 1983, following Governor Graham's successful reelection, the Navy tried again. A newspaper article in a June 1983 *Tallahassee Democrat* lightheartedly reported the outcome.

> A small but intrepid band of women on the eight member Governor's Mansion Commission appar-ently have won the war over Florida's "battleship silver," defeating the combined efforts of the U.S. Navy, a congressman, Governor Bob Graham, and the State Cabinet. . . . The governor and Cabinet, which initially took the Navy's position, beat a hasty retreat, after getting pressure from mansion supporters—including, in some cases, their wives.

In lieu of the state's silver, the commission graciously recommended that a gift of the brass wheel from the battleship *Florida* and a sterling silver coffee service from the USS *Palm Beach* be presented as gifts to the Navy. Another *Tallahassee Democrat* article summed up the situation, "If it [the U.S. Navy] continues to pursue the battleship silver, instead of accepting these alternative gifts, then heaven help the Navy. It just may have met its match." All of the silver pieces remained intact and are today a favorite of visitors to the mansion. The story of the intractable ladies adds an even greater appreciation.

GOVERNOR GRAHAM MAKES HEADLINES

During his first term of office, Governor Bob Graham was busy securing his own covenants for the preserva-tion of Florida's precious environment. Governor Askew had made significant advances in environmental legislation. Governor Graham would do the same. With his ties to farming and land development, he was singularly suited to envision these protections.

In 1979 the Conservation and Recreation Lands (CARL) program replaced the Environmentally Endangered Lands (EEL) program created under Governor Askew, with major revisions that prescribed the process for evaluating land acquisitions. In 1982, the legislature enacted the "Save Our Rivers Act," which would be funded with approximately $300 million over the course of a decade, to acquire river flood plains and water management lands. That same year the "Save Our Coasts Act" was passed, appropriating $200 million in ten years for the purchase of beaches and barrier islands.

Governor Graham dealt with his share of crises as well. In 1979, a truckers' strike gravely affected com-merce in the state. Governor Graham led steadfastly and without hesitation, bringing in the National Guard to assist in quelling the crisis. From April through October 1980 Fidel Castro allowed a mass exodus of Cubans to leave from the port of Mariel. Hundreds of thousands of Cuban émigrés arrived in Florida, largely concentrated around Miami and Key West. The "Mariel Boatlift" created critical problems in those cities as the refugees were without any means to find housing or support. The governor himself joined the Miami Police Department during the influx, witnessing firsthand the enormity of the problem. He said, "I saw how overwhelmed they were trying to deal with their regular responsibilities and these thousands of refugees arriving every day."

The state reacted quickly, housing many of the "Marielitos" in refugee camps. Governor Graham, strain-ing to provide sufficient aid and assist Miami with this unprecedented problem, went directly to the attorney

"If [the U.S. Navy] continues to pursue the battleship silver, instead of accepting these alternative gifts, then heaven help the Navy."

TALLAHASSEE DEMOCRAT, 1983

Top: "The Rainbow Connection" party for the legislature and families took place on the mansion grounds.

Bottom: Governor Graham plants a kiss on Miss Piggy during the celebration.

general of the United States and demanded that action be taken to relieve the pressure on Floridians and improve conditions in the refugee camps. In that same year, faced with race riots in Miami, Governor Graham acted decisively and, with the full cooperation from the city of Miami, ended the violence within two days.

After four years in office, Governor Graham decided to seek reelection and faced Republican challenger Congressman L.A. (Skip) Bafalis and his running mate Leo Callahan in the general election. The governor easily won reelection with 64.7% of the vote.

A Sunny Day and Much to Be Accomplished

The governor's second inauguration on January 4, 1983, was a far cry from the blustery winter day back in 1979. With sunshine and comfortable temperatures, once again former governors Reubin O'D. Askew and LeRoy Collins joined Bob Graham on the platform. Governor Askew, as master of ceremonies, drew chuckles from the thousands in the crowd when he likened Governor Graham to the unfinished Old Capitol. "Both the exterior and the interior have been remodeled," Askew said, "but there is much left to do!"

Governor Graham's address returned to the initial theme of his dreams for Florida: "We stand once more at the juncture of our dreams and our destiny. We are fully confident that we can shape the Florida we have inherited, into the Florida we envision for ourselves and for our children."

Wayne Mixson became the first lieutenant governor in the state's history to be reelected. Governor Graham made a special point of acknowledging his contributions to the administration:

> Anyone who knows Wayne Mixson knows why he makes history. This man from Jackson County is a gentleman, a scholar, a businessman, a farmer, above all a man of enormous human warmth. And Wayne has agreed to help lead our state into the future as both lieutenant governor and secretary of commerce. In this new role he will prove invaluable to the achievement of a series of specific goals we have set for our administration.

Following the inaugural ceremonies, the governor and other dignitaries led the "people's walk" to the mansion. At 4:00 P.M. the festivities began on the grounds. Hundreds of volunteers worked tirelessly to prepare for an enormous public "down-home social" with the theme "Florida's Future." Using $60,000 in surplus campaign funds, Governor and Mrs. Graham hosted an extravaganza that included hot air balloon rides on a custom-designed balloon, donated by Bob Snow of Orlando's Rosie O'Grady's restaurant. The menu (with the foods donated) included 2,000 alligator tails, 2,000 Apalachicola oysters, 1,000 grouper fingers, and 3,000 barbecued ribs. Other delicacies included 500 servings of black beans, 1,000 tamales, 500 ears of corn boiled in the husk, bagels, and hush puppies fried while you waited. The hand-made desserts included peach cobbler, flan, ice cream, Greek pastries, and lollipops. To sample everything on the menu must have been daunting even to the hungriest, but the variety of foods reflected the statewide support for Governor Graham and how far Florida had evolved in its international demographics.

During Governor Graham's second term, the efforts to refurbish the governor's mansion reached their zenith. Now intimately acquainted with the mansion, Mrs. Graham, along with the Governor's Mansion Commission and the Governor's Mansion Foundation, initiated an ambitious plan that revivified the aging home.

An Addition to the Mansion

As the dynamics of our lives change, so must the material world around us. In the past, designers of buildings could not have anticipated how this ebb and flow would accelerate. As a result many of our historic buildings have been demolished simply because they were perceived as obsolescent. Historic preservation, recognizing the need for physical adaptations to current life, introduced a concept called "rehabilitation." It simply means that changes to historic buildings may be made to create an "efficient contemporary use," but notes that the changes cannot be so dramatic that they marginalize original appearance. If this philosophy had been brought to bear in 1955, one can only think that the "obsolescent" 1907 governor's mansion, lacking sufficient space, might have been spared the wrecking ball.

When originally constructed, the northwest corner of the mansion was an open bricked terrace, covered with a corrugated steel panel for rain and sun protection. Mrs. Graham recalled that rain began during one legislative party and a legislator was caught in the leaking roof's drips.

The Florida Room has been judged the Grahams'
most successful mansion project. Architect
Herschel Shepard envisioned a light-filled space
of triple-hung windows and French doors.

The artist who arrived to hang the spectacular
mural gave strict orders that the first family could
not watch. "Quite uncharacteristically, Mrs. Graham
conceded . . . and prayed that the eccentric paper
hanger knew what he was doing!"

SELECTA MAGAZINE, 1985

The state dining room's hand-printed wallpaper mural remains one of the mansion's most admired decorative treatments. Printed from the original 1842–1843 woodblocks (just three years before Florida's statehood), the mural recreates the *Isola Bella* pattern, designed by artists Ehrmann et Zipelius for the Zuber Company of Rixheim, France. The motif (which means "beautiful island" in Italian) was inspired by the landscapes around Lake Maggiore, Italy.

Historic preservation philosophy also acknowledges a "living history" in which the contributions of successive generations are acknowledged along with those from the beginning. In this spirit the Governor's Mansion Commission undertook improvements.

James Cogar's original color scheme for the mansion was based on nineteenth-century precedents, but by 1983 the colors were faded and lifeless. The commission had many interior rooms repainted, keeping in mind the original colors but infusing them with light. In particular, the state dining room, often used for ceremonial functions, was in need of a decorative treatment that would add interest and color.

In 1985 the commission and Mrs. Graham arrived at a solution that today is one of the mansion's most admired decorative treatments: a hand-printed wallpaper mural, printed from the original 1842-43 woodblocks (just three years before Florida's statehood). The mural pattern, Isola Bella ("beautiful island", inspired by the landscapes around Lake Maggiore, Italy) was designed by artists Ehrmann et Zipelius for the Zuber Company of Rixheim, France. Dense and colorful foliage enlivens the foreground, while a *tour de force* of perspective adds depth to the scene. The landscape extends to the sky in light that could be early sunrise or the end of the day, as a subtle glow infuses the scene.

The printing of the paper required 742 woodblocks and 85 separate colors. To produce the graduating intensity of color, the background sky was brushed in by hand before the blocks were printed. When the artisan employed to hang the paper arrived at the mansion, he gave strict orders to the first family that they were not to witness the process but must wait until it was completed. An article in the 1985 *Selecta Magazine* described the first lady's reaction: "Quite uncharacteristically, Mrs. Graham conceded to this unusual request, and prayed that he, the eccentric paper hanger, knew what he was doing!" Needless to say, not only the first family but everyone who saw the completed mural was delighted.

In the meantime, the Governor's Mansion Foundation was busily acquiring other gifts that, while not as dramatic, have become an integral part of the mansion's allure. The elegance of dining in the state dining room is infinitely enhanced by the table settings. The foundation underwrote the production of sixty-seven silver water goblets emblazoned with the name of each Florida county. One additional goblet bears the name of Walt Disney's Magic Kingdom. Private companies donated Belgian lace napkins, table cloths, and placemats; Waterford crystal glasses in a Lismore pattern; and the dining room rug, which bears a flora and fauna motif. Private citizens and a not-for-profit organization bestowed gifts of porcelain by the late Edward Boehm, celebrated for his artistry.

The Grahams' most daunting (and judged most successful) accomplishment was the addition of the Florida Room at the northwest corner of the mansion. When originally constructed, that corner was an open bricked terrace, covered with a corrugated steel panel for rain and sun protection. Mrs. Graham recalled that rain began during one legislative party and a legislator was caught in the leaking roof's drips.

In 1980, state architect Derek McLean had reported that replacing the roof would cost some $32,000. As the money was not in the budget, funds would have to be reallocated. Mrs. Penner asked that a temporary canvas covering be installed while a master plan was prepared. The canvas awning was donated by a leading tent manufacturer in Sarasota.

The ASID committee continued to work with the mansion commission. During Governor Graham's second term of office, Ed Heist, who had died, was replaced by Ms. Ginny Stine from Jacksonville, who became chair. In January 1983, Mrs. Graham proposed an expansion to the mansion so that it could accommodate smaller meetings and the overflow from functions in the state reception room. At that time, Mrs. Parks was reelected chair of the Governor's Mansion Commission and was joined by Mrs. Dorothy Johnson, Mrs. Jane Aurell (daughter of Governor and Mrs. Mary Call Collins), Mrs. Grace Penner, and Mrs. Bettie Bedell. The commission sought an architect who was particularly sensitive to the requirements of historic buildings and who could maintain the delicate balance between the original building and a new addition. What better choice than Herschel Shepard, one of the pioneers in Florida's historic preservation efforts, a professor of architecture at the University of Florida, and the architect-in-charge of the restoration of the Old Capitol building?

Mr. Shepard presented his concept to the commission in April. He stated that the new room should be expressed as a light-filled enclosed space, using triple-hung windows to bring in the light and avoid extending the brick of the original residence. He suggested French doors to maintain the primarily glass enclosure but allow entry into the north gardens. This approach would not compete with the original architecture but complement it and would require the least modification to the original building. The commission enthusiastically approved the concept and appointed a committee consisting of Jane Aurell, mansion curator Jerry Newell, and Department of General Services representatives Tom Lewis and Wayne Betts.

Not surprisingly, the plan initially met mixed reviews. The budget presented to the legislature was $60,000. Unfortunately, none of the bidders proposed to construct the addition for less than $100,000. Initial criticism was based purely on the cost; most understood the need and that the addition was not a partisan project but one that would benefit the entire state. After some delay, the money was appropriated, although the construction was scaled back with the elimination of a fireplace and north portico. Construction began on September 4, 1984, and the fishpond and garden were moved further northward to accommodate the addition.

The Governor's Mansion Foundation furnished the room with comfortable furniture, using both antiques and new pieces. Decorator Ginny Stine said that in choosing, "There was nothing done that was far out, but we used fresh, inviting and interesting patterns. We wanted it appropriate, but not stodgy." One particularly interesting feature of the Florida Room is a glass cabinet that contains miniature portraits of Florida's first ladies, underwritten by Mr. and Mrs. Lewis Hall of Miami, beginning with Mrs. Spessard Holland, whose husband served from 1941 to 1945. Underwritten by the foundation, the portraits were painted by miniaturist Jane Blake in Seminole and after her death by Jeanne Dunne of Clearwater.

The guest bedroom on the north wing was improved with nineteenth-century reproduction wallpaper, new upholstery, and drapes. By the end of Governor Graham's term of office, the mansion was resplendent.

Transitions

During Governor Graham's second term of office he continued to advocate for education, and his record in environmental legislation culminated in the "Save Our Everglades Act." Personally, Bob and Adele Graham witnessed the marriage of their daughter Gwen, with the reception held at the mansion.

Governor Graham was not quite ready to leave politics and decided to run for the United States Senate against Republican senator Paula Hawkins in 1986. Graham won the race, and because he would assume his new office before the expiration of his term as governor, Lieutenant Governor Wayne Mixson had the great privilege of serving as governor for three days before newly elected Robert Martinez was sworn into office.

Senator Graham won two additional Senate terms in 1992 and 1998, and during his tenure served on a number of highly influential committees, including as chairman of the Senate Select Committee on Intelligence. Governor Graham, constantly accompanied by his devoted wife Adele, has received innumerable awards and honors. In 1982, Barry University conferred an honorary degree of doctor of laws on Mrs. Graham, and she continues to participate in innumerable charitable activities and advocate on behalf of others. Senator Graham, who recently published his book *Intelligence Matters*, is a Senior Fellow at Harvard's John F. Kennedy School of Government, and is in constant demand as a speaker. The Grahams were recently honored with the naming of the longest cable-stayed concrete bridge in the world (5.5 miles), between Clearwater and Bradenton as the "Bob Graham Sunshine Skyway Bridge." In 1980, a freighter struck the original cantilevered bridge, sending more than 1,000 feet of the bridge into Tampa Bay and killing thirty-five motorists. The new bridge, which Governor Graham fought for, was completed in 1987 and is an engineering marvel of unparalleled beauty.

The world has moved on since that wintry January day in 1979 when Bob Graham became Florida's governor, but the accomplishments of the Graham family will long be remembered. They typify a family willing to embrace change while carefully venerating and acknowledging the legacies of those who came before.

With Governor Graham's ties to farming and land development, he was singularly suited to envision environmental protections.

GOVERNOR JOHN WAYNE MIXSON
January 3–6, 1987

"I want to be
known as the
governor who did
the least damage
to Florida."

GOVERNOR

WAYNE MIXSON

If you ask former governor Mixson why his parents named him John Wayne, he will tell you that it's the other way around . . . John Wayne was named for him! This delightful man, who goes by Wayne, is a humorist without equal and leaves everyone with a smile. But to think that his well-honed humor is his only distinction would be a big mistake, as Governor Mixson distinguished himself as an effective legislator for twelve years and then as lieutenant governor in the Graham administration for another eight.

The Florida Constitution specifies that the lieutenant governor, in the event of a vacancy in the office of governor, succeeds either for the remainder of the term or during an impeachment trial or physical or mental incapacity. In a November 2005 interview, Governor Mixson said that when told Governor Graham would be stepping down, he exclaimed: "He doesn't look sick to me!" And so it was that John Wayne Mixson became the governor for three days.

Wayne Mixson was born on his parents' farm near New Brockton, Alabama, in June 1922. After high school, Mixson moved to Panama City, Florida, and worked in a paper mill. In 1942, he joined the Navy and served in a "lighter-than-air" unit placed on antisubmarine duty. Under the Navy's V-12 program, Mixson attended Columbia University in New York. He later attended the Wharton School of Finance at the University of Pennsylvania and then enrolled at the University of Florida, graduating with honors in 1947 with a degree in business administration. That same year he married Margie Grace from Graceville, Florida, the granddaughter of the town's founder. She earned her undergraduate degree from Florida State University and her master's degree from the University of Florida.

Mr. and Mrs. Mixson owned a 2,000-acre cattle and feed grain ranch near Marianna, in Jackson County. Voters elected Wayne Mixson to the Florida House of Representatives in 1967 and returned him for six consecutive terms. During those years he represented citizens in Jackson, Gadsden, Liberty, Washington, Holmes, and Walton counties. Mixson explained that he was planning to retire from politics after his last legislative term expired, when Bob Graham asked him to be his running mate. He said, "Bob owned a million dollars; I owed a million dollars!" Among Lieutenant Governor Mixson's duties after his election in 1979 was chairing a Tax Revision Commission in an effort to tax fairly and to create a better business climate.

Governor Graham appointed Mixson as secretary of commerce at the start of his second term in 1983. Mixson worked hard to create jobs throughout the state, having personally witnessed the effects that the mechanization following World War II had on so many impoverished farm workers.

During Bob Graham's two terms, Margie Mixson was of invaluable assistance to Mrs. Graham. She chaired the volunteer committee at the Florida Governor's Mansion, seeing to the myriad of details that came with public tours, receptions, and endless entertaining.

Wayne Mixson's inauguration as Florida's thirty-ninth governor was the penultimate event to culminate his twenty years of state service. That inauguration Saturday the governor-elect's day officially began at 10:00 A.M. when plainclothes officers arrived at his home and drove him and Mrs. Mixson to the new state capitol. The inauguration ceremony took place in the house chambers. None other than the stalwart and now legendary LeRoy Collins served as master of ceremonies. Both governor-elect Robert Martinez and lieutenant governor-elect Bobby Brantley and their wives were in the audience.

In both an emotional and light-hearted ceremony, Wayne and Margie Mixson were surrounded by hundreds of friends and family who came to honor this man who had given a good part of his life in service to the state. Mixson's old schoolmate from the University of Florida, and then Florida Supreme Court justice, Parker Lee McDonald administered the oath of office.

Now Senator Graham praised the sixty-four-year-old Mixson for his achievements during his long career in government. Governor Mixson followed with, "This is not the beginning, but an end of an administration," and compared himself to a copilot: "I'm bringing this flight in after a long flight where we've been a lot of places together. Bob, I appreciate this opportunity to bring her home."

After his brief nine-minute inaugural address, the new governor and Mrs. Mixson walked to the Old Capitol to greet well-wishers. The line wound up from the basement to the top of the stairs. With a broad smile Governor Mixson recalled: "Anybody who was anybody was there, legislators, former legislators, businessmen, justices. . . ."

That afternoon the Mixsons held an open house at the mansion, before they attended a reception at the home of Florida State University president Bernie Sliger, hosted by the Mixson Inaugural Committee, the Friends of Wayne Mixson, and the state Democratic Party.

The Mixsons spent Saturday night at the governor's mansion but stayed in the guest room. The next day, his staff surprised him with a special breakfast, one of the few events not open to the public. After church, Governor Mixson hosted a family luncheon at the mansion before he visited an apartment complex for the elderly. That evening the Mixsons held a barbecue for members of the staff and the inaugural committee at the mansion. Wayne Mixson acknowledged that his three days in office were largely symbolic, and in his characteristically self-effacing way remarked: "I want to be known as the governor who did the least damage to Florida."

Monday, the official start of the work week, was a busy one for Governor Mixson. He began with a cabinet meeting and then held interviews. The Mixsons hosted a business editors' luncheon at the mansion, and afterward the governor returned to the capitol. Governor Mixson continued his meetings (there was a great pressure on him to make appointments to various committees and commissions) and ended his day at 5:00 P.M.

That evening, a reception at the mansion honored Martinez and Brantley. The day ended with another reception, hosted by Governor Mixson and Jack Eckerd at the Governor's Club, to honor the in-coming governor.

For the Mixsons those three days were the opportunity of a lifetime, an unexpected reward for the faithful and loyal service of a lifetime. Governor Mixson continues to entertain and inform us in his role as an unofficial ambassador of Florida.

Inauguration
of
Wayne Mixson
Governor of Florida
January 3, 1987

For the Mixsons those three days were the opportunity of a lifetime, an unexpected reward for the loyal service of a lifetime.

Opposite: Governor and Mrs. Wayne Mixson on inauguration day, January 3, 1987.

Lower Right: Governor and Mrs. Wayne Mixson with their successors, Governor and Mrs. Bob Martinez, three days later on January 6, 1987, in the mansion's entrance foyer.

GOVERNOR ROBERT MARTINEZ
1987–1991

On Tuesday, January 6, 1987, Robert Martinez made history. He was Florida's first governor of Hispanic descent. He was also only the second Republican elected since Reconstruction. Sharing the dais with him that day were his wife Mary Jane, his ninety-nine-year-old grandmother, and his nine-month-old twin granddaughters. The governor rightfully took enormous pride in the continuity of his family's lineage.

Bob Martinez, a second-generation American, was born in Tampa on Christmas Day 1934 to parents Serafin and Iva Martinez. His grandparents had immigrated to the United States from Spain in 1906. Martinez grew up in west Tampa, in a neighborhood with deep Hispanic roots where many of the residents worked in the city's famed cigar factories. The future governor's father waited tables at the Columbia Restaurant in Ybor City.

Bob Martinez attended Jefferson High School in Tampa, where he played varsity baseball and was captain of the basketball team. During homeroom, young Martinez was lucky enough to sit behind Mary Jane Marino. In a 1989 *Orlando Sentinel* article, Mrs. Martinez revealed details of their high school courtship. In the reporter's account:

> The girl sitting in front of Bob Martinez sure had long hair. She wore it in a ponytail, and because their desks were crammed so close together, it would get in his way. So he would move it. For more than a year, relations never progressed much beyond the ponytail stage. But eventually Mary Jane got Bob to help her with her history studies, and before too long, they were holding hands in school.

They graduated in 1953 and on December 19, 1954, the former Mary Jane Marino became Mrs. Robert Martinez, when they were both nineteen years old. Mrs. Martinez came from an Italian family in Tampa, where her father ran a small grocery store and raised five children. Mr. Marino was initially not at all pleased with his daughter's decision to marry, because he wanted her to go to college, an opportunity he never had. She would do so, but not before she spent the next few years working as a dental assistant to put her husband through the University of Tampa.

During their earliest days as newlyweds, the couple lived in a two-bedroom, one-bath house next to Bob's parents. When their first child Sharon was born, the house became even more crowded. In 1961, the young family moved to the Midwest, where Bob Martinez received his master's degree in labor and industrial relations at the University of Illinois. Mrs. Martinez remembered it as a miserable time, when they lived on $25 a week, supplemented by peanut butter and canned goods sent from their parents back home.

After returning to Tampa, it was Mrs. Martinez's turn to go to school. With his encouragement, Mary Jane began her studies in education while Bob stayed home with the children and held a job as the executive director of the local teachers' union. When their son Alan was born Mrs. Martinez took a couple of years off from her college studies. After Mrs. Martinez graduated from the University of South Florida she became a librarian at Tampa's King High School.

The future governor became interested in the restaurant business and purchased the Cafe Sevilla. In 1975 Bob Martinez ran for mayor of Tampa, and although he lost, four years later he would successfully capture the office. He was reelected by a landslide in 1983.

REDUCING THE BUDGET, SAVING RESOURCES

When Bob Martinez ran for governor, the children were grown. Sharon and her husband Neil Keen lived in Tampa with their twin girls, Lydia and Emily. Their son Alan was then engaged to Shari Wilcox of Tampa and lived in the Betton Hills neighborhood of Tallahassee. Martinez ran on a platform designed to reduce the state's enormous budget, which had increased from $6.2 billion in 1979 to $16.5 billion in 1987.

Mayor Martinez faced Democrat Steve Pajcic and was elected by a margin of some 300,000 votes. In his inaugural address, as had so many other governors before him, Bob Martinez gave credit to his family

Sharing the dais with the new Governor Martinez were his wife, ninety-nine-year-old grandmother, and nine-month-old twin granddaughters.

Governor and Mrs. Martinez relax in the Florida Room during an interview on November 2, 2005. WFSU editor Charles Lockwood documents the occasion.

for their unwavering assistance in helping him meet his political aspirations: "I am honored and humbled to be here. The journey from Tampa to Tallahassee was a long one, and I would have lost my way without the love and support of my wife of thirty-two years, Mary Jane, my son Alan, my daughter Sharon, and her husband Neil. Whenever I said, 'I can't' they said 'we can' and they are the reason I am here today."

During the Martinez administration, the environmental policies begun by governors Askew and Graham were continued and enhanced. Governor Martinez enthusiastically supported the "Save Our Everglades" program, and the Florida Legislature passed the Surface Water and Environmental Act and the Solid Waste Disposal Act, adding to the protections for Florida's precious resources.

The governor made at least one appointment that would have far-reaching consequences. In December 1986 Governor Martinez appointed Dade County GOP chairman Jeb Bush as chief of the Florida Department of Commerce. Bush, thirty-three at the time, expressed his surprise at the appointment. Governor Martinez said that he was impressed by Bush's ability to speak Spanish and his extensive business experience with Latin America.

THE POWER OF PEOPLE

The governor and Mrs. Martinez shared an enduring concern for young people. Mary Jane Martinez championed the cause of finding, caring for, and preventing teen-age runaways and traveled across the state visiting shelters and raising money. Both she and the governor were greatly involved in preventing drug abuse among teens. Among his many career pursuits, the governor spent time as a classroom teacher. Mary Jane worked as the head librarian at King High School in Tampa for twenty years, before her retirement to assume the duties of the first lady. Both believed in the power of individuals to control their lives to achieve the highest possible rewards. After his election, Governor Martinez told writer Hettie Cobb for *Tallahassee Magazine*:

> When the son of a blue-collar worker can grow up to be the governor of the fifth largest state, it proves that the opportunity is open to anyone with the ambition and drive to do it. In this great country, if you apply yourself, you can achieve most anything you want.

In her role as first lady Mrs. Martinez never lost her identity as a teacher and librarian. Her keen interest in education turned to statewide issues. She was concerned about the dropout rate and the loss of parental support at school for children with two working parents. "We need to start seriously looking at parents becoming again involved in their schools, making the effort to make that visit to see your child in school, talk to those teachers."

Mary Jane Martinez's twenty years as mentor to schoolchildren, and the nurturing of her own family, evidenced itself in many ways during her residence at the governor's mansion. Docents at the mansion continue to speak of her active involvement in the tours, when she frequently joined groups of schoolchildren. The children must have been awed as the first lady of the state showed them the possibilities the world could offer.

OUTDOOR SCULPTURE AND FOUNTAIN

The Governor's Mansion Foundation and Mrs. Martinez raised substantial funds to improve the southwest corner of the mansion. Completed in May 1989, the $100,000 brick patio features a fountain that spills over from one level to the next and two free-standing gazebos. The Martinez family also made improvements to the green space just north of the Florida Room. The delightful bronze *Manatee Dance* sculpture by artist Hugh Nicholson, commissioned for the mansion, was installed at the northern terminus of the brick patio in 1990. The seven-foot-tall manatees are set into a rectangular basin, so that they are at eye-level for the children who pass by. The brick pavers and the labor to install them, as well as the landscape design and plant materials, were all donated to the mansion.

The Martinezes delighted in their granddaughters Emily and Lydia, and daughter Sharon made every effort to travel from Tampa to Tallahassee at least once a month. Mrs. Martinez remodeled one of the upstairs bedrooms as a nursery for the children. On a 1987 visit to the mansion, Barbara Bush, soon to be first lady in

Martinez added to the protections for Florida's precious resources, enthusiastically supporting Everglades, water, and solid waste initiatives.

Previous page: Governor Martinez frequently conducted state business in his office at the governor's mansion. Meeting with Governor Pedro de Silva, Spain's Governor of Justureas, and Carlos Fernandez Shane, Spain's Consul General, December 1987.

Opposite: Beaming grandmothers. Soon-to-be First Lady Barbara Bush and First Lady Mary Jane Martinez enjoy the Martinezes' twin granddaughters Lydia and Emily in the state reception room in 1987.

Mrs. Martinez
remodeled a bedroom
as a nursery for her
twin granddaughters,
whom visiting
Barbara Bush
described as "truly the
dearest, brightest little
girls I've ever seen."

THE WHITE HOUSE
December 11, 1989

Dear Mary Jane,

I hope you'll forgive the lateness of this
reply, but I do want you to know how much
I appreciate the wonderful coffee mugs you
sent for George and me. The gold Seal of
the State of Florida adds such a distinctive
touch. Thank you for your lovely gift. Your
generous friendship means so much.

George joins me in sending our best to you
and Bob.

Warmly,

Barbara Bush

Mrs. Bob Martinez
Governor's Mansion
700 North Adams Street
Tallahassee, Florida 32399

MRS. GEORGE BUSH

May 12 = 1987

Dear Mary Jane —
    How do I thank you and
Bob for opening your beautiful
home to me and letting me
tuck into your splendid guestroom.
It was so comfortable! Your
breakfast was superb and your
grand daughters were truly the
dearest brightest little girls I've
ever seen. You were so kind to
come to the coffee and the
luncheon — Especially with Deb
being sick. All in all my 18

Most warmly —
Barbara

175

Washington, seemed to dote on the children even more than their grandmother did, if that is possible. In a thank you note to Mary Jane Martinez, Mrs. Bush wrote: "Your granddaughters were truly the dearest, brightest little girls I've ever seen."

While Governor and Mrs. Martinez had to content themselves with periodic visits from their children and grandchildren, one other resident of the mansion made his presence known on a full-time basis. That would be Tampa Mascotte, the Martinezes' three-year-old basset hound.

Mascotte usually had full run of the mansion and started his day with the governor on his five-mile jog at 6:00 A.M. He was given as a puppy to the Martinezes by a Hillsborough County veterinarian in the spring of 1984 and from that moment on was their inseparable companion. Mascotte had a special weakness for bread accompanied by garnishes of cucumbers and radishes. In a November 2005 interview the Martinez family recalled the seemingly endless tales of Mascotte's mischievousness. On one occasion, Governor and Mrs. Martinez were occupied entertaining guests at a reception. For the occasion the kitchen staff set out trays of finger sandwiches, some with cucumbers and sprouts. At one point, the governor looked down to see Mascotte "sprouting" from either side of his muzzle. There was a hasty, covert scramble to discover which platter Mascotte had raided so it could be replaced.

Bob and Mary Jane Martinez beautified and extended outdoors areas with the delightful bronze seven-foot sculpture *Manatee Dance*, as well as with a brick patio whose fountain spills from level to level.

The ever-mischievous basset Mascotte loved unusual vegetables. During a reception featuring trays of cucumber-and-sprouts sandwiches, he appeared next to the governor "sprouting" from either side of his muzzle.

On another occasion, President George H. W. Bush was coming for a visit. The governor and Mrs. Martinez waited by the front door of the mansion with their faithful dog at their side. When the limousine pulled up and the President's door was opened, the normally mellow Mascotte leaped into the car directly onto the President's lap. No doubt both the President and the Martinezes were momentarily startled.

Governor Martinez faced a Democratically controlled legislature and, like his Republican predecessor Republican Claude Kirk, had some difficulty in seeing his proposed legislation passed. Governor Martinez ran for reelection in 1991 but was defeated by Democrat Lawton Chiles, former United States Senator.

Bob Martinez had little time to relax upon leaving the governor's office, as in 1991 in a most prestigious appointment, President Bush named him the director of the National Campaign Against the Use of Drugs. Following his stint as the "Drug Czar," Bob Martinez and Mary Jane moved back to their hometown of Tampa, where he now serves as director of government consulting for the firm of Carlton Fields.

Top: Mascotte, the Martinezes' basset hound, at a Halloween event with Governor and Mrs. Martinez. Mascotte sports a vest with the words "I Love Kids."

Bottom left: Mascotte stands sentry duty with red carpet during the mansion holiday tours.

Bottom right: Holiday time in a private living area of the mansion.

CHAPTER NINE

THE NINETIES
The End of an Era

he decade of the nineties ended a millennium and foreshadowed events that would occupy Americans into the twenty-first century. Worldwide conflicts escalated, particularly in the Middle East when Saddam Hussein invaded Kuwait in the summer of 1990. Easily overwhelming the Kuwaitis, Saddam proclaimed Kuwait the nineteenth province of Iraq. ¶ World reaction was swift and unforgiving as the United Nations gave Saddam a deadline for withdrawal, which he ignored. Led by the United States, a coalition of twenty-eight nations assembled troops pledged to remove the Iraqi forces from Kuwait. Americans watched the war on television as missiles lit the night sky and culminated in victory for the coalition in a matter of months. While Iraqi forces were evicted, Saddam was not captured, a dangerous failure that would prove costly in the not-too-distant future. ¶ In India in 1991, Rajiv Gandhi was assassinated, as his mother Indira Gandhi had been seven years earlier. Turmoil in Africa led to the incomprehensible slaughter of an estimated half million Tutsis by the Hutu militia in Rwanda, in 1994. ¶ There was some light in the midst of this darkness. Under the leadership of F.W. de Klerk in South Africa, apartheid ended, and Nelson Mandela, leader of the African National Congress who had been imprisoned for some twenty-seven years, was released in 1990. In Europe, the movement to create a "United States of Europe" moved forward with the Maastricht Summit in December 1991. Jacques Delors, president of the European Commission, along with Chancellor Helmut Kohl of Germany and President François Mitterrand of France, was instrumental in creating the Maastricht Treaty's provisions, which included the elimination of national barriers, institution of a single currency (the euro), and free movement of goods, capital, services, and citizens. By 1995, fifteen states had joined the European Union. ¶ The world's political seismograph went off the scale when in 1990 Germany was unified as one country. The wall separating East and West Germany was demolished, ending forty years of separation. Soon thereafter, the Union of Soviet Socialist Republics fell apart, replaced by the Russian Federation and fourteen new countries spreading from Central Asia to the Caucasus to the Baltic region. At the end of the decade, significant progress was made to defuse the centuries-old conflict between England and Northern Ireland. ¶ On the home front, former Arkansas governor William (Bill) Jefferson Clinton became president of the United States in 1992. President Clinton became the first Democratic president since Franklin Delano Roosevelt to be reelected to a second term. The Clinton administration was characterized by a

healthy economy and an emphasis on domestic programs that
increased the availability of jobs and encouraged people to break
out of the welfare cycle; the result was the lowest unemployment rate in thirty years. On the international scene, President
Clinton served as a broker in peace talks between Israel and
the Palestinian Liberation Organization that resulted in the
Oslo Accords. During his second term, after allegations of inappropriate behavior with a White
House intern, the President was impeached by the U.S. House of Representatives for perjury and
obstruction of justice, but was later exonerated by the United States Senate. ¶ Technology in the
form of cell phones and computers increasingly influenced the lives of the ordinary citizen. The
World Wide Web, initially created by the Department of Defense, became available to all, providing
undreamed-of access to information and connections around the world. ¶ With the changes in
world order, terrorism became a real threat to the United States, and anxieties, not unlike those
experienced during the Cuban Missile Crisis in the 1960s, began to occupy the thoughts of most
Americans. The threat became unbearably real as the new millennium drew closer.

Opposite top: Campaign
button for Lawton Chiles and
Buddy MacKay, Jr.

Opposite bottom:
First Lady Rhea Chiles's
inauguration dress.

Top: Official portrait of
Governor Lawton Chiles,
which hangs with other
governors' official portraits
in the main corridor of the
capitol in Tallahassee.

Bottom: Tender tribute to
a man who championed
children: outside the gates
of the governor's mansion in
December 1998.

GOVERNOR LAWTON MAINOR CHILES, JR.

1991–1995 & 1995–December 12, 1998

Lawton Chiles's inauguration in January 1991 set the tone for the duration of his administration. He called the festivities "Florida Jubilee 1991: A Celebration of Florida and Its People." The events planned around this momentous occasion were designed to celebrate the vitality of Florida's people and history and to empower individuals to help themselves. Lawton Chiles had himself become a significant part of that history as a four-term United States senator, from 1970 to 1989. Chiles served the people of Florida for nearly forty years, with only a brief hiatus after leaving the senate and running for governor. He was the consummate man of the people, effortlessly engaging everyone from all walks of life. He has been described as "folksy," "homespun," a "populist," and a "charismatic everyman." His lifetime of public service earned him a place as one of Florida's most venerated and beloved statesmen.

Lawton Chiles was born on April 3, 1930, in Lakeland, Polk County, a fourth-generation Floridian born to middle-class Americans—his father was a railroad worker and later a conductor. He was educated in public schools before attending the University of Florida and graduating in 1952. Chiles was active in student politics and was chosen for Florida Blue Key, the Hall of Fame, and Alpha Tau Omega.

Lawton Chiles had the good fortune to meet the woman who became his life partner in over forty-six years of marriage: Rhea Grafton from Coral Gables. Looking back at their relationship, one journalist said: "One never accomplished anything worthwhile without the other." The two met at a political party meeting where Rhea represented her sorority and Lawton his fraternity. Rhea Grafton was a staff member of *The Alligator* student newspaper and president of Alpha Delta Pi Sorority. Ms. Grafton was born into generations of talented family (among them Ed Grafton, a prominent south Florida architect) and is herself an accomplished painter. After her marriage, she was a co-owner of the Paradigm Gallery in Lakeland and a founding member and program director of the Polk Museum of Art.

Lawton and Rhea were married on January 27, 1951, when Lawton was a first-year law student. Rhea started working the next year to help put her husband through school. In 1953 he was called to active duty in the Korean War. Although the war was winding down, Second Lieutenant Chiles, Army Artillery officer, was a forward observer, spotting fire and then calling in the enemy's coordinates. In the artillery, it was the most dangerous place to be. Thankfully, there were only a few hostile engagements during his tour of duty, and now veteran Chiles returned home to his wife and three children in 1954.

He passed the bar exam that same year and returned to his hometown. Chiles became an instructor at Florida Southern College while he steeped himself in the affairs of the community. He was a member of the Kiwanis, the National Society of the Sons of the American Revolution, and the Polk County Association for Retarded Children.

In 1958 when Chiles was just twenty-eight, he beat the incumbent Roy Searles for a seat in the Florida House of Representatives. Chiles spent the next eight years in the state house, and then in 1966 won election to the Florida Senate, where he served another four. While a senator, Chiles became chairman of the Ways and Means Committee.

Former Florida governor Spessard L. Holland, also from Polk County, was Lawton Chiles's role model; in many ways Chiles followed in Holland's political footsteps. Holland served eight years in the state senate before running for governor in 1940. In 1946, when United States senator Charles Andrews announced that he would not seek reelection, Holland was nominated to succeed him, and upon Andrews's death, Holland was appointed to the senate in September 1946. He was elected for two more terms. In a 1997 interview

> Lawton Chiles has been described as "folksy," "homespun," a "populist," and a "charismatic everyman."

Inauguration day in the mansion. From left to right: Daughter-in-law Katherine (Kitty) Chiles, Governor Lawton Chiles, First Lady Rhea Chiles, and son Lawton (Bud) Chiles III.

Governor Chiles said of Holland: "He was the ideal of what a United States Senator looked like in my mind. He was revered by people who didn't always agree with him politically, but who looked up to him. And I looked up to him. That was my idea of a senator."

WALKIN' LAWTON SETS OUT

It was serendipitous that in 1970, Senator Holland announced his retirement and Chiles decided to run for his seat. When his quest began, Chiles was a relative unknown, and to change that he would embark upon a course that made national headlines. State senator Lawton Chiles began to *walk* the length of Florida, beginning in the small Panhandle town of Century and continuing south until he reached John Pennekamp Park in the Florida Keys. The trip covered 1,033 miles, took 91 days, and wore out five pairs of walking boots. The affectionate nickname "Walkin' Lawton" was one of the enduring consequences of his pilgrimage.

His walk was not merely a gimmick, but a unique opportunity to meet the people of Florida and hear their unedited concerns about the status of their lives and the government's influences on them. In the 1970 senate primary, Chiles ran against former governor Farris Bryant, who was enormously popular and favored to win. Bryant did win the first primary but lost the second to Chiles by a good margin. In the general election Chiles faced Republican William C. Cramer from St. Petersburg and won with 53.9% of the vote. Senator-elect Lawton Chiles, Rhea and their four children—Tandy, Lawton III (Bud), Edward, and Rhea Gay—left Tallahassee for Washington, where they would spend almost two decades.

As a freshman senator Chiles worked hard with Governor Reubin Askew to establish the 574,000-acre Big Cypress National Preserve in the Everglades to help protect its fragile ecosystem. In 1976 he was the chief sponsor of a "Government in the Sunshine" bill that required regulatory agencies to conduct their meetings in public.

In 1980 Senator Chiles fought for the Federal Paperwork Reduction Act, a cause he carried with him when elected Florida's governor. During his eighteen-year senate career, he championed children's issues by helping to create the National Commission to Prevent Infant Mortality. He expressed his concern for the elderly as chairman of the Senate Special Committee on Aging. In 1987 he became the first Floridian to chair the Senate Budget Committee.

Soon after arriving in Washington, Mrs. Chiles began a campaign to renovate a 100-year-old Victorian house near the Capitol as an "embassy" for Florida. "Florida House" opened in 1973. Through gifts of both funding and antiques, the house is an elegant showpiece of Southern graciousness. Florida House is governed by a board of trustees, with all operating funds raised through private donations. The Florida House is a center of Florida hospitality where visitors enjoy juice and snacks, find information, and may also tour this one-of-a-kind legacy.

In 1985 Chiles underwent quadruple bypass heart surgery. After his return to the senate he became increasingly frustrated by the slow pace of the federal government and decided not to seek reelection in 1988. As chairman of the Senate Budget Committee, Senator Chiles was discouraged by the impasses that met his attempts to cut federal spending. He felt Republicans and Democrats alike too often fought to preserve their own special projects with disregard for cooperation and collegiality and without an eye toward the big picture.

FROM POLITICAL RETIREMENT TO GOVERNOR

In 1989, Senator and Mrs. Chiles returned to Tallahassee, ostensibly for retirement. The senator began teaching political science at the University of Florida and heading the Leroy Collins Center for Public Policy at Florida State University. The story goes that less than a year into his "retirement," Buddy MacKay, an old friend and former member of the U.S. House of Representatives, had dinner with the Chileses and offered himself as a running mate if Chiles would run for governor.

That spring, with MacKay at his side, Senator Chiles announced his candidacy on the steps of the Florida Capitol. He defeated incumbent governor Bob Martinez with 57% of the vote. When Chiles was

Former Florida governor Spessard L. Holland was Lawton Chiles's role model. In many ways Chiles followed in Holland's political footsteps.

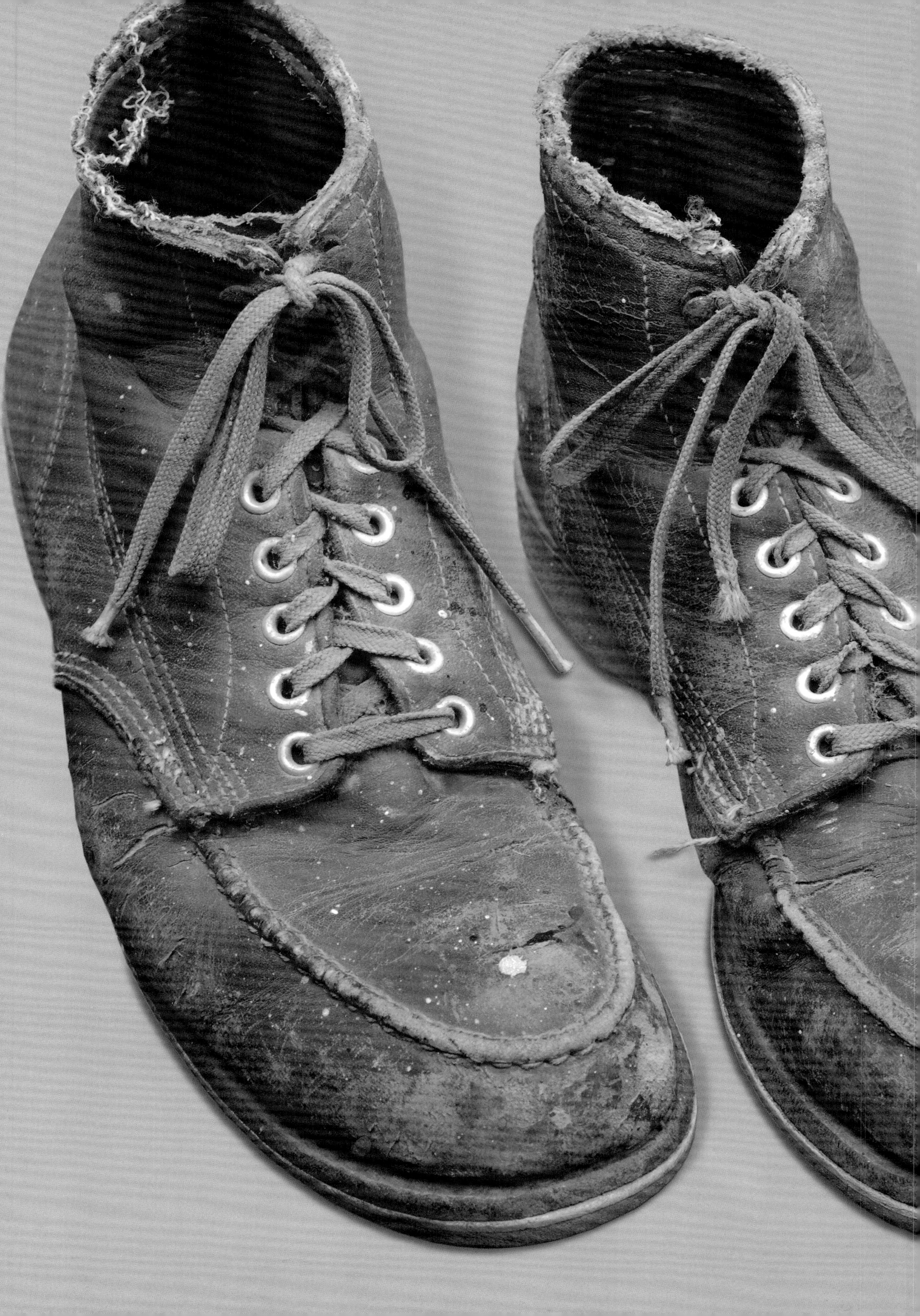

Walkin' Lawton's first cross-Florida trek covered 1,033 miles, took 91 days, and wore out 5 pairs of walking boots. No gimmick, the walk let him hear the people's unedited thoughts about their lives and government.

The story goes that less than a year into Senator Chiles's "retirement," Buddy MacKay came to dinner and offered himself as a running mate if Chiles would run for governor.

Opposite: One of five pairs of boots worn during Walkin' Lawton's cross-Florida trek.

Top: Lawton Chiles thanks voters outside the Old Capitol following his second successful election for governor.

Bottom: Lawton Chiles and Buddy MacKay campaign at a rally.

elected, the state senate was still controlled by the Democrats, and Republicans held just two of the six cabinet posts. In the house, Democrats and Republicans were almost evenly divided. That composition would change soon enough as the Republican Party began to dominate national and state politics.

The partnership between Governor and Mrs. Chiles was made even clearer during Governor Chiles's inaugural address: "On this platform today I'm blessed to have my closest confidante, my best friend, my key political advisor, the love of my life, my wife and the mother of my children. Rhea fills all these roles and she now is also your first lady of Florida."

When Governor and Mrs. Chiles moved into the governor's mansion in January 1991, their sons and daughters were grown and they held the distinction of grandparents. Frequent visits from the grandchildren called for an addition of another sort. A charming rope swing was affixed to a branch of an ancient oak on the mansion grounds. Visitors to the mansion frequently ask about it, and the swing is often photographed. Today, the swing serves as one additional reminder of Governor and Mrs. Chiles's lasting commitment to children.

Having renovated the Victorian Florida House, Mrs. Chiles was delighted to live among antiques and furnishings carefully selected by Williamsburg's first curator. In a 1997 interview Mrs. Chiles said, "I like buildings that have charm, that have history. I like the patina that things get when they've been lived in and have events in them, I like that feeling." As was their prerogative, the Chileses replaced the members of the Florida Governor's Mansion Commission with their own appointments, who would see to any improvements proposed by the governor and first lady.

Governor Chiles's first term was beset with difficulties because of a national recession that severely impacted Florida's tourist-based economy and led to a deficit of funds in the state budget. Although he introduced sweeping health care and tax reform bills, the legislature failed to act. The governor did make headway in other areas, notably the establishment of the Department of Elder Affairs, the creation of the Florida Healthy Start program for affordable prenatal and infant care, and the expansion of Everglades National Park. The governor was also successful in passing a law aimed at limiting contributions to political candidates to $500. Because of his at-times painful confrontations over national partisan politics, the governor ensured that no special interest could garner undue influence.

STORMY WEATHER

In August 1992, category 5 Hurricane Andrew took dead aim at Homestead in Miami-Dade County. With over 250,000 left homeless and some 85 deaths, the area was virtually decimated with over $30 billion in property damage. Spending over two weeks in Homestead and armed with firsthand knowledge of the suffering that followed the storm, the governor established the Emergency Management Preparedness Trust, with funds raised through a surcharge on private and commercial insurance policies. The governor also initiated an interstate support agreement with South Carolina to facilitate the delivery of services and to share resources during natural disasters. That original idea has since grown to include twenty-three states and one territory.

Meanwhile, Mrs. Chiles found that the governor's mansion was in dire need of repairs. She discovered that parts of the upstairs hardwood floor had been torn up and patched with plywood when the bedroom suites were reconfigured. Rotted wood in the floor, door, and window frames of the Florida Room needed replacement; an inefficient cooling system made parts of the residence unlivable; the kitchen roof leaked; and asbestos insulation found throughout the residence carried serious health consequences that needed to be addressed quickly.

Unfortunately these discoveries came when the state budget was slashed to reflect diminished revenues. Some perceived expenditures for the mansion's upkeep as an unnecessary extravagance. The mansion's current budget would take care of the roof repair, but the funds to replace the mechanical system, remove the asbestos, and repair the floors and windows would require an innovative approach to fundraising. While the Governor's Mansion Foundation could be a solution, Mrs. Chiles was uncomfortable with requesting

After Hurricane Andrew took dead aim at Homestead, Governor Chiles spent over two weeks amid the devastation. One result was the Emergency Management Preparedness Trust.

Wanting to beautify the east grounds, Mrs. Chiles and the mansion foundation commissioned sculptor Sandy Proctor. Of his life-sized bronze of children playing follow the leader, she loved the "sense of childlike wonder. . . . This sculpture celebrates childhood—and the child in all of us."

Top: *Florida's Finest*, silhouetted at daybreak, could easily be mistaken for life-size children playing on a log at the entrance to the governor's mansion.

Bottom left: Installation of the sculpture in the park in front of the mansion.

Bottom right: Governor and Mrs. Chiles, on dedication day in 1998, with the children who posed for *Florida's Finest*.

The Governor's Mansion
Tallahassee, Florida
1992

Christmas Eve Dinner

Salmon Canapes

Roast Wild Turkey
Montana Elk
Rice and Gravy
Green Beans
Sweet Potatoes
Cornbread Stuffing
Whole Berry Cranberry Sauce
Primrose Rolls

Pumpkin pie
Cherry pie
Margaret Chiles' Cookies

Coffee
Reception Room

Top: Christmas eve dinner menu and tree, 1992.

Bottom: Governor Chiles plays Santa Claus at a holiday party with young Marie Moyle and her parents Jon and Serena.

large donations from private citizens. After all, her husband kept his campaign contributions to just $100 per individual. Mrs. Chiles began looking at other opportunities to raise funds, saying, "There are all kinds of ways to make money, and we can do it ourselves if we just get creative enough."

The Department of General Services did find the funds to replace the heating and cooling system and to remove the asbestos in the ceilings. The work began in August 1991, and the governor and first lady moved out of the mansion for six weeks.

In 1994, as the governor approached the end of his first term, other strong winds were blowing, those of the increasing strength of the Republican Party. Governor Chiles would face Republican Jeb Bush in his reelection bid. Bush spent some $3.8 million in a seven-week media blitz, and by early October 1994, the polls showed him leading Chiles by five percentage points. By all accounts, it looked like Bush would win the gubernatorial election.

Just as in his 1970 walk across Florida, Lawton Chiles's infinitely popular appeal to the common man was resurrected toward the end of the campaign. In a debate the governor referred to himself as the old "he-coon," the wiliest raccoon in the forest. He said, "The old he-coon walks just before the light of day." The substance of that message was clear: Bush was the inexperienced upstart while Chiles was the crafty veteran who would win in the end. By the closest margin in the state's history, Lawton Chiles did just that, capturing 51% of the vote to Jeb Bush's 49%, a difference of only 64,000 votes of the nearly 4 million cast.

SECOND TERM STRIDES

On January 4, 1995, his second inauguration day, Governor Chiles stressed the importance of the individual citizen in making government work. He closed his address with these inspiring and prophetic words:

> This has been a glorious morning. It is filled with the possibilities of the future—and the excitement of choosing the path to our future. Every individual has the ability to make a vital contribution as we find our way on that path. And all of us together can raise our voices and lend our efforts to making the community of Florida better and stronger. We can embrace the challenges before us. We can walk the walk together—and we can truly make a difference. We're only here for a little while. So let's use the time we have to build the Florida of our dreams.

In the next four years Governor Chiles made significant strides in achieving the goals outlined in his address. His path was not made easy, as by 1995, for the first time in a century, Republicans controlled the senate. The Democrats clung to a 63–57 majority in the house, and three of the six cabinet members were Republican.

In fact, Governor Chiles's second term was replete with significant accomplishments, not the least of which was his war against the tobacco industry. The governor, who had constantly championed affordable health care and child welfare, was appalled with the tobacco industry's marketing to encourage smoking, leading to any number of illnesses.

Chiles first convinced the legislature to pass a bill that allowed the state to file suit against cigarette manufacturers to recoup the funds expended to treat Medicaid patients with smoking-related illnesses. In 1995, after the bill passed, the state sued the cigarette industry, resulting in an $11.7 billion settlement (later increased to $13 billion) to be paid out over twenty-five years. The governor explained, "The battle was always about more than money. It was about protecting our kids. . . . Florida can come up with ways, and I know we will, to pay for improving the health of our children."

The recurring theme of Governor Chiles's two terms was the needs of children. One of his greatest achievements was the passage of the 1998 Florida KidCare Act. The act expanded the earlier Healthy Kids program and provided health care coverage to almost 256,000 Florida children. The governor's programs also encouraged adoption and enhanced child care services, such as the Healthy Families pilot program to prevent child abuse.

Suddenly an underdog to challenger Jeb Bush, Governor Chiles sported a coonskin cap and proclaimed, "The old he-coon walks just before the light of day." When the morning dawned after the closest election in state history, Chiles was the 51% winner.

AT HOME IN THE KITCHEN

By this time Governor and Mrs. Chiles were blessed with ten grandchildren to dote upon. While their lives at the governor's mansion were more often than not devoted to business and official entertaining, there were private times. Both were at home in the kitchen, often cooking the game and fish that the governor brought home from his outdoor expeditions.

Renovations to the mansion's kitchen and butler's pantry replaced antiquated equipment and addressed the needs of the kitchen staff, who often created meals for hundreds. Jeanine Slagle, the mansion's chef, reported that turkey, deer, and quail were among the governor's favorite dishes. During the week the kitchen belonged to the staff, but on weekends, Slagle said, "It's not unusual for Governor Lawton Chiles to be puttering around the kitchen—poking his nose into the walk-in freezer and rustling up one of his favorite Italian recipes or a dish featuring game that he and his friends have brought in from the wild." The governor had quite a range of culinary skills, garnered from his experiences as a youth around the campfire and from cooking classes he took with his wife.

Mrs. Chiles embarked on a fundraising opportunity that would be both educational and entertaining. Up to this point, the literature about the governor's mansion was limited to brochures, and while they served a purpose, they did not have the breadth to describe the dynamic history of Florida's two executive residences. Using archival photographs and brilliant contemporary photography, Mrs. Chiles as editor-in-chief chronicled the story leading to the construction of the first governor's mansion and then the building of the present mansion. The book *700 North Adams Street*, published in 1977, was an immediate success. Governor and Mrs. Chiles traveled around the state for book signings, and sales raised more than $160,000.

THE ART OF CHILDHOOD

That money was put to good use in the creation of a bronze sculpture that will perpetually enhance the grounds of the mansion. The thirty-five member Governor's Mansion Foundation had embarked upon a campaign to beautify the green spaces of the mansion's east grounds, where the property terminates in a small parking lot. The foundation commissioned Tallahassee sculptor W. Stanley (Sandy) Proctor to create a piece to celebrate Florida's children. First Lady Rhea Chiles said that she wanted the park "as a balance for the formality—a place for children to run and romp and enjoy being young."

The 3,000-pound bronze entitled *Florida's Finest* depicts five children and their spaniel, precariously balancing on three fallen logs, in a game of follow the leader. The life-size sculpture is infinitely detailed and elicits the carefree joy in everyone's memories. Upon its dedication in April 1998, the first lady remarked: "Children are the state's most important natural resource. . . . There's so much violence in the world, and I think we're losing that sense of childlike wonder that Sandy [Proctor] has captured. This sculpture celebrates childhood—and the child in all of us." Judging by the response of the thousands of visitors to the mansion each year, Mrs. Chiles's description could not have been more apt. The sculpture delights everyone, both adults and children, and serves as a most appropriate testament to the Chileses' dedication to children's causes throughout their lifetimes. In 2006, sculptor Sandy Proctor was honored with induction into the Florida Artists Hall of Fame.

SHOCK AND SORROW

In November 1998, the gubernatorial race was between Jeb Bush and Lieutenant Governor Buddy MacKay. Bush won the election with 55% of the vote. Lawton and Rhea Chiles began their preparations for retirement in their newly built home in Tallahassee. And then, the unthinkable happened.

On December 12, 1998, just three weeks before his term ended, the sixty-eight-year-old Lawton Chiles, forty-first governor of Florida, died of an apparent heart attack while exercising at the mansion. As the tributes poured in, Rhea Chiles was left without the one person whose love and devotion had been a constant in her life for almost fifty years. The partnership that lasted a lifetime had come to an end, but there is perhaps no better tribute to their devotion than the formal portrait of the governor that hangs in the state capitol.

Opposite top: First Lady Rhea Chiles continues to enjoy her passion for painting at her home, December 2005.

Opposite bottom: The favorite family pet poses in the front flower bed.

that have charm, that have history. I like the patina that

hen they've been lived in and have events in them."

FIRST LADY RHEA CHILES

"God has called a great man home today. There will never b

GOVERNOR BUDDY MACKAY, DECEMBER 12

Unlike many of the formal portraits of earlier governors, the portrait of Governor Chiles speaks to the most important and influential cornerstones in his life. The painting is reminiscent of the Flemish master Jan van Eyck's *Arnolfini Wedding Portrait,* an understated testament to the bond between two people.

Governor Chiles's portrait is a *tour de force* of perspective and is filled with meaningful symbols. Behind the governor, the artist Christopher Still depicts a window revealing a rustic cabin and a raccoon crossing the grounds; beside the window, a parabolic mirror reflects Rhea Grafton Chiles in the mansion's entrance hall, facing her husband; in the foreground, looking at her and at us, is the governor himself. Referring to the portrait, the Chiles's daughter Tandy Chiles Barrett remarked, "Rhea *is* the picture."

Governor Chiles remains one of the most remembered and beloved of Florida's governors. The tributes to him are many and lasting. In May 1999, Governor Bush signed the bill which dedicated the "Lawton Chiles Trail," defined by a series of 145 signs marking the young state senator's trek across Florida in 1970. In April 2000, the University of South Florida broke ground for a $4.5 million building dedicated to reducing infant mortality and improving health care for needy mothers and their infants and young children. The building was named the Lawton and Rhea Chiles Center for Healthy Mothers and Babies.

But the governor's legacy is best borne out by the citizens of Florida who so greatly benefited from his programs. The Lawton Chiles Foundation has been established to follow the path that he blazed on behalf of America's children. The foundation continues the good work through the vast network of children's advocates and organizations that were united through his leadership and under the common goal of improving the lives of children. For this champion of children, there seems no greater legacy.

GOVERNOR KENNETH HOOD (BUDDY) MACKAY, JR.
December 13, 1998–January 5, 1999

The widely respected former United States Representative Buddy MacKay assumed the governor's office under the most tragic of circumstances. When he received the news of Governor Chiles's death, Lieutenant Governor MacKay was in Cambridge, Massachusetts. Returning immediately to Florida, MacKay was called upon to lead the state through the grieving process for one of its most outstanding leaders. Over the years, the two had been partners in politics and good friends, making MacKay's task exceedingly difficult. MacKay, like so many others, was simply shocked at Governor Chiles's unexpected passing. He told a newspaper reporter: "I have had a hard time getting my mind around it. I had been working, playing, and living with this guy for the last eight years."

At 12:35 A.M., Buddy MacKay was sworn in as Florida's forty-second governor, a post he would hold for three weeks until the inauguration of Jeb Bush in early January. At this most solemn occasion, his wife Anne and a group of close friends joined Governor MacKay. Following his swearing in, he made only this brief, but emotional statement: "God has called a great man home today. There will never be another like him."

Buddy MacKay was born in Ocala, Marion County, on March 22, 1933, the son of third-generation citrus farmers. He was educated in public schools and then matriculated at the University of Florida, where he earned two undergraduate degrees in 1954. In 1955 he began a three-year tour with the Air Force, holding the rank of captain. He then attended law school at the University of Florida and in 1960 married Anne Selph. While in college MacKay was inducted into the University of Florida Hall of Fame, the most prestigious honor a student could earn.

Admitted to the Florida Bar in 1961, MacKay moved with his wife to Ocala to begin his practice. His long political journey began in 1968 with his election to the Florida House of Representatives, where he served until 1974, when he was elected to the Florida Senate. MacKay served until 1980, when he ran unsuccessfully for the United States Senate.

Opposite: Governor Lawton Chiles and Lt. Governor Buddy MacKay celebrate victory atop the rooftops of downtown Tallahassee.

Just three years later, Buddy MacKay won a seat in the United States House of Representatives, beginning his first term on January 3, 1983. He won reelection two times, and during his career in the house worked with other congressmen to gain control of the burgeoning national budget.

When Lawton Chiles announced that he would not run for reelection to the U.S. Senate in 1988, Buddy MacKay successfully won the Democratic nomination for the position. But in the closest election in Florida's history, Republican Connie Mack III defeated him. MacKay's political career was far from over, as this chronicle attests.

A Seamless Team

In his first inaugural address, Lawton Chiles spoke of his regard for his lieutenant governor:

> Buddy MacKay has to the most qualified and talented Lt. Governor this state has ever had. He also has a tremendous partner in his wonderful wife Anne. At the outset of our campaign, there were some who did not fully appreciate the special relationship that I have with Buddy MacKay. Today, the Chiles/MacKay people are beginning to understand the benefits to our state if we function as a team utilizing every speck of talent both of us possess. Rhea and I consider ourselves especially lucky to have Anne and Buddy with us on this great adventure.

Governor Chiles gave MacKay a great deal of responsibility, assigning him to co-chair the Florida Commission on Education, Reform and Accountability. The commission identified over 120 low-performing schools and was charged with improving them. The Chiles administration characterized MacKay as a

different kind of public servant, with "a 27 year record of service based on finding common-sense solutions to the problems facing Florida's families" (*This Time the People Won: The Chiles/MacKay Years, 1991–1998*). In his second term Chiles charged MacKay with reducing the number of the state's rules and regulations by 50% within the next two years. Immediately after assigning MacKay to this Herculean task, the governor added, "Good luck."

Lieutenant Governor Buddy MacKay was just a little over a month from his defeat in the gubernatorial race when Governor Chiles's death ironically catapulted him into the governor's office. To attain the office in this way was excruciatingly difficult for the MacKays and they declined moving into the governor's mansion. Governor MacKay's duties in those last three weeks would be to see to the passage of bills high on Governor Chiles's list. But before that, he would honor the man he was closest to for so many years.

His first official act came on December 14 when he issued an executive order declaring a statewide day of mourning, closing all state offices in remembrance of Lawton Chiles. The formal executive order eloquently extolled the former senator and governor's lengthy accomplishments. In a statement made on that same day, Governor MacKay put it plainly, and from the heart:

> Sad as this time is, and even as we mourn the death of this great man, this is also a time to celebrate the gentle and lasting ways he changed our state and the lives of its people. The joy he found in living and giving so much of himself to others is a shining example to anyone who truly values family, friends and community.

In this most difficult time, Governor MacKay proved himself every bit the consummate statesman.

Buddy MacKay and Lawton Chiles had been a seamless team. Chiles charged Lieutenant Governor MacKay, among many big responsibilities, with reducing state rules and regulations by 50%. The governor kindly added, "Good luck."

"I have had a hard time getting my mind around it. I had been working, playing, and living with this guy for the last eight years."

CHAPTER TEN

THE MILLENNIUM BEGINS
New Challenges and a Renewed Commitment

In the months before the world entered the twenty-first century (abbreviated as Y2K for the year 2000), fears of potentially chaotic effects on computers dominated the globe. Many computer experts warned that the "millennium bug" would bring the world to its knees. Because computers used only two digits to designate the current year, the year 2000 would be interpreted as 1900, causing the collapse of the global computer network that relied on time-based calculations. ¶ Those fears proved false, as the millennium began with only a few computer glitches, planes continued to fly, and power grids around the world continued to operate. The biggest technological failure came because of jammed circuits when too many people tried to make cell phone calls. The *New York Times* reported the global scene on January 1, 2000:

> Though technically the millennium is still a year off, it hardly mattered. In Times Square and across the United States, in Europe, Asia, Africa, in cities and towns all over the world, bells pealed, crowds shrieked and surged, skyrockets soared into the night, fireworks burst into supernovas, 'Auld Lang Syne' rang out, lights pulsed, loved ones and friends embraced, and the music and champagne flowed.

While the world avoided near disaster on that front, another more sinister threat would change our lives forever. On September 11, 2001, terrorists attacked the World Trade Center in New York and the Pentagon in Washington. While the horror unfolded on live television, Americans learned that their formerly secure world was no longer. In the days that followed, reports of random anthrax attacks added to the fear. At airports, National Guard troops patrolled the concourses in full battle gear bearing M16s on their arms. In Florida the state's lifeblood, the tourist industry, virtually disappeared. ¶ Gradually, confidence returned as a new government agency, the Department of Homeland Security, enacted safeguards for American security. In 2003, the nation went to war in Iraq, ostensibly to rid the world of weapons of mass destruction and to relentlessly pursue terrorists whose activities threatened the world at large. That same year, Americans wept when the space shuttle *Challenger* exploded during its reentry over Texas. ¶ In the face of these events, Americans drew together, revealing a sense of patriotism and unity akin to the mood during the Second World War. Today, although that unity of purpose is challenged as factions earnestly seek to end the war in Iraq, the pervasive optimism so long associated with the American people remains unscathed.

Governor and Mrs. Bush, with children George P., Noelle, and Jebby on the mansion grounds early in the first term of office.

LET'S GO Jeb!

GOVERNOR JOHN ELLIS (JEB) BUSH
1999–2003 & 2003–2007

As the new millennium began, Governor Jeb Bush was just one year into his tenure as Florida's governor. It would be his fate to see the state into the twenty-first century, a passage during which Floridians, while revering the accomplishments of the past, looked ever more optimistically toward the future. The governor's quest for excellence in all people began at its source, with the governor himself, as he worked tirelessly through two terms to make a difference.

John Ellis Bush was born into an extraordinarily influential family on February 11, 1953, the third of George Herbert Walker Bush and Barbara Pierce Bush's six children. George H.W. Bush (United States president 1989–1993) was the son of Prescott and Dorothy Walker Bush, a highly successful and politically inspired family. Jeb Bush's grandfather was an investment banker who was elected to the United States Senate from Connecticut and served from 1952 until 1963.

Given this background, Jeb Bush (nicknamed from early childhood) is in a position to talk from firsthand experience about excellence and public service. Jeb was the first of the Bush children to be born in Midland, Texas, following the family's move from New England in 1948. It was from Texas that his father entered the political arena. Jeb's education, in addition to public schools in Texas, included a secondary school education at his father's alma mater, the Phillips Academy in Andover, Massachusetts.

In 1971, at just seventeen, Jeb Bush went to Mexico as an exchange student from the academy, where he taught English and polished his Spanish. Unbeknownst to him, that trip would have the greatest impact on Jeb's life, as there he met his future wife, the beautiful Columba Garnica Gallo. Mrs. Bush remembers their initial meeting as if it were yesterday. One Sunday night, while driving with her sister and her sister's boyfriend (another Phillips Academy student), they stopped briefly in the town square to talk with Jeb and a group of other students. "Jeb was the only one who came back and said again, 'What did you say your name was?'" she smilingly recalled. Some four days later, Jeb asked Columba for a date and was invited for dinner at her home. It was then that the diminutive 5-foot-tall Columba glimpsed the full 6-foot, 4-inch height of her handsome suitor. The match was made for a lifetime.

Columba Gallo was born in Leon, Guanajato, Mexico, in 1953. Even as a small child, she was inspired by the arts. Her dream became leaving her small town for Mexico City, where she could steep herself in the culture she so appreciated and begin her own career. Leon, a 400-hundred-year-old shoe manufacturing capital in central Mexico, was simply too small to contain this delightful and talented young woman. However, nothing could have prepared her for the life she would lead as the future wife of Florida's governor, the daughter-in-law of a president of the United States, and the sister-in-law of today's president. Years later Mrs. Bush said: "I did not ask to join a famous family, simply to marry a man that I loved. With that decision came a responsibility beyond anything that I could imagine."

Jeb returned to the United States, smitten, and love letters flew back and forth between them. Bush was then enrolled at the University of Texas at Austin. He chose Latin American studies as his major, citing the inspiration of his high school Spanish literature teacher. Bush spoke perfect Spanish, which would figure prominently in his later political interests, as he bridged the demographic gap for the country's growing Hispanic population. Jeb Bush graduated Phi Beta Kappa in 1973, finishing four years of course work in just two and a half years. The first time Jeb asked Columba to marry him she refused, though she relented soon enough. The couple was married at the university's chapel on February 23, 1974.

Jeb Bush began his career with the international division of the Texas Commerce Bank and in 1977 was sent to Caracas, Venezuela, to open a new operation. Bush was there for a little more than two years, returning home to work on his father's unsuccessful bid for the Republican Party's presidential nomination in 1980.

Following that campaign, Jeb Bush moved his young family to Miami and began an association with Armando Codina, a young Cuban immigrant and self-made millionaire. The two formed a partnership, and

"I did not ask to join a famous family, simply to marry a man that I loved.

With that decision came a responsibility beyond anything that I could imagine."

FIRST LADY COLUMBA BUSH

"It was so cold [inauguration morning], everyone left. I think I
was the last one there. I finally left just as the elephants from
the Ringling Brothers circus came over the horizon."

GOVERNOR JEB BUSH

The Inauguration
of
Jeb Bush
as Governor of Florida
and
Frank T. Brogan
as Lieutenant Governor of Florida

January 5, 1999

eventually Bush became president and chief operating officer of the Codina Group. Miami-Dade County was a close equivalent to late nineteenth-century New York, as it had become an ethnic melting pot, largely through the mass exodus of Cubans who left their country when Fidel Castro seized power in 1959.

The Latin American flavor of the city of Miami was welcomed by Mrs. Bush, whose mother and sister both lived there. While she raised their three children—George P., Noelle, and Jeb, Jr.— Bush excelled in the real estate business and continued his involvement in politics. In 1984 he became chairman of the Dade County Republican Party. With the end of Bob Graham's two terms, the 1986 gubernatorial election had no incumbent, and Tampa mayor Bob Martinez won the Republican nomination.

Jeb Bush proved of invaluable assistance to the Martinez campaign, as he communicated in Spanish with potential constituents in Miami-Dade County, where almost half of the population was Cuban. When Martinez was elected the first Hispanic governor of the state, he appointed Bush as his secretary of commerce. Governor Martinez explained that he was impressed not only with Bush's bilingual abilities, but also with his experience in international business relations. The appointment brought the Bush family to Tallahassee.

Secretary Bush served for eighteen months, traveling extensively and emphasizing Latin American business links and high technology. He found that the experience shifted his interests from the federal to state level. "I saw up close, the enormous possibilities of the [governor's] office," Bush said. "My interest in federal issues waned as I saw the institutional gridlock take hold in Congress." He left his position as commerce secretary early to participate in the 1988 presidential campaign, won by his father against Democrat Michael Dukakis, governor of Massachusetts.

In 1989, Jeb Bush successfully served as campaign manager for Ileana Ros-Lehtinen, the first Cuban-American elected to congress. Then, in 1990, Bush chaired Governor Martinez's unsuccessful reelection campaign against Lawton Chiles.

By 1994, Jeb Bush decided to seek the Republican nomination for governor. He won the primary against a total of *six* candidates, with 45.7% of the vote, and began a highly effective campaign with his choice for lieutenant governor, Tom Feeney from Orlando. A Republican tide had swept the nation that year, and the polls showed Bush running ahead of Governor Chiles for much of the campaign. It was not until the very end that Chiles made a successful rally for a narrow win.

The high-energy campaign that kept Jeb Bush on the road put a strain on the family. After his defeat in the election, Mr. Bush made a commitment to spend more time with them, sold his share in the real estate development company, and became involved in policy and charitable interests. In 1995, he started a nonprofit organization called the Foundation for Florida's Future, with a mission to influence public policy at a grass roots level. He volunteered at Miami Children's Hospital, the United Way, and the Dade County Homeless Trust. Jeb Bush's interest in education was a constant in his life, and along with T. Willard Fair, the president and CEO of Greater Miami Urban League, he founded the Liberty City Charter School, the first charter school in Florida. On the personal side, Mr. Bush made the decision to convert to Catholicism and join his wife, a devout Catholic, in worship.

Thus in the intervening years between his runs for governor, Jeb Bush cultivated another dimension to his already capable, compassionate personality. For the 1998 gubernatorial election, he was more than ready for the challenge against Democrat Buddy MacKay. Though MacKay had earned a significant reputation while lieutenant governor, he garnered only 44.7% of the votes to Bush's 55.3%. Governor-elect Jeb Bush and his lieutenant governor Frank Brogan would be inaugurated the following January.

Opposite: A jubilant new governor during his first inauguration on a chilly January morning, 1999.

Governor Bush with two of his brothers on inauguration day, 1999: George W. Bush (left), then governor of Texas, and Marvin Bush (center). A year into his governorship, older brother George would be elected 43rd president of the United States.

A Statewide Celebration

The Bush family celebrated the inauguration with events across the state. The festivities moved from Miami's Bayfront Park to Orlando's Universal Studios and finally to Tampa's Convention Center, where the inaugural ball was held. The idea behind a series of events was the governor-elect's belief that "people shouldn't have to come to Tallahassee to be heard." Bush remembers arriving in Tallahassee very late the night after the ball and then being up at 6 A.M. to test the microphones in front of the capitol. "It was very cold, six degrees that morning, and coming from south Florida, we really felt it." Along with his wife and children, the governor's mother, father, brothers and sister were all there lending their support and expressing their pride in Jeb's accomplishments. "It was pretty stupendous," the governor recalled. After his swearing in, a parade wound through the streets of Tallahassee. "It was so cold, everyone left. I think I was the last one there. I finally left just as the elephants from the Ringling Brothers circus came over the horizon."

The Bush family found Tallahassee very different from the megalopolis of Miami, with its decidedly Latin flavor. The move to Tallahassee as the chief executive of the state allowed Governor Bush and his family more time together. In describing the Bush family's life, a *Tallahassee Democrat* reporter observed: "They go to the movies. They eat out regularly. There are early tee times on Sundays, afternoon Mass on Saturdays. They try to spend time just hanging out at home."

Of course, what seemed like an ordinary suburban life denied the real truth—that the first family was constantly under scrutiny and that private times were rare. When Governor and Mrs. Bush moved into the governor's mansion, Governor Bush remarked, "The place I love is the house I get to live in," and enthusiastically added, "I love my work. I really love my job. I think people think that sounds corny, but it's really true. I love doing what I'm doing. I feel so privileged and so fortunate to do what I do, and I give everything I've got."

The governor's energy and hard work have become legendary. After spending a twelve-to-sixteen-hour work day, Governor Bush spends an hour at dinner, relaxes a bit, and then begins again. He personally answers the hundreds of e-mails he receives, often late into the evening.

In his first term, Governor Bush set out on a rash of initiatives. They included reducing the state work force, linking new growth to the availability of classrooms (concurrency), improving long-term health care for nursing home patients, eliminating the intangibles tax on savings, reducing the teacher shortage, creating higher academic standards, and initiating tax-supported private school vouchers. Another of his programs, called One Florida, was designed to increase opportunity and diversity in the state's universities and in state contracting without using policies that discriminate or that pit one racial group against another. The program did stir emotional protests and cost Bush some support from African-Americans.

The governor's educational plan, which focused on improving Florida's declining performance in public schools, created the greatest controversy. The Bush-Brogan A+ Education Plan mandated standardized testing, eliminated social promotions, and tied schools' funding and incentives to students' performance in the Florida Comprehensive Assessment Test (FCAT). The plan also provided for publicly funded vouchers that students in schools with a failing grade could use to attend private school.

The controversy over his bold programs left the governor undeterred. He explained, "We've had some controversies, but I'd be kind of disappointed if everything was just moving along hunky-dory around here. That means we're probably not pushing the envelope out far enough. I view my role as an agent of change, and I really do feel there's a window here that's unique in history."

The Nation Watches and Waits

In fact, Florida was thrust into the global spotlight during Bush's first term of office. In the November 2000 presidential contest between his brother George W. Bush and Vice-President Al Gore, the race was so close that no clear winner was declared. While it appeared that Gore had won the greatest number of popular votes nationally, the dispute centered on Florida's twenty-five electoral votes. Although votes were close in other states, Florida's controversy focused on the accuracy of the vote counts in a number of Florida's coun-

"They go to the movies. They eat out regularly. There are early tee times on Sundays, afternoon Mass on Saturdays. They try to spend time just hanging out at home."

TALLAHASSEE

DEMOCRAT

Between his runs for governor, Bush steeped himself in a whole new dimension of service: nonprofit organizations and volunteer work in education, health care, homelessness, and grassroots policy.

Governor Jeb Bush, Florida's 43rd governor, relished the work of the office over which he presided during his eight-year tenure.

Governor Bush acted decisively during 9/11: evacuating the tall Florida Capitol Complex and Department of Education building, lifting turnpike tolls, closing universities, and putting disaster officials on stand-by.

Governor Bush first learned that terrorists had struck the World Trade Center from freelance journalist Maureen Walsh in Tallahassee, moments before the start of his 9:00 a.m. cabinet meeting on September 11, 2001.

ties. A hand count of votes began, along with legal challenges of the recount's validity. After rulings from the Leon County Circuit Court followed by the Florida Supreme Court, the case was sent to the United States Supreme Court. The high court ruled in a 5–4 decision that the hand counting of ballots was unconstitutional because it was being conducted in different counties under different standards. On December 13, Vice-President Gore conceded the election victory to Texas governor George W. Bush, who became the forty-third president of the United States.

All the while that this played out, the scrutiny on Florida's elections process was intense. Governor Bush was assailed about his objectivity, despite the fact that he had recused himself during the recount debacle. The election highly polarized segments of the community and created some hostile backlash.

After September 11, 2001, Americans drew together, revealing a sense of patriotism and unity akin to the mood during the Second World War.

The president-elect, the vice-president, and Governor Bush all sought reconciliation amid the potentially devastating effects of national partisan politics.

Less than a year later, on September 11, 2001, the unthinkable "9/11" happened. That morning terrorists in hijacked planes flew into the Twin Towers of the World Trade Center, causing their collapse in the worst terrorist attack in United States history. A third plane flew into the Pentagon, while a fourth crashed in rural Pennsylvania after the passengers overcame the terrorists, ultimately sacrificing themselves. The death toll came to nearly 3,000.

In Florida, Governor Bush called the attacks "irrational acts by cowards." Bush ordered the evacuation of the twenty-two-story Florida Capitol Complex and the tower that housed the state's Department of Education. Tolls were lifted on Alligator Alley and the Florida Turnpike, universities and colleges were closed across the state, and the governor called the state's disaster officials into the Emergency Operations Center, where they were brought into a stand-by level. While the governor did not feel personally threatened, he did feel that the heightened security was warranted. As he said, "The proper thing is to be prepared." After the attacks of September 11, Florida, the nation, and the world changed forever, and the nation would face the startling realities of its vulnerabilities.

As the public's fear of air travel caused the largest passenger drop in the airline industry's history, Governor Bush took to the skies. On September 27, Governor Bush traveled by commercial air to Boston and Chicago to urge travelers to visit Florida. He wanted to reassure people that air travel was safe and convenient, countering the dramatic downturn of Florida's tourism industry.

TOWARD A SECOND TERM

As the year progressed, the governor decided to seek reelection in November 2002. In a race that received national attention, Governor Bush defeated Tampa attorney Bill McBride with 56% of the vote. He became the first Republican governor to win reelection in the state's history, and in January 2007 he becomes only the second governor to serve two complete four-year terms (Reubin Askew in the 1970s was the first).

> Faith is grounded in humility, gratitude, and generosity; an acknowledgement that through life we have been given a gift that is wholly unearned and never fully understood. It requires the difficult acceptance that we are loved, despite our flaws, just as we should love others, despite theirs. In our darkest hours, it is what sustains us. In our final darkness, it will bring us light. — Governor Jeb Bush, January 8, 2003

With his hand firmly planted on the Bible given him by his father—and used to swear in his father and brother as presidents of the United States—Jeb Bush was sworn in for his second term as governor of the state of Florida. In his address, Governor Bush was especially reflective.

> Can it be that only four years ago we paused under these oaks to talk about the future with enthusiasm and, in hindsight, an innocence that was unique to that day? Only four years, yet a generation's wisdom learned in that time . . . [W]e come here today as a people, as a community; as a state that has for the first time in our modern experience united behind common goals that elevate all of us, and the least of us.

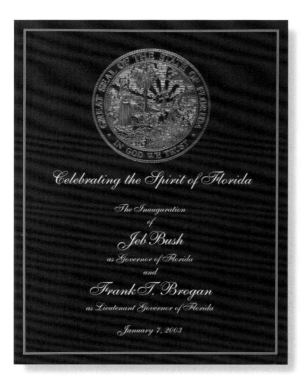

Celebrating the Spirit of Florida

The Inauguration
of
Jeb Bush
as Governor of Florida
and
Frank T. Brogan
as Lieutenant Governor of Florida

January 7, 2003

With so many of his first-term promises kept, Governor Bush reaffirmed his commitment to the people of Florida. He quoted LeRoy Collins, the man whom Bush considers Florida's greatest governor, saying, "Governor Collins said that the proper role of government is to make sure we navigate the ship out of the harbor, but not beyond the horizon where it can no longer be seen by those on shore." When asked in a February 2006 interview why he considered Governor Collins Florida's greatest governor, Governor Bush said, "He had integrity; he would be willing to go against the grain. He had the courage of his convictions, and he acted on them. He wasn't restrained by the here and now. A lot of politicians don't take the risks; I think he was a real risk taker."

As he began his second term, Governor Bush never settled back and rested on his previous accomplishments; instead he moved forward to others. The administration would again be affected by tragedy when on February 1, 2003, the *Columbia* space shuttle broke up upon reentering the Earth's atmosphere, resulting in the deaths of all seven crewmembers. In

"Our principles must endure beyond that person [the next governor] and those who come after. They must be intractably rooted in a culture that demands excellence, not adequacy; that exults in the individual, not government; and that through compassion, rather than compulsion, provides solace and support for the most vulnerable among us."

GOVERNOR JEB BUSH, INAUGURAL ADDRESS, 2003

"I applaud the efforts of Florida's emergency operations personnel, first responders and volunteers, who have worked tirelessly over the past six weeks to assist those affected by these devastating storms. I also thank our federal partners for their support in these difficult times."

GOVERNOR JEB BUSH, SEPTEMBER 22, 2004

Opposite: Governor Bush managing one of many devastating hurricanes during the 2004–2005 hurricane seasons at the Emergency Operations Center in Tallahassee. Lt. Governor Toni Jennings stands at far right.

Top: A welcome sight over the state's coast was captured by photographer Clint Krause on August 14, 2004, fourteen days after Hurricane Charley hit Florida. Photo courtesy of *The News-Press* (Fort Myers, Florida).

Bottom: Governor Bush, commander-in-chief of the Florida National Guard, greets reserve units which mobilized during several unprecedented hurricane seasons.

Wonderful and varied art exhibits in the governor's mansion,

open to the people, are part of Columba Bush's legacy.

March the United States and Britain went to war against Iraq. In the midst of these disheartening events, the governor continued his visioning for Florida.

When Lieutenant Governor Frank Brogan resigned early into the governor's second term to become the president of Florida Atlantic University, Governor Bush appointed former state senate president Toni Jennings as the first woman ever to serve as Florida's second highest executive. In 2004 and again in 2005, Florida was struck by a series of deadly hurricanes, creating havoc followed by costly rebuilding. The governor created a regionally based emergency response system to better manage similar disasters in the future.

AN ARTFUL FIRST LADY

The first lady has shone during her husband's second term in office. With her children grown, Mrs. Bush could concentrate more on her role as first lady, but also on her work with charities and her own creative energies. Always a private person, Columba Bush is intensely interested in promoting the arts and in keeping children away from substance abuse. Her compassion and empathy are expressed in all of her work.

As a part of her *Arts for Life!* initiative, the first lady began Florida's Arts Recognition Program, which not only honors but also supports, through scholarships, high school seniors who excel in music, media, dance, theater, and the visual arts. Mrs. Bush, working in unison with the Governor's Mansion Foundation, came up with the idea to create a special holiday ornament, depicting some quintessential aspect of Florida and the mansion's history, in order to raise funds for the scholarships. The first ornament was created in 2003 and features Florida's great seal, set into a domed decal within a gold frame of sabal palm fronds, Florida's official state tree. The program is enormously successful, due in large part to Mrs. Bush, who inspires others to cultivate their talents.

Mrs. Bush is also cofounder of the Children's Cultural Education Fund of the Ballet Folklorico Nacional de Mexico, which performs for children at no cost. The forty-year-old ballet company was founded by ballerina Silvia Lozano, and the troupe travels across the world as ambassadors of Mexican culture. Mrs. Bush is a spokesperson and member of the Informed Families of Florida, a nonprofit organization dedicated to preventing drug abuse in children; a member of the board of Columbia University's Center on Addiction and Substance Abuse; and a cochair of the National Institute on Alcohol Abuse and Alcoholism's Leadership to Keep Children Alcohol Free.

Being born and spending her youth in Mexico has left Columba with strong feelings regarding her culture and the demeaning effects of discrimination. Her love for her native country and its people continues and instills others with pride for their Mexican cultural heritage. Mrs. Bush once remarked, "I love the food, the people, and the beautiful countryside."

In April 2002, she joined the Florida Coalition against Domestic Violence to open the very first shelters for victims of abuse in Mexicali and Mexico City. While there, Mrs. Bush spent time with abused young women and children, sharing her compassion and concerns.

Mrs. Bush holds the title of the national Madrina for the Substance Abuse and Mental Health Services Administration.

In that capacity she helps empower Latinas to turn away from drugs and alcohol, while at the same time she raises awareness of the vast contributions Hispanic-Americans have made to Florida's heritage.

The diminutive Columba Bush is passionate about art. The enthusiasm cultivated as a youth in Mexico she has shared with others as first lady. Over the years, Mrs. Bush has promoted the exhibition of art works in the mansion, inviting the people of Florida to enjoy them. The paintings displayed present a panorama of artists and styles: surrealist painter Salvador Dali and contemporary painter Romero Britto, featured during Hispanic Heritage Month, as well as important African-American art from the prestigious Barnett-Aden Art

Continued on page 218.

First Lady Columba Bush is intensely interested in promoting the arts and keeping children away from drug abuse.

Opposite top: Mrs. Bush's passion for the arts is shared with visiting students during one of the many art exhibitions she organized in the state reception room.

Top: Governor and Mrs. Jeb Bush greet visitors at one of hundreds of official receptions they hosted in the state dining room.

Bottom: First Lady Columba Bush is a tireless ambassador for the arts. Here she hosts a musical program conducted and performed by Japanese children during their goodwill trip to the mansion in spring 2005.

Top: First Lady Columba Bush hosts the Annual Docent Luncheon, a time-honored tradition which began in the 1970s. Pictured with Mrs. Bush is Mrs. Marylou Madigan, a faithful docent who retired and was thanked for her decades of service at the November 2, 2005, luncheon.

The Florida Room at dusk during the 2005 holidays. Commemorative holiday ornaments, from left to right: (2003) The Great Seal of the State of Florida; (2004) The USS *Florida* Silver Punch Bowl; (2005) *Manatee Dance*; (2006) The 50th Anniversary of the Governor's Mansion. Ornaments continue to be available at local gift shops and online at www.floridashistoryshop.com.

Mrs. Bush began Florida's Arts Recognition Program to award scholarships to high school seniors.

The sale of special state holiday ornaments, very popular with the public, funds the successful program.

*To Joshua –
a great chef !
Thanks for taking
care of my family!
Barbara Bush
January 6th 2003*

The Governor's Mansion staff and volunteers are an

integral part of life at the Governor's Mansion, helping

to make the mansion a family home.

Opposite top: Joshua Butler, mansion chef, makes a final check of his holiday reception buffet preparations. Since joining the mansion staff at age 19 during the Chiles administration, Chef Josh has prepared dinners and receptions for thousands of guests during his eight-year tenure with the Bushes. The governor's mother, First Lady Barbara Bush, is among the many admirers of his great culinary skills.

Opposite bottom: Jerome Cummings, mansion manager, was honored with a surprise luncheon in the mansion courtyard on the occasion of his thirtieth anniversary in April 2004. He is pictured at center with his wife Connie and family, as well as former governors and first ladies with whom he served. "Without Jerome," stated Lt. Governor Toni Jennings on that day, "[the mansion] wouldn't be the same."

Bottom center: A faithful team of volunteer FTD floral designers have chaired the floral team for twelve years, donating untold hours of service prior to and during each holiday season. Left to right: Jill Weishaupt, Steve Roberts, Nell Roberts, Danny Sexton.

Bottom right: Professional FTD floral designers arrive in mid-November from throughout Florida to prepare the interior and exterior, public and private areas of the governor's mansion for the hectic holiday season. In years past, local volunteers decorated the mansion.

THE FLORIDA GOVERNOR'S MANSION LIBRARY

When Governor and Mrs. Collins opened the newly constructed governor's mansion to the public for their first look in January 1957, the mansion interior was yet to be completed. The mansion was unfurnished, the grounds unplanted, and the newly painted interiors still in the process of curing. In 2006, the mansion reached the venerable age of fifty and is now listed in the National Register of Historic Places.

Far from being static, history is ever evolving, and the Florida Governor's Mansion reflects dynamic forces that have added nuances to its physical character. As Governor Jeb Bush leaves office in 2007 after two terms as governor, the Florida Governor's Mansion will be the subject of yet another distinction, the addition of a library. It will be the first major architectural improvement to the mansion since the addition of the Florida Room under the Graham administration in 1985.

With the gift of the bronze sculpture *Manatee Dance*, the Martinez administration began a tradition in which each first family contributes to the residence upon their departure. Governor and Mrs. Chiles commissioned the bronze sculpture *Florida's Finest* that is now such a beloved part of the grounds.

On June 30, 2005, the Governor's Mansion Commission recommended the Library Legacy Project to the Florida Cabinet. With the cabinet's approval, the Governor's Mansion Foundation trustees began fund-raising efforts in earnest.

The library will house a collection of books by Florida authors, celebrating the talent and diversity of the state from its very beginnings as a territory of the United States. The rich interiors, to include wainscoting on two walls and a coffered ceiling, will provide a contemplative and quiet space to appreciate the volumes.

The foundation was successful in their search for an architect with the vision and experience to meld the new library seamlessly into the existing mansion, defining it as a new element while maintaining historical continuity. Tallahassee architect Robert Ferren, principal of Ferren Architects, was selected to design the addition. Because of their overarching concerns to protect and preserve the integrity of the mansion's original architecture, the foundation also created an Architectural Review Committee, comprising Herschel Shepard (designer of the Florida Room), Carlos Alfonso (a Florida Governor's Mansion Foundation trustee), Walt Marder (with the Division of Historical Resources), and Mark Bertolami (director of FSU Facilities Planning), all outstanding Florida architects with knowledge and expertise in historic buildings. A local interior designer, Ms. Kenan Fishburne, with the company Main Street Design, Inc., was selected to complete the interior and choose furnishings.

To select a location that would not disrupt the initial impression of the building from its main façade, the design team's task began with the examination of the existing building footprint. Given the topographical eccentricities of the site, and the space available, they selected a location at the rear (west side) on the north end, adjacent to the Florida Room and north gardens.

The library, measuring approximately 30 feet by 25 feet, will extend westward from the existing state reception room. The only alteration necessary to the original building, to provide access to the room, is the conversion of two existing windows into doorways. From there, the library's rectangular footprint will extend; the plan also adds an open portico that can be accessed through either the library or the Florida Room. Great care was taken to ensure the compatibility of proportion, materials, and fenestration while accommodating the special requirements of a library.

Governor and Mrs. Bush relax in the Florida Room and reflect upon life in the mansion during their interview with author Ellen Uguccioni in February 2006.

Following repeated discussions and refinements, the Governor's Mansion Commission and Foundation lent their *imprimatur* to the design. Ground was broken in March 2006, for completion in the fall. The library will be dedicated to the people of Florida during the final months of the Bush administration.

In the life of Florida, the governor's mansion reflects the progress and aspirations of the state. It stands as symbolic testimony to the resilience and dynamism of its people, gazing backward, while ever striding forward.

"... this library will highlight Florida books by Florida authors. It is the first addition to the residence in over twenty years, and it will reflect the emphasis which our governor and first lady have placed upon literacy and education during their tenure."

AMBASSADOR AND MRS. ALFRED HOFFMAN, JR.,

FLORIDA GOVERNOR'S MANSION FOUNDATION TRUSTEES

Collection and the Paul Jones Collection, shown during Black History Month. Important solo exhibitions (with educational catalogs and teacher lesson plans) featured Naples, Florida, painter Jonathan Green and Eustis-born artist Hughie Lee-Smith (February 2005 and 2006, respectively).

Whatever free time Mrs. Bush finds is usually spent with her husband. She particularly enjoys cooking with him on weekends in the mansion kitchen and going to the movies. The Bushes, who celebrated their thirtieth anniversary in 2004, continue to set aside Saturday as "date night." Both Governor and Mrs. Bush are very fond of their two pets, Marvin, a black Labrador, and Sugar, the Siamese cat. Marvin, the first dog, can usually be found wandering through the mansion, out on the grounds, or asleep in his bed in Mrs. Bush's office. Marvin has also provided the Bushes with some excitement, as he escaped from the grounds on two occasions.

On one such occasion, the Bushes learned that Marvin had been picked up and brought to a Tallahassee animal shelter. While Marvin did make it home safely, the governor, with a grin spreading across his face, explained why he was picked up in the first place: "Marvin doesn't bark, although he sometimes howls when he has an interesting dream. He probably forgot to tell them who he was."

At the end of 2006, the Bush family will make their preparations to leave the Florida Governor's Mansion. While there, the mansion became their home, imbued with humor, a sincerity of purpose, and the dreams of its distinguished residents. The mansion's history since 1957 has corresponded with the cycles of life, with triumphs and tragedies, with personal bests and with falls from grace. Above all else, it reflects Florida's own special history. Governor Bush put it this way:

> I'm very proud to be a Floridian. I'm a Floridian by choice like most Floridians are, and it's the best place in the world. I think it's important to be proud; I'm a Texan by birth, so I know what it is to exaggerate. Our history goes back to the earliest settlements in the Americas. That is amazing.

The Florida Governor's Mansion continues to stand as testament to a state that has transformed itself from one of the most isolated places in the continental United States to the fourth-largest state in the nation. The Florida Governor's Mansion is, and will continue to be, the People's House.

Marvin, the Bushes' Labrador retriever, was one of the most popular parts of a visit to the mansion grounds. Indeed, Marvin's name was derived from the governor's affection for his brother of the same name. First dog Marvin lived the last happy eight years of his eleven-year life at the Florida Governor's Mansion.

"He (Marvin) was always a star at mansion events. All the kids loved him. It was always a treat to go downstairs to meet mighty Marvin...he'll be fondly remembered as the kindest, gentlest dog a family could have."

AUTHOR'S ACKNOWLEDGEMENTS

Surely, it must be every Florida historian's dream to come face to face with history, to address legendary figures one-on-one, and to experience every nuance of tone, facial expression, laughter, and sadness. It has been my extraordinary privilege to have that opportunity as the author of *First Families in Residence*.

The road to the realization and completion of this book is the result of the vision of many, first and foremost, of the Trustees of the Florida Governor's Mansion Foundation, to whom I am eternally indebted. In particular I wish to acknowledge the support of trustees Dawn Hoffman and Kathleen Shanahan, Carole Smith and Cliff Brown, whose personal support was evident from the very beginning. The artistic merit of any book is not due solely to its author, but to the team whose patronage, constant encouragement, limitless humor, constructive criticisms, and enormous talent put it all together. I would be remiss not to thank Fred Gaske, Florida's State Historic Preservation Officer, whose recommendation for the project helped set events into motion.

Carol Graham Beck, the curator of the Florida Governor's Mansion (whom I am proud to call friend) exhaustively saw the process through from start to finish. Her rare insight, keen observations, savvy mediations and genuine warmth and wit are largely responsible for the product. Floridians are indeed fortunate to have such a professional caring for our iconic Florida home.

The "dream team" I worked with in the production of this work includes former state historic preservation architect Walt Marder, whose diverse talents gleaned illuminating bits of information about the mansion and its residents from the entire state and nation; Dee Dee Celander, a designer *extraordinaire* who envisioned how the book would look; Ray Stanyard, a photographer *non-pareil*; and Ellen Ashdown and Susanne Hunt, the principal editors whose careful reading and astute (and sometimes painful) suggestions made the book eminently more readable.

To friends and family, particularly Mrs. Norma Hall who insightfully read the entire manuscript making vital edits, and to you the reader, my thanks for truly making this 50th Anniversary Edition a welcome addition to Florida's infinitely interesting history.

THE GOVERNOR'S MANSION COMMISSION

Chair: Carole Smith. **Members:** Dorothy Alfonso; Jane Aurell; Mike Bullock; Emilia DeQuesada; Tim Dimond; Fred Gaske; LeeAnn Korst; Carol Price. **Ex officio:** Mrs. Columba Bush.

THE GOVERNOR'S MANSION FOUNDATION TRUSTEES

Ambassador Alfred Hoffman; **President:** Dawn Hoffman; **Vice-President:** Dorothy Alfonso; **Secretary:** Kathleen Shanahan; **Treasurer:** Carol Dover.

Board Members: Mr. and Mrs. Carlos Alfonso; Mr. and Mrs. Bill Becker; Mr. and Mrs. Paul Bradshaw; Mr. and Mrs. Bobby Brantley; Mr. and Mrs. Clifton Brown; Mr. and Mrs. David C. Brown II; Ms. Jerry Buchanan; Mr. and Mrs. Keith Clayborne; Mr. and Mrs. Jay Crouse; Mr. and Mrs. Courtney Cunningham; Mr. and Mrs. Walt Dover; Mr. and Mrs. Tre Evers; Mr. Willard Fair; Mr. Marty Fiorentino; Ms. Vivian Freas; Dr. Lois Gerber; Mr. and Mrs. Mark Guzzetta; Rev. and Mrs. R.B. Holmes; Mr. Mark Kaplan; Mr. and Mrs. Art Kennedy; The Honorable and Mrs. Bob Martinez; Dr. Dorsey Miller; Mr. and Mrs. Gary Morse; Dr. and Mrs. Harold Nippert; Mr. and Mrs. Tom Petway III; Mr. and Mrs. Sergio Pino; Mr. and Mrs. Tom Rush; Mrs. Carlos Salman; Ambassador and Mrs. Mel Sembler; Ms. Kim Binkley-Seyer; Mr. and Mrs. Daryl Sharpton; Mr. and Mrs. Ned Siegel; The Honorable and Mrs. Jim Smith; Mr. Denver Stutler; The Honorable and Mrs. John Thrasher; Ms. Miffie Uhlfelder; Dr. and Mrs. Erwin Vasquez.

Acknowledgements

The members of the Florida Governor's Mansion Foundation wish to thank the following individuals for the generous donation of their time, resources and talents.

Florida's First Families 1956–2006: Collins, Bryant, Kirk, Askew, Graham, Mixson, Martinez, Chiles, MacKay, and Bush families, especially Mary Call Collins, Jane Collins Aurell, Mary Call Collins Proctor, Darby Collins; Jane Aurell Menton; Cecilia Bryant, Adair Bryant Simon; The Honorable and Mrs. Claude Kirk, Adriana Dolabella, Claudia Kirk Barto, Erik and Kristen Kirk; The Honorable and Mrs. Reubin Askew, Kevin Askew; The Honorable and Mrs. Bob Graham, Gwen Graham; The Honorable and Mrs. Wayne Mixson; The Honorable and Mrs. Bob Martinez, Lydia Keen; The Honorable and Mrs. Buddy MacKay; Mrs. Lawton Chiles, Jr.; The Honorable and Mrs. Jeb Bush; and The Honorable Toni Jennings, Lieutenant Governor of Florida.

Florida Governor's Mansion Foundation Supporters
Co-Chairs: Ambassador and Mrs. Alfred Hoffman.
Supporters: Mr. and Mrs. Carlos Alfonso; Mr. and Mrs. Bill Becker; Ms. Shannon Bennett-Manross; Reginald and Tiffeny Brown; Mr. and Mrs. Vern Buchanan; Ambassadors Sue and Chuck Cobb; Hayden and Angela Dempsey; Mr. and Mrs. Walt Dover; Earl and Karen Durden; Diana and Llwyd Ecclestone; Mr. Walter Forehand; Mr. Mark Guzzetta; Mr. and Mrs. Lewis Hall, Jr.; Mr. Philip Handy; Ms. Ann Herberger; Mr. Michael Hightower; Mr. and Mrs. Sol Hirsch; Mr. Bart Hudson; Ms. Carole Jean Jordan; Mark and Sherry Kaplan; Ms. Lynda Keever; Ruben Jose and Patricia King-Shaw, Jr.; Ms. Debie Leonard; Alan and Laura Levine; Mr. Scott Lutgert; Mr. and Mrs. Gary Morse; Jim and Kelly Magill; Stuart Miller; Ms. Ruth O'Donnell; Mr. Charlie Parker; Mr. and Mrs. David Pike; Ms. Cheryl Riddick; The Honorable Julio Robaina; Mr. and Mrs. John Rood; Francis and Kathleen Rooney; Ambassador and Mrs. Mel Sembler; Jim and Dayle Seneff, Jr.; Kathleen Shanahan; The Honorable Jim and Carole Smith; Mr. Chris Sullivan; Ms. Susan Towler; Dr. and Mrs. Erwin Vasquez.
Organizations and Corporations: Blue Cross and Blue Shield of Florida; Communication Service Centers; The Community Foundation in Jacksonville; Florida League of Cities; Florida Restaurant & Lodging Association; Florida House; GrayRobinson, P.A.; The Lennar Corporation; Thomas Howell Ferguson; Republican National Committee; Republican Party of Florida; Volunteer Florida Foundation. **Publications:** *Architectural Digest*; *Florida History & the Arts*; *Florida Trend*; *Southern Living*.

Florida Department of State/Florida State Archives Staff: Gerard Clark; Miriam Gan-Spalding; Jody Norman; Adam Watson.

Florida Department of State/ Division of Historical Resources Staff: Dr. Jeana Brunson; Fred Gaske; Susanne Hunt; Robert Jones; Barbara Mattick; Kieran Orr; Dr. Carl Shiver.

John and Mable Ringling Museum of Art: Dr. Stephen Borys; Laura Carlin; Clarissa Fostel; Dr. Aaron de Groft; Françoise Hack-Lof; Tess Koncick; Michele Leopold; Michelle Scalera; Heidi Taylor; Dr. John Wetenhall.

Tallahassee Trust for Historic Preservation: Mike Wing; Lee Yawn.

University of Florida Press and University of Florida Library Staff: Head Librarian Derry Perez.

Governor's Mansion Architectural Oversight Committee: Carlos Alfonso; Mark Bertolami; Walt Marder; Herschel Shepard.

Florida Library: Robert Ferren (Ferren Architects); Elizabeth Ferren; Cynthia Ingle; Kenan Fishburne (Main Street Design); Kim Newell; Beverly White; Bill Weldon (All-State Construction); Charles Arant; Marlin Keller; Kenny Pique; Walter Vidak; Durrant Whiddon.

Research: Jane Aurell; Kara High; Marylou Madigan; Dr. Jan Matthews; Arva Parks; Serena Moyle; The Breakers Hotel, Palm Beach, Florida (Jennifer Genco and Ann Margo Peart); The College of William and Mary; The Hermitage; The Honorable and Mrs. Jim Smith; WFSU-TV: Deborah Lindgren; Charles Lockwood; Beth Switzer.

FTD Holiday Décor Floral Team
Chairpersons: Nell and Steve Roberts; Danny Sexton; Jill Weishaupt. **Floral Designers:** Raven Arbella; Peter Berden; Stan Brock; Beatriz Cardozo; Shea Curtis; Carol Duncan; Elaine Fulford-Gillis; Gerry Gemski; Annabelle Marin; Richard and Becky Martinez; Denise McDonald; Ed Oman; Myra Jean and Everett Nutting; Bonnie Rocks; Christine Vasconcelo.
2003–2006 Holiday Ornaments: Opus Design Group and Photo Fabrication Engineering (Milford, Massachusetts): Pete Gacicia, Deb Stenstream, Sue Pasck, Doug Pyron.

Florida's History Shops: Susan Stratton; Courtney Chappell; Marlisha Jackson; Stephen McLeod.

Mary Brogan Museum of Art and Science:
Chucha Barber, Jose-Luis Aguirre-Diaz, Michelle Smith Grindberg; Cynthia Hollis; Shannon Mahoney.

My Favorite Things Gift Shop: Lauren Teal; Nancy Nystrum; Joanna Ward.

Florida Restaurant and Lodging Association: Brittany Dover; Carol Dover; Sandy Moore; Deborah Spradley; Mike Truelove.

Governor's Mansion Education Team
Co-Chairs: Sharon Burnette; Dr. Ron Yrabedra. **Members:** Perry Albrigo; Jason Austin; Susan Baldino; Jane Barranger; Carol Graham Beck; Victoria Bell; Blake Bieber; Hugh Butler; Joan Cassels; Dr. Anthony Chow; Mary Beth Clark; Dana Edwards; Susie Henderson; Pamela Jones; Blair Limcangco; Carol Ann Mathews; Tony Miller; Hugh Nicholson; Evelyn Pender; Velinda Root; Pamela Shrestha.

Florida Governor's Mansion Docents
Chair: Tonie Vogt. **Members:** Peggy Allen; Sue Anstead; Betty Ashlock; Susie Backerman; Susan Baldino; Victoria Bell; Andrea Bonilla; Florence Brainerd; Mary Ann Braswell; Fran Brower; Ellen Bryant; Janele Bullard; Marie Cantwell; Sandy Cartee; Joan Cassels; Delyne Chapman; Tanja Clendinen; Vivian Corgan; Jan Cuddington; Pep Culpepper; Harriet Dickson; Galen Dillow; Rita Driggers-Healy; Leslie Elliott; Bev Ewald; Sue Flowers; Ann Foster; Lu Frye; Gloria Gant; Fay Grimes; Jane Harding; Jayne Harmon; Jan Harrell; Billie Harrison; Ginny Harrison; Dr. Helen Hatchett; Susie Henderson; Kara High; Dot Hinson; Maureen Hurlbut; Evie Hutchinson; Anne Johnson; Dr. and Mrs. Ivan Johnson; Marilyn Johnson; Pam Jones; Mary Kehrer; Patricia Kitchen; June MacDonald; Nancy MacDonnell; Dolores Maddox; Marylou Madigan; Mary Madsen; Sue Mancuso; Ida Manning; Shirley Marshall; Jean McCully; Ruth McDonald; Rhonda McMahon; Mary Middlebrooks; Margie Mixson; Ruth Moon; Nell Morse; Serena Moyle; Ginny Musick; Lynn Nilson; Debi Olenick; Marilyn Overton; Dr. George Palmer; Charlotte Palmer McNab; Janice Perkins; Mary Warren Perkins; Dorie Pilkey; Doris Pollock; Carol Price; Jane Pruitt-Fletcher; Mary Radcliffe; Jackie Rennick-King; Barbara Robertson; Maggie Rogers; Maxine Sandvig; Van Scherff; Nelle Sewell; Evelyn Shackelford; Leila Shuffler; Kim Skelding; Millie Smith; Mary Solomon; Robin Spellman; Pat Stephens; Mary Ellen Strongoski; Florazelle Teele; Sara Turner; Miffie Uhlfelder; Jane Villa; Michelle Webster; Linda Wells; Debora Williams; Marilyn Williams; Sylvia Williams; Dee Youngman.

Additional Individuals: Lee Adams; Gretchen Bachner; Carol Graham Beck; Gina Bevino; Kristin Bonnell; Jim Boyd, Jr.; Bill Butler; Joshua Butler; Sharon Burnette; Gail Campbell; Stacy Campbell; Cristal Cole; Jerome Cummings; Shane Desguin; Kelley DiSalvo; James Dow; Travis Eisenhauer; Alia Faraj; Brian Gaynor; Traci Gerrell; Vicki Goins; Mike Granger; Wendy Grant; Lon Green; Jennifer Grice; Betty Hampton; Analise Harshbarger; Jean Hartman; Mark Hendrick; Amos Herring; Guy Hill; Keith Howell; Shae Humphries; Mark Kaplan; Damien Kelly; Spencer Kraemer; Don Ladner; Henry Lockwood; Luvina Lynn; Dorine Martin; Leon Martin; Angela Matiyak; Nansi McDonald; Liza McFadden; Mac McNeill; Tina Millard; Samuel and Sylvia Mills; Ashley Miracle; Seth Montgomery; Kim Murphy; Richard Nichols; Kris Parks; Chris Pate; Chris Prichard; Carolanne Roberts; Ricardo Rolon; Sandy Shaughnessy; Bruce Slager; Bob Swanson; Logie Thomas; Bond Thornton; Justin Timineri; Eric Tournay; Sara Turner; Darrick Waller; Kevin Waters; Ashlyn Welker; Tracey Van Hook; Jennifer Von Chamier; Maureen Walsh; Annie B. Williams; Lorine Williams.

First Families Book Team: Ellen Ashdown; Carol Graham Beck; Dee Dee Celander; Susanne Hunt; Walt Marder; Kathleen Shanahan; Ray Stanyard; Ellen Uguccioni.

SELECTED BIBLIOGRAPHY

Blackman, Lucy Worthington. *The Women of Florida*. 2 vols. Jacksonville: Southern Historical Publishing Associates, 1940.

Clements, Patricia L. *Legacy of Leadership*. Tallahassee: Sentry Press, 2005.

Cozens, Eloise N. *Florida Women of Distinction* Vols. 1 and 2. New Smyrna Beach: Coronado Publishing, 1957.

Evans, John E. *Time for Florida: Report on the Administration of Farris Bryant, Governor, 1961–1965*. Self-published,1965.

Forgey, Max. "The Old Planners' Almanac: A Chronology of Growth Management, Environmental Policy, and Property Rights in Florida." August 2004. Florida Department of Community Affairs, Division of Community Planning, dca.state.fl.us/fdcp/DCP/publications/max.pdf.

Gannon, Michael, ed. *The New History of Florida*. Gainesville: University Press of Florida, 1996.

Menton, Jane Aurell. *The Grove: A Florida Home Through Seven Generations*. Tallahassee: Sentry Press, 1998.

Mormino, Gary R. *Land of Sunshine, State of Dreams: A Social History of Modern Florida*. Gainesville: University Press of Florida, 2005.

Morris, Allen, comp. *The Florida Handbook*. Series. Tallahassee: Peninsular Publishing Company, 1947– .

Tebeau, Charlton W. *A History of Florida*. Coral Gables: University of Miami Press, 1971.

Tebeau, Charlton W. and Ruby Leach Carson. *Florida: From Indian Trail to Space Age*. Delray Beach: Southern Publishing Company, 1965.

Archival Documents

Governor's Mansion Advisory Council. Minutes, 1965–1981.

Governor's Mansion Archival Records, c. 1955–2005.

Governor's Mansion Collection. Florida State Archives.

Governor's Mansion Commission. Minutes, 1957–2005.

Governor's Mansion Foundation. Minutes, 1982–2005.

Frank B. Moor Collection. Florida State Archives.

Author Interviews

Governor and Mrs. Reubin O'D. Askew, February 3, 2006.

Ms. Cecilia Bryant and Ms. Adair Bryant, November 2, 2005.

Governor and Mrs. Jeb Bush, February 4, 2006.

Mrs. LeRoy Collins, November 3, 2005.

Governor Robert Graham (telephone interview), June 14, 2006.

Mrs. Robert Graham and Mrs. Arva Moore Parks McCabe, December 15, 2005.

Governor Claude Kirk (telephone interview), December 16, 2005.

Mrs. Claude Kirk, Mrs. Claudia Kirk Barto, Ms. Adriana Dolabella, December 15, 2005.

Mrs. Mary Lou Madigan, September 28, 2005.

Governor and Mrs. Robert Martinez, November 2, 2005.

Governor and Mrs. Wayne Mixson, November 2, 2005.

Secretary of State Jim Smith, September 28, 2005.

ARCHIVAL PHOTOGRAPHY CREDITS

The following photographs appear through the courtesy of the following collections:

Florida Governor's Mansion Foundation Archives: Pages 2-3, 4-5, 6-7, 8-9, 10-11, 12, 13, 14, 16, 18, 20 (Governor's Palace), 22, 44, 45, 49, 52, 54 (brick detail), 56, 57, 58, 59, 60, 62-63, 64-65, 68-69, 70-71, 72-73, 74-75, 77 (invitation), 78-79, 80-81, 83, 84-85, 96 (recipe book), 99, 111 (upper photo), 120 (pamphlet),122 (invitation), 131, 134 (brochure), 140-141, 144, 147 (gala), 150, 152-153, 154-155, 156, 165, 169 (photo only); 170-171, 175, 176-177, 179 (portrait), 185, 186 (top photo and menu), 189, 208 (catalogs), 209, 212-213, 214-215 (floral staff), 228. *Florida Department of State/Florida State Archives*: Pages 8, 9 (snow scene), 26 (Osceola), 29, 31, 34, 36, 37, 38, 39, 40-41, 42,43, 46-47, 50 (Collins family), 51, 53, 54, 59 (column detail), 60 (furniture details), 61, 66-67, 77 (photos only), 84 (governors together), 86, 87, 88, 91, 92-93, 94, 97, 98-99 (all photos), 101, 102-103 (photos), 105 (inaugural), 106-107, 109, 111 (lower photo), 112-113, 116-117, 118-119, 120-121 (photos), 122 (photo), 123, 124, 127, 128 (top photo), 129, 135, 149, 158 (letters), 172-173, 177, 183, 190, 192, 197, 198-199, 201, 202-203, 204-205, 206-207 (large and small photos), 209, 210-211, 214-215 (chef and manager), 219. *Visual Resources Collection, J. D. Rockefeller Library, Williamsburg, VA*: Page 20. *Florida Department of State/Division of Historical Resources*: Pages 24-26, 26 (mission), 208 (Mrs. Bush). *Florida Department of State/Museum of Florida History*: Pages 30, 32, 86 (button), 101 (gowns), 114-115, 133, 138-139 (hat and dress) 146, 158-159 (artifacts), 178, 182-183 (shoes), 205 (artifact). *NASA*: Page 102. *Tallahassee Democrat*: Page 50 (mansion photo). *University of Florida, Smathers Library*: Page 105 (cartoon). *Governor and Mrs. Claude Kirk*: Pages 128, 129, 132. *Governor and Mrs. Reubin Askew*: Pages 136, 139, 140-141, 145. *Senator and Mrs. Bob Graham*: Pages 157, 161 (photo by Mark Block). *Governor and Mrs. Wayne Mixson*: Pages 168, 169 (program). Associated Press: Page 179 (photo by Don Edgar). *Lawton "Bud" II and Kitty Chiles*: Page 180. *Serena and Jon Moyle*: Page 186. *Governor and Mrs. Jeb Bush*: Pages 194-195, 198-199, 201, 202-203, 204-205, 210-211, 214-215 (chef and manager photos), 219. *The News-Press* (Fort Myers, FL): Page 207 (photo by Clint Krause). *Chef Joshua Butler*: Page 215. *Ferren Architects P.A. (Tallahassee, Florida)*: Pages 216-217. *Main Street Design (Quincy, Florida)*: Page 217 (interior detail). *Office of the Governor* (Mrs. Bush): Pages 208-209.